Books by Vernon Coleman include:

The Medicine Men (1975)
Paper Doctors (1976)
Stress Control (1978)
The Home Pharmacy (1980)
Aspirin or Ambulance (1980)
Face Values (1981)
The Good Medicine Guide (1982)
Bodypower (1983)
Thomas Winsden's Cricketing Almanack (1983)
Diary of a Cricket Lover (1984)
Bodysense (1984)
Life Without Tranquillisers (1985)
The Story Of Medicine (1985, 1998)
Mindpower (1986)
Addicts and Addictions (1986)
Dr Vernon Coleman's Guide To Alternative Medicine (1988)
Stress Management Techniques (1988)
Know Yourself (1988)
The Health Scandal (1988)
The 20 Minute Health Check (1989)
Sex For Everyone (1989)
Mind Over Body (1989)
Eat Green Lose Weight (1990)
How To Overcome Toxic Stress (1990)
Why Animal Experiments Must Stop (1991)
The Drugs Myth (1992)
Complete Guide To Sex (1993)
How to Conquer Backache (1993)
How to Conquer Pain (1993)
Betrayal of Trust (1994)
Know Your Drugs (1994, 1997)
Food for Thought (1994, revised edition 2000)
The Traditional Home Doctor (1994)
People Watching (1995)
Relief from IBS (1995)
The Parent's Handbook (1995)
Men in Dresses (1996)
Power over Cancer (1996)
Crossdressing (1996)
How to Conquer Arthritis (1996)

High Blood Pressure (1996)
How To Stop Your Doctor Killing You (1996, revised edition 2003)
Fighting For Animals (1996)
Alice and Other Friends (1996)
Spiritpower (1997)
How To Publish Your Own Book (1999)
How To Relax and Overcome Stress (1999)
Animal Rights – Human Wrongs (1999)
Superbody (1999)
Complete Guide to Life (2000)
Strange But True (2000)
Daily Inspirations (2000)
Stomach Problems: Relief At Last (2001)
How To Overcome Guilt (2001)
How To Live Longer (2001)
Sex (2001)
We Love Cats (2002)
England Our England (2002)
Rogue Nation (2003)
People Push Bottles Up Peaceniks (2003)
The Cats' Own Annual (2003)
Confronting The Global Bully (2004)
Saving England (2004)
Why Everything Is Going To Get Worse Before It Gets Better (2004)
The Secret Lives of Cats (2004)
The Cat Basket (2005)
The Truth They Won't Tell You (And Don't Want You To Know) About The
EU (2005)
Living in a Fascist Country (2006)
How To Protect & Preserve Your Freedom, Identity & Privacy (2006)
The Cataholic's Handbook (2006)
Animal Experiments: Simple Truths (2006)
Coleman's Laws (2006)
Secrets of Paris (2007)
Cat Fables (2007)
Too Sexy To Print (2007)
Oil Apocalypse (2007)
Gordon is a Moron (2007)
The OFPIS File (2008)
Cat Tales (2008)
What Happens Next? (2009)
Moneypower (2009)
Bloodless Revolution (2009)

Catoons From Catland (2009)
101 Things I Have Learned (2010)

novels
The Village Cricket Tour (1990)
The Bilbury Chronicles (1992)
Bilbury Grange (1993)
Mrs Caldicot's Cabbage War (1993)
Bilbury Revels (1994)
Deadline (1994)
The Man Who Inherited a Golf Course (1995)
Bilbury Pie (1995)
Bilbury Country (1996)
Second Innings (1999)
Around the Wicket (2000)
It's Never Too Late (2001)
Paris In My Springtime (2002)
Mrs Caldicot's Knickerbocker Glory (2003)
Too Many Clubs And Not Enough Balls (2005)
Tunnel (1980, 2005)
Mr Henry Mulligan (2007)
Bilbury Village (2008)
Bilbury Pudding (2009)

as Edward Vernon
Practice Makes Perfect (1977)
Practise What You Preach (1978)
Getting Into Practice (1979)
Aphrodisiacs – An Owner's Manual (1983)

with Alice
Alice's Diary (1989)
Alice's Adventures (1992)

with Donna Antoinette Coleman
How To Conquer Health Problems Between Ages 50 & 120 (2003)
Health Secrets Doctors Share With Their Families (2005)
Animal Miscellany (2008)

The 100 Greatest Englishmen and Englishwomen

Incisive biographies of the one hundred most influential English men and women of all time; individuals who made the most significant contribution to life in England and who changed the world, making it a better, wiser place

Vernon Coleman

Published by Blue Books, Publishing House, Trinity Place, Barnstaple, Devon EX32 9HG, England.

ISBN: 978–1–899726–18-9

A catalogue record for this book is available from the British Library.

Printed by CPI Antony Rowe

Dedication

To Donna Antoinette
Always in my heart
Always on my mind

Contents List

Introduction

Historians around the world agree that England has produced far more great men and women than any other country in the world. No other country comes close. When it comes to producing men and women of genius, England is, and always has been, the greatest country in the world. (It is, please note, England and not Britain which gave the world the greatest number of geniuses. Shakespeare, Newton, Dickens, Churchill, Darwin, Hooke, Bacon *et al* were all born in England. They were English first and British second. The Industrial Revolution was born in England, not Britain.)

I decided to write this book in order to inspire people to be proud of their English heritage. It has been politically correct for some time now to attack England, to sneer at her achievements, her culture and her history, and to oppress her people. The establishment and the media, regard it as wonderful for individuals to celebrate their Scottish, Welsh or Irish heritage. But to celebrate your English roots? Well, that's racist isn't it? If the politically correct critics find it impossible to avoid some modest praise then they make sure that it is Britain, and not England, that they praise.

I decided at the outset that my criteria for inclusion in this book would be strict and simple: to be included in *The 100 Greatest Englishmen and Englishwomen* individuals had to be born in England. This is, I realise, a much tougher criterion than is usually accepted. (It is, these days, perfectly possible to represent England at sport without being born in the country). This rule meant that I had to exclude many people I'd have liked to consider. For example, neither of those 'typical' Englishmen, the actors who first gave flesh to Sherlock Holmes and Dr Watson, was born in England. Philip St John Basil Rathbone, was brought up in England but born in Johannesburg while Nigel Bruce, probably the most English of all

Englishmen, was born in Mexico because his parents happened to be on holiday there when his mother went into labour. And, in addition to having affected England in their own time, their achievements had to have made the world better for generations after them, to have affected the whole world and to be still relevant today. And so although gardeners Lancelot 'Capability' Brown and Gertrude Jekyll had a big influence on the English landscape their influence on the rest of the world was not so great.

They should, moreover, have been individuals who made a significant and continuing contribution throughout their lives (rather than a single, albeit spectacular, achievement) and been people who initiated change rather than participated in the process of change. At one end of the spectrum, Thomas a Becket may be a saint but his role was incidental rather than constructive. He did not change the lives of ordinary people either in his life or after it, either in England or around the world. His arguments with Henry VIII were significant at the time, but they produced nothing of consequence and his death, although hugely tragic, was an embarrassment to the King rather than a history-changing event. Thomas Linacre, scholar and physician, taught St. Thomas More and was physician to Henry VII and Henry VIII but his greatest claim to fame is that he introduced the first rules ensuring that doctors should be licensed. It was Linacre who stopped clergymen and barbers practising medicine and claiming to be doctors. But there was an inevitability about this and no flash of genius involved. The Earl of Sandwich invented the sandwich (he had been gambling all night and was peckish so ordered a piece of meat to be placed between two slices of bread so that he didn't have to leave the gaming table) and thus in one brief moment, which combined hunger and passion, created the world's fast food industry. And then, at some very different point on the spectrum, there lies Jerome K. Jerome. Jerome wrote *Three Men in a Boat*, the funniest book in the English language, and his style defines English humour more effectively than any other writer (even P.G.Wodehouse, whose extraordinary talent was too individual to be definitive of Englishness but who is on my list for the quality and uniqueness of his vast oeuvre). But the rest of Jerome's work is disappointing and even pedestrian in comparison to *Three Men in a Boat* and even though that one book created a genre it seems invidious to include an author for just one book when there is no room for prolific and important greats such as Henry Fielding, Aldous Huxley, Evelyn Waugh and Arnold Bennett. Anthony Trollope, the English author who invented the idea of writing a series of novels following the adventures and lives of the same characters came close to my list. Trollope worked for the Post Office (and invented the pillar-box) and in addition to his daily work wrote for three hours every day. He even had a special desk made to clip onto his saddle so that he could write as he wandered around the countryside inspecting rural post offices. But his work, although entertaining, did not have the global appeal of Wodehouse or the social influence of Dickens.

If having a disease named after you merited a place on this list then my 100 would be filled with doctors. There are many English physicians after whom diseases are named. My list would have included Thomas Addison, Richard Bright, Thomas Hodgkin and James Parkinson for example. But I looked for doctors whose works affected the world in a much greater way and found medical men such as Lister, Snow and Linacre: all of whom had a massive impact during their own lives and continue to have a massive impact today.

I decided that the people on my list should be individuals who exhibited the English virtues of strength and determination and who loved their country. Indeed, many of them loved England so much that they risked their lives for her, and for their fellow countrymen. I have tried throughout to look at individuals through the mores and standards of their time. Today, patriotism is unfashionable among the storm-troopers of the politically correct; the apologists for the European Union (EU) who regard any hint of English nationalism as dangerously backward-looking. It wasn't always so.

I've avoided the temptation to include masses of kings and queens. If you are a royal, or born rich and powerful, you have to do more to prove your worth than if you start out impoverished and poorly educated. It's pretty easy for a king to change things. All he has to do is pass a law or start a war. Elizabeth II doesn't make this list because although she has reigned for a long time she has done and said nothing to stop the nation being swallowed up by the fascist bureaucrats of the European Union. She could have done a good deal more and I suspect that the two Queens who do make my list, Elizabeth I and Victoria, would have done.

A remarkable number of English people showed astonishing amounts of courage and persistence. What country would not be proud to have such men as Defoe, Cobbett, Paine, Tyler, Wycliff and Lilburn as its own?

I was initially astonished at the number of people in my list who spent at least part of their lives in prison. The explanation, of course, is that many great men and women are intrinsically rebellious and, therefore, especially likely to get into trouble with the authorities. And, after all, no one ever did great things by agreeing with the establishment; no one ever changed things for the better without having original ideas. And original ideas are always an anathema to the establishment.

Some who played a major part in world events do not appear here because of their lack of loyalty to England. For example, I considered putting Annie Besant on my list.

It was an Englishwoman, Queen Victoria, who created the Empire. And it was an Englishwoman, Annie Besant, who helped to give impetus to the move to give constituent countries of the Empire, strengthened and organised by their association with England, their independence.

Annie Wood was born in Clapham, London in 1847 and, by the time she was 30, had married Frank Besant and become a well-known writer and an important speaker for the National Secular Society. In 1877, she and her husband were prosecuted for publishing a book about birth control by Charles Knowlton. The scandal made the couple famous. Anne then joined the Fabian Society and the Social Democratic Federation. She helped organise the Bloody Sunday riot and the London matchgirls strike of 1888. In 1890 she became interested in theosophy and rather lost interest in left wing politics. In 1908, she became President of the Theosophical Society and steered the society away from Buddhism and towards Hinduism. None of this would have given Annie Besant a place in my top 100. It was what happened next that changed the world.

Besant's interest in Hinduism took her to India, where she became involved in local politics and joined the India National Congress. At the time this was little more than a debating society which met annually to consider political issues. In 1914, she formed the Home Rule League to campaign for dominion status within the Empire.

She deliberately chose to do this just as England entered the First World War because she believed that England would be vulnerable and susceptible to pressure. It was hardly the action of a patriot. In 1917, while the war still raged, she was arrested and interned at a hill station. As a show of defiance she flew a green and red flag in the garden. Her arrest provided a focal point for those who wanted long-term independence for India, and the India National Congress and the Muslim League threatened protests if she were not set free. One of the individuals campaigning for Besant's release was a 48-year-old lawyer called Mohandas Gandhi, who had, three years earlier, returned from leading Asians in a peaceful struggle against racism in South Africa.

Back in London the Government was forced to make significant concessions. England had given India a political structure, law, democracy and freedom, a bureaucracy (and cricket). But the cuckoo was ready to leave the nest and it officially announced, for the first time, that the ultimate aim of English rule was self-government for India. England started to make the necessary moves. Besant was released and that same year she was elected President of the India National Congress.

After the end of the First World War she continued to campaign for independence for India until her death in 1933. It is no exaggeration to say that Annie Besant was the mother of modern India. And it was Annie Besant, an Englishwoman, who started the pattern of countries within the Empire seeking their independence. Her impact on England, on India, on other countries of the Empire and on the world was considerable.

But she certainly showed no signs of loving her country and, it could be argued, that a less generous nation might have had her shot for treason.

Other well-known names didn't make my list because fame alone isn't a measure of influence or significance. I didn't include Mary Woolstoncraft or the Pankhurst women (there were three of them, Emily, Sylvia and Christabel) because the hard groundwork in the battle for women's liberation had been started much earlier by people like Daniel Defoe and John Locke and, especially, by the determination, courage and work of Aphra Behn. I considered Elizabeth Garrett Anderson for my list. Anderson was the first woman licensed as a physician in England in 1865. Despite being denied admission into a number of medical schools, she was not deterred. She soon discovered that the Society of Apothecaries did not forbid her from taking her examinations. Shortly after she began practising, Elizabeth founded a dispensary for women in London. Not only was Elizabeth England's first female doctor but she was also England's first female mayor. She was elected Mayor of Aldeburgh in Suffolk in 1908. She, far more than the publicity-seeking Pankhursts and the rather worthy Mary Wollstoncraft, helped prove that women deserved the rights they so rightly craved. She doesn't appear on the list because other women elsewhere in the world had already broken down these particular barriers and so she was not leading the way. (Incidentally, Elizabeth Blackwell, the first woman doctor in America, was born in Bristol.)

Sometimes I considered that an individual's great contribution had been cancelled out by some less praiseworthy action or incident in their lives. So, for example, I considered Jeffery Amherst for my list. In 1760, he directed the campaign that captured Quebec and Montreal and secured Canada for England. However, his tenure as commander in chief of the army was rather marred by the fact that he managed to lose a war with rebellious American colonialists. Gaining Canada put a feather in his cap. Losing America took it out again.

Despite the fact that I had strict criteria when choosing my 100 names, my problem was not finding 100 great Englishmen and Englishwomen, but in choosing 100 from the many names available. When considering explorers and adventurers I tried to seek out individuals who had made their mark by influencing the world in some way. If I had considered simply heroic exploits then Shackleton and Scott, the arctic explorers would have been high on my list. As, indeed, would Sir John Hunt the leader of the first expedition to conquer Everest and Amy Johnson, the brilliant and charismatic, pioneering aviator who was the first woman to fly alone to Australia. She set numerous long distance flight records during the 1930's and flew in the Second World War as part of the Air Transport Auxiliary. She died serving her country.

The inclusion of some of the people in this book may surprise you. But, when you have read of their achievements, I think you will agree that they are worthy of inclusion. On my searches through numerous libraries I was often surprised to discover that people whom I had not thought of as English were indeed, born in England. For example, I admit that I was surprised to discover that the composer Frederick Delius was a Yorkshireman and that the composer of the Planet Suite, Gustav Holst, Gustavus Theodore von Holst (aka Gustav Holst) was born in Cheltenham Spa. The national anthem of the United States of America was written by John Stafford Smith, an Englishman. I wonder how many people will be as surprised as I was to discover that T. E. Lawrence (Lawrence of Arabia) was born in Tremadoc, Caenarvonshire, Wales and that David Lloyd George, the professional Welshman and former Prime Minister, was born in Manchester, Lancashire, England.

I sought individuals who changed the world but I have tried to find people whose contribution was chronic rather than acute – in other words people who made a series of contributions, rather than a single contribution. But occasionally, an invention, a discovery or a creation demands respect and inclusion. It is, of course, possible to argue that if X hadn't invented Y, then someone else, say Z, would have eventually invented it. Probably so. But it wasn't the someone else. It was X. And if X hadn't invented it when he did, but Z had invented it a decade or two later, then the history of the world would have been changed.

My basic rule that those who appear in my 100 had to be born in England meant that I had to exclude the Duke of Wellington (born in Ireland), George Orwell and Rudyard Kipling (both born in India) and Florence Nightingale (born in Italy). Raymond Chandler grew up in England but was born in the United States of America. Bob Hope, Cary Grant (born Archibald Leach), Elizabeth Taylor, Boris Karloff (originally William Pratt) and Alfred Hitchcock are just a few of the Hollywood names who are often thought of as American but who were, like Charlie Chaplin, born in England. Stephen Leacock, usually thought of as the only Canadian humorist, was born in Swanmore, Hampshire. And Peter Roget, who is often thought of as French but rightly appears in this book, was an English physician who was born in London and died in Worcestershire.

I was enormously disappointed that my self-imposed rules meant that I had to exclude Wing Commander Guy Gibson VC DSO DFC, one of the bravest Englishmen ever to have fought and died for his country. Gibson doesn't qualify for my list because, although his family moved to Cornwall when he was six, he was born in India.

England has had a great many military heroes (Leonard Cheshire and Douglas Bader to name but two of the more recent ones) but it is difficult to find one more archetypically English, or more truly heroic, than pipe-smoking, dog-loving Wing Commander Gibson. Gibson was the inspired and inspirational Royal Air Force leader who commanded the raid on the Moehne-Eder dams in Germany during the Second World War – the famous Dam Busters Raid. It was an impossible raid. In order to make sure that the famous bouncing bombs designed by Barnes Wallis hit their targets the pilots had to fly so low that on occasion their wheels touched the water and crew members would complain that they were getting soaked. When his plane had dropped its dam-busting cargo, Gibson continued to fly around the heavily defended dams, deliberately attracting German flak, so that the other planes under his command could drop their bombs with less risk of interference.

Time and time again Gibson exhibited levels of courage that bring a lump to the throat and which trigger an intense sense of patriotic pride and respect in the heart and mind of the reader. He, and the pilots who flew with him, flew heavy, relatively primitive bombers just a few feet off the ground. The mortality rate among RAF bomber crews during the war was horrendous. Most of these young crews measured their life expectation in weeks or months. Gibson led the bombers who took part in the most daring air raid ever conducted. It was brilliantly conceived and brilliantly executed and it raised the spirits of a besieged nation. Gibson became a hero. The authorities thought him too valuable a hero to be risked on any more raids. They promoted him, filled his chest with medals and turned him into a propaganda tool. He was sent on tour to America. But Gibson was unhappy. He fought to get back into an aircraft. And at the age of 25, he died in his plane towards the end of another successful bombing raid. His book *Enemy Coast Ahead* is surely the most realistic, and certainly the most modest, true story of wartime ever written and one of the most moving autobiographies ever published. English history is full of heroes and heroines, and Gibson would have made a fine 'known' soldier; standing alone to represent the many. No one on earth knows precisely how many Englishmen and Englishwomen have died for their country, and to protect the lives and freedom of people of other nations. But of all those who died in war it is difficult to think of anyone braver, more dignified, or more typical of the English virtues than Guy Gibson, the leader of the Dam Busters raid. How awful it is that the nation he and so many others died to save has been betrayed into EU slavery.

There are numerous surprises in this book. And evidence too that the English were responsible for inventing many things often credited to others (usually the Americans). The electric lamp, the internal combustion engine, the cinema, the steam engine, the car, anaesthetics, the factory and the production line, the first manned flight, champagne, photography, the guillotine, the first railway, the electric telegraph – all these are usually credited elsewhere but were, in truth, and as I show in this book, the inventions of Englishmen. Adam Smith's economic theories were first propagated by William Petty a whole century earlier. Englishmen gave the world the first police force and the first postal service. Countless sailors around the world have good reason to be grateful to Samuel Plimsoll, who helped overcome resistance to the Merchant Shipping Act which brought in such reforms as a loading limit for cargo ships. A Plimsoll line was marked on the hull of every cargo ship, showing the maximum depth to which the ship could be safely loaded. This practice, started in England, spread around the world. Francis Crick, an Englishman, was co-discoverer of the double helix structure of deoxyribonucleic acid (DNA), the basic building block of all living cells. And it was, I must not forget, an Englishman, Tim Berners-Lee, who invented the World Wide Web.

(I'm still not convinced that the Internet is a 'good thing', which has benefited mankind, and so the undoubtedly brilliant Mr Berners-Lee does not appear on my list. So far the Internet seems to me to be little more than a cesspool of bigotry, libel and pornography; a market place for thieves, tricksters, failures and exhibitionists; a noticeboard for those driven by hatred and envy and a dark world populated by the half-witted, the ineffectual and by people who believe that all copyright is theft but who will happily sell their unwanted books for a penny each and make a few pence by overcharging for the postage and packing. The Web has killed whole industries and contributed massively to unemployment, poverty, misery, abuse and theft but, unlike the Industrial Revolution, has done nothing whatsoever to improve the quality of our lives by taking over backbreaking physical labour or mind-numbingly repetitive tasks. Show me someone who has benefited from the World Wide Web and I will show you 1,000 whose lives have been considerably diminished. Propaganda means that it is almost impossible to obtain accurate, reliable information from the Internet unless you are already an expert in the subject you are researching and I firmly believe that the world would be a better, happier and richer place if the Internet had never been invented and the computer confined to doing sums. Maybe I'll be proved wrong but I don't feel ashamed of my caution. After all, the Chinese are still trying to draw conclusions about the implications of the French Revolution.)

The English were the first to invent the free press and modern democratic government. The English invented the jet engine, hovercraft, the steam engine, railways, the telegraph, the lawn mower, nuclear physics, postboxes, buses, satellites, submarines, knitting machines, the flushing toilet, the slide rule, the syringe, matches, the seed drill, the tuning fork, the diving bell, the jigsaw puzzle, carbonated water and the universal joint, the pencil eraser, the fire extinguisher, the electromagnet, the dynamo, the computer and computer software, plastic, traffic lights, the light bulb, the steam turbine, the vacuum cleaner, the crossword puzzle, the mass spectrometer, the telephone, polythene and cats' eyes in the middle of the road. It was Englishmen who discovered the circulation of the blood, the existence of red blood cells, binary stars, the laws of gravity and motion, orbiting comets, hydrogen, vaccination, atomic theory, chemical electrolysis, the law of conservation of energy, diamagnetism, planet Neptune, absolute zero temperature, the theory of evolution by natural selection, the existence of electrons and neutrons, hormones, concrete, sewing machines, Tarmac and radar. If you are beginning to think that doesn't leave much for the citizens of any other nationality to invent, you're absolutely right. Over the last 250 years English scientists and engineers have been responsible for around four out of every five major inventions, discoveries and new technologies.

My aim in writing this book has been a simple one: to enable readers to learn the basic details about the most important men and women in English history and how and why their contributions deserve to be remembered. Some of the people in this book are far less well-known than they ought to be, thanks to the prejudices and bigotry of so many academics, historians and commentators. I hope that even ardent historians will find surprises here and that when you've finished reading about my 100 heroes you will know, and understand, a great deal more about England, English history and the people who made England great. These are men and women who, in one way or another, honoured themselves and their country and made the world a better place for the rest of us. These men and women were unique and irreplaceable. They all made gigantic contributions to life on earth. These men and women were all giants. They were giants of their time and they are giants of our time. We should be grateful for their lives, celebrate their work and be proud that they were English.

Vernon Coleman

P.S. My wife, Donna Antoinette, helped enormously in the preparation of this book. She helped me with the vast and seemingly unendingly difficult business of selecting the entries, she helped considerably with the research and collation of information and she helped prepare some of the profiles. The project turned out to take far more time and energy than either of us had suspected when I began, and without her help I would have wilted long before the book was finished. When writing about people who lived several hundred years ago it is often difficult to find the truth without a good deal of detective work. Too much of history is seen through the eyes of historians whose views are coloured by prejudices and modern expectations. There is often confusion about dates and places (with the birth dates for some figures being particularly difficult to find accurately) but Donna Antoinette and I have done our best to ensure that everything in the book is correct. Naturally, any errors which might have crept in are all my own work and I take full responsibility for them. But a sweeping bow or dainty curtsey (as appropriate) and a hearty round of applause for Donna Antoinette, please.

P.P.S. To make it easier to find the people in the book I have printed them in alphabetical order rather than according to their dates of birth.

P.P.P.S. As a starting point for discussion and argument I have ranked my Top 100 in a section at the back of this book. It is, of course, my ranking. There are no rules which make one individual more heroic or more special than another, or which make the contribution of one person more substantial than that of someone from a different age. But lists of this kind are, undeniably, enormous fun. And, as far as I know, there are not quite yet any EU rules which insist that history books and biographies cannot be fun to read.

Alfred the Great (849-899)

Born in Wantage in Berkshire, Alfred was the fifth and youngest son of King Aethelwulf. At the age of four he was taken to Rome to be confirmed by Pope Leo IV. He succeeded his brother as King in 871, when he was 22 years old. It wasn't a good time to take charge. The Viking invaders had landed in the north and the east of England and Wessex was under constant attack. The invasion and the threatened conquest continued for several years and Alfred was the only leader to refuse to submit to the invaders. Then, in 878 a Danish army invaded Wessex. Alfred and his army were sent into hiding in the Somerset marshes, at Athelney, before thrashing the invaders at the battle of Edington in Wiltshire. Alfred had planned his comeback battle while in hiding and it was while he was in Somerset, plotting his return, that the famous story about the burnt cakes began.

While fleeing the Vikings, Alfred was given shelter by a peasant woman. She had no idea who he was and asked him to watch some cakes which she was cooking on the fire. But Alfred was busy thinking about how to fight the Vikings and had too much on his mind to concentrate on the cakes. He accidentally let them burn and was told off by the woman when she returned home to find cinders instead of cakes. When she eventually realised the identity of her visitor the woman was mortified and apologised profusely. But Alfred, being a gentleman as well as a king, insisted that he was the one in the wrong and that he was the only one who needed to apologise. There is also a story that Alfred disguised himself as a minstrel in order to get into the camp of the Vikings and to discover their plans.

In the peace treaty that followed the leader of the Danes agreed to be baptised and to withdraw his army from Wessex while Alfred, in turn, recognised the Danes as the rulers of East Anglia and a good deal of Mercia.

But the battles continued.

Alfred repelled another invasion attempt in 885 and in the following year he captured London – which even then was a rich and important city. In an attempt to stop the invasions he built a ring of fortified strongholds around his kingdom, formed a proper army and created a fleet (the first English navy).

Alfred's military strategy worked. By the end of his reign he had created a strong nation. He had also begun a campaign to conquer all the other English kingdoms that were not occupied by the Vikings and he had declared himself the King of all England. His successors in Wessex re-conquered the remaining territories held by the Vikings.

(Alfred's best-known predecessor, Offa, whose birthdate is uncertain but who died in 796, had declared himself first King of Mercia and then King of the English. He had built a massive earthwork to mark the boundary between his kingdom and Wales. The boundary 'fence' was 120 miles long and 25 feet high. Shortly before his death Offa, inspired by the prospect of a powerful position within an early European Union, had signed some sort of early commercial treaty with Charlemagne of France and had allowed the Pope to take more control over the church in England. But Offa's hold on the English nation, which had been strengthened by his marrying off his daughters to the rulers of Wessex and Northumbria, was tenuous and fragile and there is no record that Offa cared overmuch for England or its people. He seems to have been driven by a lust for power rather than a vision of a strong and united England.)

Alfred promoted education and learning in general, inspired the production of the *Anglo-Saxon Chronicle* (a collection of annals chronicling the history of the Anglo-Saxons) and ensured that manuscript copies of the *Chronicle* were made and distributed throughout England. He encouraged all the arts and created an excellent and fair legal system. Alfred himself was an educated man and translated numerous books from Latin into Anglo Saxon.

Alfred was a humble, pious, honourable man and a great soldier. He was England's first real King and, without a doubt, the greatest. If any one man can be credited with creating the nation of England, it must be Alfred.

Sir Richard Arkwright (1732-1792)

Though it would be much later before it hit the rest of the world, the Industrial Revolution was in full swing in England in the second half of the 18th century. One of the industries most deeply affected by the Revolution was the manufacture of cotton. Several Englishmen invented ways to improve the spinning and weaving of cotton but of these one stands out above the rest: Richard Arkwright.

Arkwright was born in Preston in Lancashire, which had become the centre of the English cotton industry. He was the youngest of 13 children. His parents were so poor that they could not afford to send him to school. Instead they arranged for him to be taught to read and write by his cousin, Ellen. He became apprenticed to a barber in Kirkham and in 1750, he set up a shop as a barber in Bolton. In addition to cutting hair he also became a wigmaker and a dealer in hair and invented a secret process for dyeing hair which dramatically increased his profits. The profits from the waterproof dye he invented for wigs gave him the money to start his first factory.

In 1767, he moved back to Preston where he patented the famous spinning-frame. It was the very first machine in the world which could produce cotton-thread of sufficient strength to be used in the manufacture of cloth. His early mechanically-powered, cotton-spinning machines were driven first by water and later by steam.

In the same year he was forced out of Preston by opposition to his machine. He went to Nottingham and set up his first mill, driven by horses. He patented the water-frame in 1769. In 1771, he went into partnership with Jedidiah Strutt (a wealthy hosiery manufacturer and the improver of the stocking-frame) and set up a larger factory at Cromford Mill in Derbyshire. He continued to take out fresh patents for improvements to his equipment and spent £12,000 perfecting his machine.

In his new factory in Derbyshire, Arkwright faced two main problems.

First, employees feared that the machines would destroy their chances of employment, and in 1779 an angry mob broke into the factory and destroyed the equipment which they believed would affect their ability to earn a living. The destruction was carried out under the eyes of a military and police presence which failed to stop the invasion. But, despite the problems, Arkwright persisted and in the end his machines increased production so much that the factory grew and so did the number of people he employed.

The second problem Arkwright faced was that his commercial success inspired rival manufacturers to steal his patent. In 1781, he took out prosecutions against nine different manufacturers to try to protect his own business. But the outcome was disastrous. Complaints were made and in 1785 his patents were cruelly cancelled so that anyone could use his invention. At that time 30,000 people were employed in factories which used his patents.

But, before that, the firm he had built had expanded dramatically. He had opened a mill at Chorley (which subsequently became one of the most industrialised towns of the Industrial Revolution) and by 1774 he employed 600 workers. At a time when the average businessman was a blacksmith with a boy to operate the bellows that was a lot of employees. Arkwright was invited to start a business in Scotland, and he duly established the cotton industry there too. He also made a good deal of money from licensing his intellectual rights.

In 1787, Richard Arkwright was knighted and became High-Sheriff of Derbyshire and three years later, still an innovator, he introduced the steam engine into his factory in Nottingham. He built factories in Bath, Matlock, Manchester and elsewhere. He died, a rich man, in 1792 at the castle he had built overlooking his Cromford mills, though the castle was only completed after his death. He was one of the richest men in England.

Arkwright is usually remembered for having combined machinery (specifically his spinning frame – later renamed the water frame), semi-skilled labour and cotton and for being a leading figure in the Industrial Revolution. But his inventive genius and his organisational skills made him even more than all that; he was also the creator of the modern factory. More than a century before Henry Ford used factories to build cars, Arkwright, in many ways the spiritual father of the Industrial Revolution, had, for better or worse, invented mass production.

Charles Babbage (1791-1871)

Charles Babbage, an employee of the Royal Mint and a Professor of Mathematics at Cambridge University, is the man who invented the computer. Even the Americans (not good losers in the 'we were first' stakes) acknowledge that Charles Babbage was the first person to build a programmable calculating machine – a machine which had a separate programme of instructions which could be stored in a memory and used at will.

Babbage, born in London, the son of a banker, was an enthusiastic researcher and inventor. He once had himself lowered into Mount Vesuvius to take a closer look at what was going on and he had himself baked in an oven at 265 degrees Fahrenheit for five minutes. (He said there was no great discomfort). He invented coloured spotlights for use in theatres though, sadly, they were judged a fire hazard and never used. He invented the cow catcher too.

Babbage's first two computers were called the Difference Engine (invented in 1823) and the steam powered Analytical Engine (1834). The machines were designed to be built with brass gears rather than silicon chips. Babbage's first programmer was Lady Ada Lovelace, the daughter of Lord Byron.

The Difference Engine was used to calculate mathematical tables but, sadly, Babbage never managed to build his improved computer, the Analytical Engine. The problem was that Babbage had got ahead of mechanical engineering skills: no one could build the parts needed to the necessary level of precision. However, in 1991 the Science Museum in London used Babbage's plans to build the first Analytical Engine. It worked just as Babbage had predicted – perfectly. The world's first really effective, electronic computer was not built until 1946 – over a century after Babbage invented it.

Babbage was inspired to design and build the world's first computer because he found inaccuracies in calculation tables for the movements of the moon and the planets. Realising that the inaccuracies were due to human error, he decided to try to make a machine that could make the calculations for him. His first device compiled and printed sheets of logarithms.

Babbage was a far more interesting character than the average modern computer 'nerd'. He stood for Parliament twice but failed to get a seat. He campaigned vociferously for Babbage's Act, designed to deal with the noise made by unruly neighbours. Unfortunately, Babbage's neighbours (against whom the Act was directed) responded by hiring fiddlers, drummers and stilt walkers to walk to and fro outside his window.

Since Babbage's death, English computer experts have continued to lead the world. Alan Turing, the English mathematician who worked on the principle of the digital computer, is widely regarded as the father of the modern computer. And the World Wide Web was invented by another Englishman, Tim Berners-Lee, who with his colleagues, created a communications protocol called HyperText Transfer Protocol (HTTP) and then released a text-based Web browser for public use in 1991.

Francis Bacon (1561-1626)

Bacon began life with great advantages. His father, Sir Nicholas Bacon, was Lord Keeper of the Great Seal, the chief law office of England. As Lord High Chancellor Sir Nicholas was a successor of Sir Thomas More. Francis Bacon's mother was also in a position to pull a good many strings. Her sister married Lord Burghley, Queen Elizabeth I's Prime Minister and Treasurer. So Francis Bacon's father was Lord High Chancellor and his uncle was Prime Minister. Not a bad start in life.

It was a very different upbringing to that of William Shakespeare, the contemporary with whom Bacon is so often linked.

At the age of 13 Bacon went to Trinity College, Cambridge. By the time he was 15 he was back in London, studying law. He was a thoughtful, self-confident, enormously ambitious boy who determined early on that he wanted to do great work that would be beneficial to the human race and that would ensure that he would always be remembered. Watching his father at work in the court he learned that intrigue was the key to worldly prosperity.

When he was still a teenager (probably between 16 and 18 years old) the well-educated Bacon travelled to the English Embassy in Paris where he worked as a junior secretary. Shortly after his arrival there his father died, leaving young Francis only a relatively modest bequest. This was, to be blunt, a disappointment to a young man with great ambitions.

Bacon's fundamental ambition was a very simple one. He was driven by the desire, the need, to know how to know, to teach others how to acquire knowledge and to use that knowledge 'to command nature'. He was passionate about this in the way that other men are passionate about golf, football or trainspotting. It was his single, real driving force. He wanted to be rich and powerful because he knew that without money and power he could not do the one thing on earth that he believed to be worth doing: investigate the world and show others how best to learn. His one huge weakness was that he neither would nor could contemplate the idea of a frugal independence. He was, and needed to be, a man of the world just as much as an alcoholic wants and needs alcohol. As a result Bacon could be, and often was, a flatterer, a hypocrite, a hand-wringing acolyte and a pitiful 'yes man'.

Put simply, Bacon realised that if he were to achieve his ambitions he would need money. And he knew that the only way to obtain enough of the stuff was to obtain an admission to the nation's 'affairs'. He felt that he could not, and would not, realise the great things he believed himself capable of, and qualified to reach, unless he became well-off and influential in a merely material way. Sadly, like a lot of men and women who believe that in order to do great things it is necessary first to become financially independent, he spent a good part of his life wasting his time and energy on obtaining money and power, and relatively little of it doing the things he really wanted to do.

'I may truly say,' he later admitted, rather sadly, 'that my soul hath been a stranger in the course of my pilgrimage.'

Bacon had hoped that his uncle, Lord Burghley, would open some doors for him. And the uncle came through. When Bacon was 23 years old, Burghley helped his nephew become a member of parliament. Francis Bacon was to remain a member of the House of Commons for over 30 years.

Throughout history lawyers have often dabbled in politics. The one thing the law and politics have in common, an absence of any great regard for justice and the truth, means the two professions fit easily, comfortably and profitably together. Lawyers have often been among the most ruthless and grasping politicians. Francis Bacon was an unashamed opportunist and could, on occasion, be as ruthless as the next lawyer. For example, he was good friends with the Earl of Essex (who had given him a valuable piece of land in payment for his support and advice) but, when Essex fell out of favour at court and instead found himself a defendant in the Court of the Star Chamber, Bacon played an active role in ensuring that Essex was found guilty; he readily admitted that the Queen's favour was more important to him than that of Essex. In the end Bacon played a major part in ensuring that Essex was executed for treason.

And although Bacon urged that the Government be tolerant in all matters of religion (arguing that the aggressive persecution of minorities was unstatesmanlike as well as inhuman) he remained, generally, careful not to upset too many people by voicing political views which were not popular with those in power. He argued that the best way to force one's views on those in authority was by appearing to agree with them, and avoiding any declared disagreement with them. 'Avoid repulse,' he said, 'never row against the stream.' He knew, and admitted, that 'the best way to get on in life is to accommodate oneself to the ways of great men'.

But, despite all this ruthless expediency, Bacon, who was above everything else a proud Englishman (one of the things he most often thought about was 'the greatness of his country'), made copious notes about what should be done to secure and increase England's greatness and how to make the forces of Elizabeth's great and growing empire work together without jealousy. He was always looking for ways to unite the aims and sympathies of the Crown, Parliament and the people.

He drew up schemes of inquiry, sources of help and cooperation (from within and without the country) and suggested endowing a university college specifically for inventors and thinkers. He could on occasion be almost recklessly brave in standing by his principles. For example, although he had well-placed relatives and friends and should have been a shoe-in for a lucrative position at court or in the Government, Bacon wrecked his chances of winning a prize appointment by bravely opposing a Parliamentary tax bill which Queen Elizabeth supported rather enthusiastically. Bacon was courageous in doing this because his extravagant lifestyle meant that he was constantly in debt and couldn't easily afford grand, independent gestures. (He was once arrested for debt.)

When Queen Elizabeth died in 1603, Bacon became an adviser to King James I. By now he had learned to be more circumspect in sharing his views. To begin with he continued to argue that the country should be tolerant in matters of religion. But when he saw that this was unpopular and dangerous he turned around and supported persecution. He never did much believe in democracy and at this time of his life he was clearly not well-endowed with moral fibre. The lawyer in him had taken over.

His cunning and lack of principles were well-rewarded. In 1606, at the age of 45, he had married the daughter of an alderman in the city of London who had brought with her a good dowry and in 1607 the now wealthy Bacon became solicitor general. In 1613 he became attorney general. And in 1618 he was appointed Lord Chancellor of England and was appointed a baron. In 1621 he became Viscount St Alban. Things were going well.

But then his life rather fell apart.

It was Bacon's own fault. His greed and need for money led to his downfall. Throughout his life he always spent more than he earned, and more than he had.

After his marriage he had built, decorated and furnished a huge mansion where he maintained a vast retinue of servants. Despite the generous dowry that had arrived with his wife it was more than Bacon could afford.

And it was money troubles which finished his dazzling career.

Constantly broke he had accepted 'gifts' from litigants who had appeared before him when he had sat as a judge. This was common at the time but even so it wasn't exactly legal. Like so many who rise to the heights, Bacon lost the ability to differentiate between right and wrong in his personal dealings. He did what many men in power have done: he convinced himself that he was doing the 'right' thing. He was underpaid and had no private means and yet he expected to be able to live lavishly. He was confident that he could defy temptation and indeed there is no proof (nor was there ever any suggestion) that he as a judge allowed himself to be influenced by the gifts he received. But (and the But is the size of Mount Everest and decorated with neon lights) he had laid himself wide open to suspicion, criticism and arrest. He was foolish, vain and, in a word he would have understood, 'unmanly'. He was, perhaps, an echo of his times and King James. He lacked character and spine.

His problem was made worse by the fact that although he was popular and efficient he had, in climbing up to the top, trodden on many corns. He had enemies galore and many of them held grudges. He had introduced reforms and had tried to bring order into the nation's management. Such actions are rarely popular.

The result was that when the charges of impropriety started, they quickly grew into a flood. Bacon was overwhelmed by it all. Shamed and ashamed he declined to stand trial and instead chose to confess. There was no evidence that his decisions had been affected by money; but there was plenty of evidence that he had taken money. (Ironically, his most violent critics and accusers were the individuals who had given him money and then lost their cases. They complained that they had paid bribes and got nothing for it.)

Unlike modern politicians who are caught doing something naughty Bacon was man enough to take his punishment. He was filled with shame and became ill. He was a broken man; mentally and physically destroyed. Humiliated. He held up his hands and confessed (though he constantly argued that none of the bribes had influenced his decisions). He admitted his guilt in writing and refused to submit a defence.

He was dismissed from the post of Lord Chancellor, fined £40,000, barred from holding public office and put into the Tower of London for life. Within two months he had fallen from the very top to the very bottom.

Even though the King eventually granted him a pardon (from both the fine and the imprisonment) Bacon's political career was over. Shortly before he died he described himself as the 'justest judge that was in England these fifty years' but he knew he had done wrong. He described the sentence as 'the justest censure in Parliament that was these two hundred years'.

However, a new career had begun some time earlier. And it is because of this other career that he is remembered today, and a worthy member of my chosen 100. Bacon was well-read (Machiavelli was one of his favourite authors) and although he was an ambitious and successful politician it is as a writer and philosopher that he is now remembered. He is, indeed, now widely regarded as the father of all modern philosophers.

Bacon had started writing long before his political career hit the buffers. After all, it was for the freedom to write books that he fought to survive political life and make money. His first major book was his collection of essays (entitled, appropriately, *Essays*) which first appeared in 1597. These essays are penetrating reflections on human nature and conduct; the work of an experienced observer. Bacon enlarged and improved his essays up until his death. The first edition contained 12 essays. The most complete edition contains 59 essays.

Next, in 1605, came his book *Advancement of Learning*, a popular encyclopaedia of thought and knowledge for which Bacon surveyed and assessed all areas of information and explained where he believed progress was most essential.

It is Bacon's writing on the philosophy of science that defines his greatness most vividly. His next major book after *Advancement of Learning* was the *Novum Organum* (the New Instrument,) which was published in 1620. Despite the fact that he was struggling to cope with the demands of the nation, and his world was about to fall apart around his ears, he edited and rewrote the book twelve times. After his shaming he put all his energy into writing. And although his disgrace must have been painful his enforced removal from public life was hugely advantageous. No more would the greatest thinker of his age waste his life on trivialities.

It was his book the *New Instrument* which truly changed the world.

Up until Bacon, scientists and other thinkers had relied upon the system of deductive logic espoused by Aristotle. But Bacon realised that we only gain new knowledge by observing the world, collecting facts and then using inductive reasoning to draw conclusions from our collected facts. Bacon believed that the scientist should act as an interpreter of nature and that knowledge can only be derived from experience and experiments. He believed that experiments had to be carefully planned and that the resulting evidence had to be carefully assessed. Only when the facts had been obtained, he believed, should conclusions be drawn.

His 'big idea' was that the systematic examination of the facts was the first thing to be done in any scientific investigation and that until this had been done, faithfully and impartially, with all the appliances and all the safeguards that experience and forethought could suggest, all generalisations, all anticipations from mere reasoning, had to be adjourned or postponed.

Bacon believed that if men followed this plan then knowledge valuable beyond that ever imagined could be obtained.

He was, of course, absolutely right.

Bacon spoke with clear authority and he persuaded future generations that the patient, intelligent, persevering cross examination of facts, and careful study and assessment of the results, was the only way to obtain worthwhile knowledge. He worked on this idea for 40 years and wrote about it many times.

This may all sound obvious to us now. But in the 17th century it was not at all obvious and it was not the way most men thought. Bacon believed that if men followed his plan, there were no bounds to what human thought could accomplish. Bacon was no great scientist. But, in his own words, he rang the bell which called scientists to order. He was the father of modern science and modern philosophy. His great contribution to science was to create the idea of empirical thought − the principle that we should build up our knowledge by using our senses to observe what happens around us (whether it is happening by accident or because of something − an experiment − we have devised). Ever since Bacon's time, all good scientists, in countries all around the world, have followed the English method as created and codified by Francis Bacon. He was, without any doubt, one of the very greatest philosophers of all time, well worthy of a seat alongside Aristotle.

For his last book (*The New Atlantis*) Bacon combined his own new scientific method with the setting of Thomas More's book *Utopia*. In this book Bacon argued that the prosperity and welfare of people depends upon scientific research.

Bacon was the first modern philosopher. He believed in God but his approach was entirely secular. He was rational and he was an empiricist. He had a sound basis in classical learning, a great literary style and an enormous interest in, and sympathy for, science and technology.

It is true that other men had recognised the importance of

experimentation and the potential value of science. But Bacon was the first writer to describe these thoughts effectively and influentially. When the Royal Society of London was founded in 1662, the founders named Francis Bacon as their inspiration. And although he was no scientist, Francis Bacon never avoided a chance to experiment.

It was an experiment which killed him.

In March 1626, he climbed out of his coach on a freezing cold day in Highgate and collected snow for an experiment on preserving food in cold storage. He bought a hen from an old woman, and had her kill it, and he then stuffed the dead hen with snow. Suspecting that meat might be as well-preserved in snow as in salt, he wanted to observe the effect of cold on the preservation of flesh. He was 65 years old and frail and he caught a chill. He was taken to a nearby house where he was put into a damp bed. The result was that a few days later he died of bronchitis. He did, however, live long enough to see that his experiment had worked.

His final words, in a letter he dictated to his absent host, were: 'I was likely to have had the fortune of Caius Plinius the elder, who lost his life by trying an experiment about the burning of the mountain Vesuvius. For I was also desirous to try an experiment or two, touching the conservation and induration of bodies. As for the experiment itself, it succeeded admirably.'

It was a fine epitaph for a true Renaissance man.

When he died Bacon left behind a will in which he left money to friends, retainers, the poor and to public institutions. In his will he made it clear that he hoped the money he left would help improve the service provided by those institutions. But Bacon's incompetence with money followed him beyond the grave. When his assets were realised he did not leave enough to pay off his debts. None of his bequests could be met.

Bacon was a scholar, essayist, historian, scientific author, lawyer, philosopher and politician. He reached great heights. But he couldn't manage his money.

There are many people who believe that Bacon wrote Shakespeare's plays. I don't. How on earth would he have found the time? Bacon was a great man, a genius, but there simply weren't enough hours in the day, days in the year or years in his life.

Moreover, unless Bacon had mastered an entirely different literary style to fit in with an adopted name there is no way that he could have written Shakespeare's plays. 'Bacon could no more have written the plays of Shakespeare than Shakespeare could have prophesied the triumphs of natural philosophy,' wrote R.W.Church, Dean of St Paul's, in his definitive biography of Bacon, published in 1884.

But, even without having written the plays, Bacon is well worth his place in England's most magnificent one hundred. He is, after all, generally accepted by philosophers and historians around the world as the father of modern science.

Roger Bacon (1214-1294)

Probably born in Somerset, and educated in Oxford and Paris, Roger Bacon was one of the most extraordinary men who ever lived. A Franciscan monk, he was an original thinker at a time when original thought was rare and dangerous. His reputation for knowledge and wisdom in many areas (including science, philosophy, medicine, magic and alchemy) resulted in him being given the nickname Doctor Mirabilis. He was a mathematician, physicist, chemist, physician, astronomer, geographer, comparative philologist and philosopher. He was a loyal servant of the church and prepared an encyclopaedia of knowledge for the Pope.

While other academics throughout Europe were still studying and dissecting the ancient, woefully outdated and inaccurate Greek texts about medicine, Roger Bacon was one of the first men to insist that chemicals could be used medicinally and that alchemy had a role to play in human pharmacology. He found himself battling the entire establishment. Galen had favoured herbal medicines and the medical establishment revered the works of Galen. The Church strongly objected to Bacon's theories because it seemed dangerously sacrilegious for a monk to suggest that the will of God could be influenced with the aid of a handful of chemicals. Herbs were tolerable, they came direct from God. But chemicals, which had to be refined and mixed, were definitely not acceptable. Bacon ensured his unpopularity by moaning that: 'Medical men don't know the drugs they use, nor their prices.'

Bacon did not confine himself to the study of drugs and their effect on human patients. He is credited with having designed the earliest versions of the magnifying glass, the telescope and the microscope. He is believed to have invented gunpowder and the first spectacles. He also prophesied powered flight, locomotives and underwater exploration with the aid of submersible machines. He performed a great many original scientific experiments. As a result, his work was rejected and he was censored and imprisoned. Roger Bacon was one of the first scientific martyrs of the Renaissance.

His views on the importance of mathematical proof and his early ideas about following method in experimentation are strikingly modern. The importance of his books on mathematics, logic and philosophy, widely ignored or suppressed during his lifetime, was recognised in later centuries.

Robert Baden-Powell (1857-1941)

Robert Stephenson Smyth Baden-Powell was a brave hero who walked straight from the pages of *Boys Own Paper*. He was the sort of soldier who made England great; the kind of man who would fight to the death without a murmur of protest. He was quintessentially English.

During the siege of Mafeking, which made his name, Baden-Powell sent out dry, laconic messages that could have only ever come from an Englishman. 'All well. Four hours bombardment. One dog killed.' was the extent of one of them.

Today, comedians and politicians sneer at England and English virtues and they laugh especially loudly at Baden-Powell's type of Englishman.

But between the two Great Wars, Baden-Powell was regarded as an Edwardian soldier-saint; a great hero to be admired and respected.

It was after the Second World War that wave after wave of anti-Englishness washed away traditional respect and replaced it with a contempt for everything that had once been regarded as magnificent.

Commentators and historians whose experience of warfare and

inconvenience is limited to queuing for tickets on the London Underground, snigger at Baden-Powell and dismiss him as a racist, a hypocrite, an incompetent military buffoon, a closet homosexual, a philistine, a reactionary, a fascist and an imperialist. (Odd, isn't it, that the politically correct should regard it as just and proper to accuse a man of being a 'closet homosexual', and not see the bigotry in the accusation.)

In the modern world no scornful epithets are too rancid to be used on Baden-Powell, and his appearance in this book, and on this list of great English heroes, will doubtless trigger much fluttering of hands and dabbing of feverish anti-English brows. Guardian reading pseudo-intellectuals will send their Filipino maids for the smelling salts. Baden-Powell was, after all, a man who never grew up politically; a man whose life was one long adventure; a man who believed that cricket was more than a game.

But not even the mincing armies of the politically correct, and the European Union's massed battalions of state-registered England bashers, can alter the facts: Robert Baden-Powell was a genuine military hero whose valour at Mafeking cannot be questioned.

Moreover, he created single-handedly a world-wide scouting movement with tens of millions of members and organisations established in over a hundred countries.

When Baden-Powell died in 1941 one obituary summed things up very well: 'No Chief, no Prince, no King, no Saint was ever mourned by so great a company of boys and girls, of men and women in every land. No other leader in the history of men gathered under one banner, in his own life-time, so great a multitude of followers of all ages, or all races, of all colours, of all creeds.'

Maybe it's simple jealousy that drives those who sneer loudest.

The siege of Mafeking (the town has since changed the spelling of its name to Mafikeng) took place in 1899-1900. A British military garrison, under the command of the then Colonel Robert Baden-Powell, held out against a vastly superior Boer force for 217 days until reinforcements could arrive. During the siege Baden-Powell sang and whistled music-hall ditties to keep up the spirits of his troops. His amateur theatricals and practical jokes kept his men alert and alive.

The defence of Mafeking was, and still is, one of the great heroic defences of all time. It is forgotten now but when Mafeking was finally relieved, the people of England sang and danced in the streets in celebration. Baden-Powell was a great hero.

His adventures took him around the world. He chased brigands in Afghanistan. He explored the interior of Brazil. He spied in Montenegro. Everything was adventure. He could have been a character devised by Rudyard Kipling, Alexandre Dumas, Fenimore Cooper, Robert Louis Stevenson or Conan Doyle.

And then the boy who had never really grown up created a boy's kingdom: the Boy Scouts. It was a movement complete with initiation rites, secret ceremonies and signs, curious litanies, totem poles and funny hats. It was an organisation which gave every boy the right, nay the responsibility, to carry a penknife with an attachment for removing the stones from horses' hooves. The scarf and toggle might not always be worn but the penknife could always be carried. It was a kingdom in which honour and loyalty were everything. The motto 'Be Prepared' (based on the BP initials) became a stirring challenge for millions of adolescents, though it's important to remember that Baden-Powell's scouting movement was all about fun as well as honour.

Christened Robert Stephenson, after one of his godfathers (the son of George Stephenson, the man who had built The Rocket, the first successful steam locomotive), Baden-Powell was appointed a General after Mafeking. He was just 43 and the youngest General in the British army.

But his next moment of greatness was something quite different: after the army, his love of woodcraft and nature led him to found the Boy Scout movement. The principles were simple, honest and always honourable. He preached service and kindness and his aims were well meant.

His critics claim that there were deep, dark motives behind the scouting movement but Baden-Powell was no Machiavellian genius. He was a simple man with simple tastes. And the Boy Scout movement is what it always seemed to be: an opportunity for boys to have fun and to enjoy adventures, even if most of them are make-believe.

When the Boy Scout Movement celebrated its 21st birthday (birthday, note, not anniversary) scouts from all over the world were invited to contribute one penny (or its equivalent in their currency) towards a gift to the Founder and Chief Scout, who was by then Lord Baden-Powell. And at a special 'coming of age' Jamboree that year, Baden-Powell was presented with a Rolls Royce motor car and a trailer caravan – bought with the pennies donated by enthusiastic scouts.

(Baden-Powell, when asked what present he wanted had said, with typical simplicity and modesty, that he would like a new pair of braces as his old ones were almost worn out. He was given the braces too.)

Few stories better illustrate the way Baden-Powell was regarded by millions.

The scouting movement was so popular that there was a problem: girls wanted to join. Baden-Powell feared that this would make the movement 'sissy' and so he and his sister, Agnes, dreamt up the Girl Guides. He defined the guides as 'jolly people who enjoy themselves...a happy sisterhood who do good turns to other people.' The Girl Guide movement was designed to promote home-making and mothercraft.

Baden-Powell died in Kenya, loafing and enjoying the sunshine. He had retired there in 1938 (though he'd offered to return home the following year if England needed him) and he died still a boy at heart. He didn't enter a second childhood; he had never grown up. How appropriate that he had founded the largest and most successful youth organisation in the history of the world.

Mrs Isabella Mary Beeton (1836-1865)

The name 'Mrs Beeton' has reached iconic status in England. Whenever I hear the name I think of a rotund, efficient, middle-aged woman, energetically trying out different recipes and educating the nation through her various books on cooking and running a household correctly.

In fact, Mrs Isabella Mary Beeton was a rather slender, fairly attractive woman who never really had a great interest in cookery and who was dead by the time she was 28. But her famous book, *Beeton's Book of Household Management* had an enormous impact and changed the way people did things in the home. That's why Mrs Beeton is included here.

Isabella Mary Beeton, was born in 1836 in Cheapside, London. Her parents were Benjamin and Elizabeth Mayson. Sadly, Isabella's father died four years later, while her mother was expecting her fourth child. To ease the domestic burden, Elizabeth sent her two eldest children to live with relatives for a while. Isabella was sent 350 miles away to live with her 79- year-old clergyman grandfather; a move that must have been very traumatic for a small child.

Less than three years after the death of Isabella's father, her mother married widower, Henry Dorling, who had four children of his own. Isabella returned to the new family home and the couple, who now had eight children between them, proved remarkably fertile. By the time Elizabeth was 47, they had a staggering total of 21 children. Isabella was the second eldest, her stepbrother, Henry, was the eldest by a year. Being the eldest female of so many siblings must have contributed enormously to Isabella's organisational and house management skills, and helping her mother to look after the increasing brood no doubt gave her a sense of responsibility from a young age.

Shortly after her mother's marriage to Henry Dorling, the seven-year-old Isabella moved with her newly expanded family to her stepfather's home in Epsom, Surrey. Henry Dorling was Clerk of Epsom Racecourse and leaseholder of the Grandstand at Epsom. To cope with the ever-growing family, some of the children were sent to live at Epsom Grandstand in the care of Isabella and her grandmother.

After having attended school in Islington, Isabella was, at the age of 15, sent to school in Heidelberg, Germany for two years. At Heidelberg, Isabella learnt to speak French and German very well and also became extremely proficient at the piano. In fact, her increasingly wealthy stepfather helped nurture his stepdaughter's musical talent by paying for private piano lessons.

After returning home Isabella married publisher, Samuel Orchart Beeton in 1856. Her new husband was the English publisher of the anti-slavery novel, *Uncle Tom's Cabin* by Harriet Beecher Stowe. Samuel used some of the money he had made from *Uncle Tom's Cabin* to launch magazines such as *The Englishwoman's Domestic Magazine* and *The Boy's Own Magazine* (both of which he founded, edited and published). Sadly, Isabella's family did not like her choice in husband.

Her stepfather did not think that Samuel Orchart was good enough for the stepdaughter whom he looked upon as his own. The bitter family feud was never resolved in their lifetimes.

After their honeymoon, the Beetons moved into their first home together, on the Woodridings Estate in Hatch End. It was in that house that Mrs Isabella Beeton wrote *Beeton's Book of Household Management*. As well as being packed with recipes, it was an essential guidebook on how to run a Victorian household. Less than a year after they got married, their first child Samuel Orchart was born, but died three months later. After a series of miscarriages, their second son also named Samuel Orchart was born in September 1859 but, sadly, he too died – he was just three-years-old when he died of scarlet fever on New Year's Eve.

In 1857, nine months after her marriage, Isabella began providing copy for one of her husband's publications, *The Englishwoman's Domestic Magazine*. She contributed regular articles on cooking and household management. In the same year, Isabella Beeton began work on the iconic book that was to immortalise her name and make her famous.

Despite having had a few pastry-making lessons from the local baker after she returned home from her school in Heidelberg, Isabella hardly knew anything about baking or cookery. She wrote to a friend to tell her about her idea of writing a cookery book and asked for ideas about how to embark on such a project. Isabella's friend wrote back advising her to compile the book using recipes taken from good cookbooks. And so Isabella did just that.

The book was published in monthly instalments and first appeared on the market towards the end of 1859. The instalments were published as a single volume in 1861 and the book was called *Beeton's Book of Household Management*. It was described as being 'Edited by Mrs Isabella Beeton'. The original cover of the book, never described Isabella as the author of the book, she was simply listed as the editor.

When writing the book, Isabella wisely adopted a rather matronly tone, not something you would expect from a young woman in her mid-twenties. The book sold 60,000 copies in its first year and was the first cookery book in the country to use colour-plates of some of the finished dishes. Although Mrs Beeton copied other people's recipes, she was the first to put the list of ingredients at the start of her recipes and she was the first to tell readers the time for which dishes should be cooked.

In 1862, the Beetons moved house into accommodation above Samuel's offices in the Strand. They lived there for two years and, in that time, Isabella gave birth to her third baby in December 1863. This time the baby, another boy, lived to celebrate his 83rd birthday.

In the spring of 1864, the Beetons moved from their home above the offices in the Strand to Mount Pleasant, a farmhouse in Greenhithe.

Tragically, less than a year later, the now famous Mrs Beeton was dead. She died on 6 February 1865, within a week after giving birth to her fourth child. The Dorlings, who by now despised Samuel, blamed Isabella's premature death at the age of 28 on her husband, believing that he made her work too hard.

Shortly after his wife died, Samuel Beeton, who was never very competent at handling his financial affairs, found himself in deep financial trouble. His most successful publication was his late wife's book so to him it made sense to let the world believe that the author of *Beeton's Book of Household Management* was still alive. About a year after the death of Mrs Beeton, rival publishers bought the copyrights to Beeton's publications and, over the years, many new titles appeared bearing Mrs Beeton's name. These new titles mostly contained bits taken out of *Beeton's Book of Household Management* and re-packaged. Over the years, many revised editions of the book were produced and by 1906, *Beeton's Book of Household Management* was twice the size of the original.

Even now, a century and a half after her death, the name Mrs Beeton is still well known. The impact her book had on households everywhere has been phenomenal. Mrs Beeton's book, with its delicious recipes and invaluable domestic advice has been a great source of guidance and reassurance to millions of women over the years. Mrs Beeton did much throughout her short life to help improve the domestic lives of people all over England (and the rest of the world) with her invaluable advice. The woman who wrote one famous book (and who copied most of it from other people's books) inspired a global industry of cookery books, self-help books and advice books.

In 1877, 12 years after his wife's death, Samuel Beeton, also died. Both Mr and Mrs Beeton are buried at Norwood Cemetery in South London.

Aphra Behn (1640-1689)

Born in Wye, near Canterbury in Kent, Aphra Behn is probably one of the least well-known people in this book. But she deserves her place here just as much as anyone else. She was a novelist, playwright, poet, traveller, adventurer and spy. She was the first woman to earn her living as an author and to do so she had to fight huge prejudices and overcome traditional assumptions about the role of women in society. By doing what she wanted to do, regardless of the expectations of those around her, she did far more for the rights of women than many better known activists who operated centuries later.

Born Aphra Amis, her father, John Amis, was a relative of Francis, Lord Willoughby of Parham, the administrator of several British colonies in the West Indies and South America. While Aphra was still very young, Mr Amis set off with his family to Surinam to take up a post he had been promised there. Unfortunately, he didn't reach his destination alive but died during the long sea journey.

His widow and children, including Aphra, stayed in Surinam for a few years. While still a young girl Aphra met an enslaved negro prince called Oroonoko who would, in due course, be the subject of her most successful novel. The family returned to London in 1663, shortly after the Restoration of the Monarchy. Charles II was now on the throne and London society was thriving. In England, the young Miss Amis met and married a Dutch merchant called Behn who died shortly afterwards, leaving the unfortunate Mrs Behn quite penniless. He died in 1665, probably of the Great Plague.

Having now been left in dire straits by the deaths of two men, the still young Mrs Behn, a penniless widow, decided to look after herself. She met Sir Thomas Killigrew who introduced her to the second Duke of Buckingham and the young prince who would become King James II of England. There is no precise record of the nature of her relationship with these powerful men, or how she met them, but it is known that at the suggestion of Killigrew she agreed to go to Antwerp as a spy. She travelled with her brother, a maid and Sir Antony Desmarches, who was a secret agent of considerable experience. The aim was that she would mix in smart society and send back naval and political information. Her code name was Astrea – which she later used as a pen name when she wrote poetry. However, the Government was very ungrateful to their first female spy and the bureaucrats got so far behind in paying her salary that she had to pawn a ring to survive. She appealed for her money to be sent, but it was 1666 and London was in chaos. She was sent just fifty pounds, which only covered half her accumulated debts at the inn where she was lodging. Broke once again, she returned home to England where she was immediately put into prison by her unsympathetic creditors. Once she was out, Killigrew persuaded her to go Venice on another spying mission. It was her last.

She abandoned the profession of spy at the age of 30, and decided to write a play. Although Charles II allowed women to act (and took one actress, Nell Gwyn, as a mistress) women simply didn't write plays, or indeed anything else, for money. They might write to entertain themselves. But not as 'professionals'. Mrs Behn, more in need of money than social approval, just ignored the rules.

Her first play, a comedy, was written in 1670, and was a huge success. It was considered rather coarse but then most of the plays on the stage at that time were rather raunchy. *The Forc'd Marriage* went down extremely well. King Charles II had abolished all the rules restricting what dramatists could and could not say and as a result plays were often outrageous, rude or satirical, and sometimes all three. Behn's plays certainly were. One of her famous lines was: 'One hour of right-down love, is worth an age of living dully on.' That was pretty near the knuckle for the late 17th century.

Aphra Behn, playwright, was on her way and quickly became one of the most popular writers of Restoration Drama. Six months after *The Forc'd Marriage* had opened she followed it with *The Amorous Prince*.

Behn took advantage of the freedom she had to attack all the social conventions that prevented women living as equals to men. Although her plays were written three centuries ahead of the bra-burning days of the 20th century they contained messages which were just as powerful as any of those favoured by 20th century supporters of liberation for women. However, she had the good sense to make sure that her plays were also funny and entertaining. And so they were profitable.

Over the next decade or so she wrote a number of plays, all of which were comedies. The titles included *Sir Patient Fancy*, *The Feign'd Courtezans* and *The City Heiress*. After meeting and having an affair with John Hoyle, a lawyer, rogue and keen duellist, she wrote a play called *The Rover* which was another huge success. She also wrote poetry and a collection of these appeared in 1684. In 1685 she wrote a coronation ode for King James II. In 1688, fed up with the savagery she was experiencing from critics who disapproved of her plays, she started writing novels. *Oroonoko, the Royal Slave*, based on the slave she'd met in Surinam, appeared in a year when she published not one, not two but three novels. *Oroonoko* is a romantic, adventure story about a slave revolt led by an African prince. Aphra Behn was one of the first authors in the world to have the sensibility and courage to attack the slave trade. (William Wilberforce didn't get involved in the anti-slave trade campaign for another century.) She was also one of the world's first writers of fiction.

In 1689, Mrs Behn followed up this amazing industry with another novel entitled *The History of the Nun*, or *The Fair Vow-Breaker*. She translated many books from the French and she wrote the once famous, if scandalous, *Love Letters from a Nobleman to his Sister*. Book critics, more accepting than the drama critics had been, praised her skills in writing plot and intrigue and were also full of praise for the wit of her dialogue.

At the still young age of 50, Aphra Behn became ill and, after being treated by what sounds like a rather useless doctor, she died. She was buried in Westminster Abbey, a fact which tells us all we need to know about her status at the time.

Long after her death, Virginia Woolf wrote these lines about Mrs Behn: 'All women ought to let flowers fall upon the tomb of Aphra Behn, for it was she who earned them the right to speak their minds.'

How sad it is that she is largely forgotten today.

Jeremy Bentham (1748-1832)

Jeremy Bentham, philosopher and social reformer was born in London, the son of a lawyer. He was a child prodigy and as a toddler was allegedly found sitting on his father's desk engrossed in a book about the history of England. He began studying Latin at the age of three. He entered Oxford University at the age of 12 and became a barrister at the age of 15. (The idea of ending up in court being defended by a 15-year-old seems rather scary today but things were different then.)

Bentham was a firm proponent of utilitarianism. In his books *A Fragment on Government*, which was published in 1776, and *Introduction of the Principles of Morals and Legislation*, which was published in 1789, Bentham argued that the objective of all legislation should be 'the greatest happiness of the greatest number'. He developed what he called a 'hedonic calculus' to enable him to work out the effects of different actions.

Bentham travelled widely throughout Europe and Russia in order to study different forms of government and was made an honorary citizen of the French Republic in 1792. He published a vast number of papers and books on social reform, politics, penal reform and economics and spent his life studying the problems which face legislators, and helping to construct an ideal legal system. He was closely concerned with the functions of government, the true meaning of liberty and the purpose of civilisation. He argued that mankind is governed by two motives: avoiding pain and finding pleasure. In support of his claim that all legislation should promote 'the greatest happiness of the greatest number', he pointed out that since punishment involves pain, and is therefore evil, it should only be used 'so far as it promises to exclude some greater evil'.

He was not simply a theoretician. He spent enormous energy working on ways to put his theories into practice and worked long and hard on developing effective forms of law reform. He planned a special prison (the Panopticon) and a special school (the Chrestomathia) and helped to found the Westminster Review. He was a firm advocate of democracy and believed that education should be available to everyone – rich and poor.

John Stuart Mill regarded Bentham as one of mankind's great

benefactors and said of him: 'He had neither internal experience nor external; the quiet, even tenor of his life, and his healthiness of mind, conspired to exclude him from both. He never knew prosperity and adversity, passion nor satiety; he never had even the experiences which sickness gives; he lived from childhood to the age of eighty-five in boyish health...How much of human nature slumbered in him he knew not, neither can we know.'

Jeremy Bentham inspired the formation of University College, London and his skeleton (appropriately clothed) is preserved there.

William Blake (1757-1827)

Poet, artist and visionary William Blake never went to school (his father was a tradesman with little money) but taught himself a good deal about literature and The Bible. He also taught himself several languages. In his early teens he trained as an engraver at the Royal Academy and eventually, in 1784, opened a print shop in London. He developed his own innovative method of producing coloured engravings and began to publish his own, specially illustrated, books of poetry. The books he published included *Songs of Innocence* (1789), *The Marriage of Heaven and Hell* (1793), *Songs of Experience* (1794) and *Jerusalem* (1804-1820).

Blake was inspired by his mystical ideas about the struggles of the human soul and about heaven and hell. He firmly believed that imagination was the most important human experience and that it deserved constant encouragement. He often had visions of angels and ancient figures from bible stories. Whether writing or drawing he ignored all conventions. Blake's work owes nothing to any other artist.

Jerusalem, his third major epic work to deal with the fall and redemption of mankind, is perhaps the best known of his poems. It is certainly the most richly decorated and has been made into the hymn of the same name.

Blake also published a series of 22 watercolours which were inspired by the *Book of Job*.

William Blake was often regarded as mad by his contemporaries.

But this was never a medical diagnosis. He was regarded as mad partly because of his exceptional talent, partly because he was so determined and single-minded and partly because he was utterly unworldly. He didn't seem to care for material things; spending his life in poverty. The public had little interest in the wonderful books he produced but that didn't stop him. He just kept writing, drawing and publishing. He neglected himself and lived in terrible surroundings but that didn't matter. He lived only to write books.

Today Blake is generally regarded as having created one the most original and unique bodies of work in the world. He was a revolutionary who, in order to avoid ending up in prison (or being transported to Australia), confined himself to screaming and raging in his work and in his prophecies.

William Blake was one of the great English individuals, a true English eccentric, a mystic, a visionary and a prophet. He is sometimes regarded as one of the earliest and most significant figures in the Romanticism movement but he was much more than a figure in a movement. Blake was simply Blake. He was daringly original in a uniquely English sort of way.

Boudicca (15-61) (aka Boadicea)

Although the former queen's name is often spelt as Boadicea, it now seems clear that the correct spelling is Boudicca. The name 'Boadicea' seems to have slipped into common usage because Alfred Lord Tennyson spelt it that way in a famous poem, though to be fair the good lord could blame William Cowper who wrote a poem called Boadicea a quarter of a century before Tennyson was born.

Contemporary reports suggest that Boudicca was a huge woman, tall and well-built, who had a loud voice and a piercing glance. She had red hair which she wore long (it hung below her waist) and she invariably wore a golden necklace around her neck. She was rarely seen without a spear in her hand.

Boudicca is remembered today because she was one of the few native English citizens to have the courage to resist the Roman invasion. She had been married to King Prasutagus of the Iceni tribe in East Anglia and her husband had negotiated a deal enabling him to rule his part of England as a nominally independent ally of Rome. When he died, King Prasutagus left the kingdom jointly to his daughters and the Roman Empire but the Romans decided to ignore the King's will and subsequently behaved rather despicably towards his family. The Romans stole his lands, called in loans, raped his daughters and flogged Boudicca. Generally speaking, they treated Boudicca and her family extremely badly and Boudicca, not a woman to allow people to push her family around, wasn't prepared to take the ill-treatment lying down. She led an uprising of the whole Iceni tribe and while the Roman armies were busy killing the Welsh residents of the island of Anglesey in North Wales, she and her army burnt the Roman town of Camulodunum (Colchester), where there was a temple to the former Roman emperor Claudius, and set off to attack Londinium (London) and Verulanium (St Albans). While doing all this Boudicca and her army thrashed a Roman legion – the IX Hispana. This was a little like Bilbury Thirds beating Manchester United.

Hearing of this significant embarrassment the Roman legions which were still in Wales turned their chariots round and hurried back to England, hoping to rescue Londinium, a major settlement that had been established twenty years earlier. Realising however that he didn't have enough men to defend Londinium, Gaius Suetonius Paulinus evacuated it and abandoned it. Boudicca and her army then duly destroyed it. They also destroyed Verulanium. It is estimated that Boudicca killed around 80,000 Romans and their followers in destroying these cities. The damage Boudicca did was so great that the emperor Nero considered withdrawing all Roman troops from the island of Britain.

However, Suetonius Paulinus re-grouped in the West Midlands and his well-trained, and by now rather desperate and red-faced Roman legions, managed to defeat a presumably exhausted Boudicca at the Battle of Watling Street, which took place near Fenny Stratford. Rather than allow herself to be captured Boudicca poisoned herself. She and her army had fought bravely and had very nearly defeated the mighty Romans.

For centuries Boudicca was more or less forgotten but her fame rose to legendary status just before and during the Victorian era. Queen Victoria was frequently portrayed as a modern day Boudicca;

something which did not displease her. Poems by William Cowper and then Alfred, Lord Tennyson (who was Queen Victoria's Poet Laureate) confirmed Boudicca's status. Ships were named after her and statues built in her memory. In particular, a huge bronze statue of Boudicca with her daughters in her war chariot was commissioned by Prince Albert and stands near to the Houses of Parliament in the city she had once destroyed. Numerous books, films and songs have been based on her life.

Joseph Bramah (1748-1814)

Born a farmer's son in Yorkshire, Joseph Bramah had an accident that left him lame when he was just 16 years old. Unable to work on the farm, he was apprenticed to the village carpenter and subsequently became a cabinet maker in London. He eventually became one of England's greatest inventors. His work contributed enormously to the success of the Industrial Revolution.

Bramah's first successful invention was for a water closet that didn't freeze in cold weather. It had a hinged flap that sealed the bottom of the bowl. Bramah manufactured his water closets at a workshop in Denmark Street in London. His company continued to make the Bramah patented water closet for many years and an example can still be seen (fully functioning) in Queen Victoria's former home, Osbourne House, on the Isle of Wight.

The year 1784 was a big year for Bramah (whose father originally spelt the family name 'Bramma').

First, he married Mary Lawton, who came from Barnsley. They set up home together in London, initially in a house in Piccadilly though they later moved to Pimlico. Second, he designed a new lock for which he received a patent. He also started the Bramah Locks company to manufacture his locks. Their attraction was their resistance to lock-picking. On 21 March in 1798 the official journal of the House of Commons reported that Parliament had decided: 'That leave be given to bring in a Bill for vesting in Joseph Bramah his executors, administrators and assigns, the sole use and property of his invention of a new kind of lock for doors, drawers and other purposes.'

From 1790, Bramah's London shop had a lock mounted on a board containing these words: 'The artist who can make an instrument that will pick or open this lock shall receive 200 guineas the moment it is produced.'

(The challenge was finally met in 1851 by a locksmith called Hobbs who was awarded the prize. He took 51 hours, spread over 16 days, to open the lock. The lock was quickly redesigned.)

In order to manufacture his locks, Bramah needed precision-tooled parts. And so he started manufacturing tools with which to make those parts. Together with an employee called Henry Maudslay he designed a number of machine tools.

The invention for which Bramah is best remembered is undoubtedly the hydraulic press – which is today also known as the Bramah Press. The hydraulic press still has many uses and is widely used in industry for forming metals and for other tasks where a large force is needed. Presses are manufactured in many styles and sizes and in capacities ranging from 1 ton to 10,000 tons. They all work in the way Bramah designed them to work.

Although it is the hydraulic press which puts Bramah into our top 100, the Yorkshireman produced a number of other useful and important inventions. He created a beer engine, used at the bars of public houses, a type of fountain pen, the machine used for automatically printing bank notes with sequential serial numbers and a paper-making machine.

Early in the 19th century, Bramah invented a hydrostatic press which could uproot trees. In 1814 he was supervising work with the machine in a forest in Hampshire when he caught a cold. The cold turned into pneumonia and he died shortly afterwards.

William Brockeden (1787-1854) Devon

Brockeden was a watchmaker's son who invented the compressed tablet and inadvertently founded the modern pharmaceutical industry.

Born in Devon, Brockeden trained as a watchmaker (like his father) but also earned money as an author and an artist. It was in his capacity as an artist that he made the discovery that was to revolutionise the preparation of medicines and enable apothecaries to replace pill-rolling apprentices with efficient, reliable tablet-making machines.

Infuriated by the fact that he could not obtain drawing pencils which were free from grit, Brockeden had the idea of compressing pure powdered graphite in a die between two punches. Realising that his invention could have other uses, he wisely took out a patent for a device for the 'shaping of pills, lozenges and black lead by pressure in a die'. (The graphite pencil had been invented earlier and in 1546 the first lead pencil had been made in England when a source of pure graphite was discovered at Borrowdale in Cumbria. The graphite was so pure that writing sticks could be cut straight from the mine. But no other pure source of graphite was ever found and Brockeden's invention enabled decent pencils to be made from impure graphite.)

In 1844, a few months after Brockeden's patent was granted, the *Pharmaceutical Journal* announced: 'We have received a specimen of bicarbonate of potash compressed into the form of a pill by a process invented by Mr Brockeden and for which he has taken out a patent. We understand the process is applicable to the compression of other substances into a solid mass, without the intervention of gum or other adhesive material.'

The invention was immediately successful on both sides of the Atlantic. The big advantage was that every pill made by Brockeden's method contained the same quantity of ingredients. Inevitably, there were many who dismissed machine-made tablets as nothing more than a passing fancy, and one disgruntled apprentice wrote to the *Pharmaceutical Journal* asking whether he had trained for three years only to spend his future writing out labels and wrapping up bottles of factory made tablets. Even at the end of the nineteenth century, the *Pharmaceutical Journal* published an editorial stating that, 'Tablets have had their day...and like every other form of drug preparation that has preceded them, will pass away to make room for something else.'

However, the medical profession and the public found tablets attractive and too simple to resist. They were easier to take and to carry around than powders or mixtures, and customers soon realised that the efficacy of individual tablets did not vary much. When machines began to turn out tablets by the thousand, the popularity of Brockeden's invention was confirmed. Within a few years of the registration of Brockeden's patent, small companies making compressed tablets had sprung up all over the world, and apothecaries had discovered that it was easier and cheaper to buy their finished tablets from a specialist supplier rather than to rely on the pill-rolling skills of an apprentice. Thus the Industrial Revolution had its first direct effect on the medical profession and upon the medicines its members prescribed. Brockeden, the watchmaker from Devon, had single-handedly given birth to the pharmaceutical industry.

Isambard Kingdom Brunel (1806-1859)

Isambard Kingdom Brunel, renowned as a genius working in iron, was born in Portsmouth, Hampshire, the son of the engineer Sir Marc Brunel. Unlike many of the engineers and scientists who played a vital part in the Industrial Revolution, the young Brunel received a sound education (partly in England and partly in France) before entering his father's employment.

His first job was taking full charge of the Thames Tunnel being dug at Rotherhide. He was just 20 years old at the time. His father, Marc Brunel, who had started the tunnel, got the idea for the boring tool used in the construction of the tunnel from the destructive worm teredo navalis. The tunnel, which involved driving a horizontal shaft from one side of the river to the other, was eventually opened to the public in 1843, after costing nearly £500,000, a huge sum at the time. The vast cost meant that when it was built the tunnel, though an engineering success, was considered a commercial failure. The building of the tunnel nearly cost the young Brunel his life because he was injured when the tunnel flooded and spent six months recuperating.

(Marc Brunel, Isambard's father, was a spectacularly successful engineer in his own right. He was almost comically absent-minded and was renowned for forgetting his own name and climbing into the wrong coach. He was also accused of mistaking other men's wives for his own though how much of this was unintentional is now a mystery. The author Arnold Bennett would have doubtless called him a Card.)

At the age of 26, Isambard Kingdom Brunel was appointed Engineer to the newly created Great Western Railway. The bridges, tunnels and stations he planned are still used today by modern high speed trains travelling between London and Bristol, and his bridges now safely carry trains which are ten times as heavy as anything Brunel envisaged. He chose a broad gauge for the tracks so that the trains could travel safely at high speed. This was a controversial decision but Brunel argued that the then popular narrow gauge was a leftover from the mine railways that George Stephenson had built, and he proved that the broader gauge provided a safer and more comfortable ride, as well as allowing for larger carriages and thus greater capacity. Unfortunately, in 1892, the broad gauge was abandoned in England because most of the country's railway lines had by then been laid according to Stephenson's gauge.

The Great Western Railway is a magnificent tribute to Brunel's genius. Paddington Station in London is a Brunel creation and there is an excellent statue to him beside Platform 1. The Box Tunnel, which was the longest railway tunnel in the world at the time, is orientated so that the rising sun shines all the way through it on Brunel's birthday. Brunel was so meticulous that he even designed the specification for the locomotives to be used on his railway, which runs along the coast at Dawlish in Devon and is one of the most dramatic and best loved stretches of railway line in the world. Throughout his remarkably short life Brunel continued to build railways. He built lines in Ireland, Italy and Bengal.

Brunel saw the railway from London to Bristol as the first step in creating a link between London and New York and to complete the link he subsequently built ships to cross the ocean. The 'Great Western' was the first real ocean-going steamship ever built and the 'Great Britain' was the first large ship to be driven by screw propellers. The third huge ship he built, the 'Great Eastern', had an unprecedented five funnels and was so big that it remained the largest ship on the seas for half a century. Each vessel was a major step forward in shipbuilding. The 'Great Eastern' played a vital part in laying the first lasting transatlantic telegraph cable in 1865.

Brunel's other work included tunnels, buildings, viaducts and docks. His notebooks and sketchbooks show that he involved himself in every detail of his creations. For example, he surveyed the entire length of the route between London and Bristol himself.

For the Crimean War, Brunel designed a hospital of prefabricated parts that could be shipped out to the Crimean and reassembled on the battlefield. The hospital arrived complete with its own drainage system and its own air conditioning. He even designed new guns for use in the war.

The Clifton Suspension Bridge, 700 feet long and 200 feet above the River Avon, had the longest span of any bridge in the world when it was built. It still stands today and carries over four million vehicles each year. The Royal Albert Bridge, at Saltash in Cornwall, is another lasting monument to Brunel's genius.

Even Brunel's occasional failures were brilliant and imaginative. His 'atmospheric' railway, which had coaches drawn along by vacuum power, was way ahead of its time and cost Brunel a good deal of his own money. But it was a great idea.

Brunel's designs revolutionised the world of engineering and public transport. Sadly, he endured years of ill health before dying of a stroke at the tragically early age of 53. Few men have achieved so much in so little time.

John Bunyan (1628-1688)

Born in the village of Elstow near Bedford, John Bunyan's family had been farmers and tinkers for generations. The young Bunyan seemed destined to work on the farm, and do a little tinkering, as his parents had done. He had very little education.

Then the English Civil War started in 1642. On his 16th birthday John Bunyan joined the army. He fought in Cromwell's Parliamentary army during the English Civil War which took place between 1642 and 1647 and then he returned to his native village and married.

During the war his horizons were widened and he met many people he would never have met if he had remained a farm boy. He became interested in the idea of Puritanism, which was a strict form of Christianity popular among those fighting the King.

When he married, Bunyan read two books belonging to his wife (one was called *The Practice of Piety* and the other *The Plain Man's Pathway to Heaven*) and these had a huge impact on him.

He renounced vice and ungodliness, confessing that he had been 'a ringleader among those enjoying the delights of sin', and joined a Baptist congregation in Bedford. The still young Bunyan soon became a preacher himself.

However, it wasn't a good time to start a new life as a preacher because, after the Restoration of the Monarchy in 1660, Puritans weren't allowed to preach in public. Indeed, Puritan worship was banned completely.

Bravely and stubbornly Bunyan repeatedly disobeyed the law and as a result spent eleven years in prison. It was while he was incarcerated that he began to write. His first book was *Grace Abounding to the Chief of Sinners* and is the story of his own conversion to Christianity. Bunyan reveals himself as an emotional man, constantly terrified that he would be punished by God. He explains how when he became angry after his father remarried he quickly realised his sinfulness and was overwhelmed with remorse. He explains that as he stood in the church tower he was convinced that the bells would fall on him, condemning him to everlasting punishment. The book shows him to be passionate, earnest, intense and imaginative. These were the qualities which made him such a successful preacher and author.

During his long prison sentence he wrote nine books. Ironically, Bunyan was eventually released from prison as a result of the Declaration of Indulgence, which was intended by Charles II for the relief of Catholics.

During a later, shorter term in prison he wrote the first part of *The Pilgrim's Progress*, probably the most famous and moving book with a religious theme ever written. The book is an allegory about the problems and hazards of trying to be a good Christian in a corrupt and evil world. The hero of the book, Christian, is followed from the City of Destruction to the Celestial City.

After the publication of *The Pilgrim's Progress* Bunyan was allowed to preach without hindrance until his death.

Bunyan's other books include *The Life and Death of Mr Badman*, *The Holy War* and *A Book for Boys and Girls*. He wrote a sequel to *The Pilgrim's Progress*, in which he told the story of Christian's wife and children and reintroduced the eternally memorable characters of Greatheart, Standfast and Valiant.

It is, of course, *The Pilgrim's Progress* which marked Bunyan as a writer of genius. It is, in part at least, an autobiographical book but it is second only to The Bible as the world's biggest-selling and most everlastingly popular religious book. It was in a tenth edition by 1685 and since then it has been continually in print in almost every language in the world. The characters in Bunyan's masterpiece are drawn from every day life. The book may be a fantasy but the people are all utterly believable and all recognisable, and the simple story is dramatic and gripping. Bunyan's aim was not to create a work of art but merely to teach the religious truths which he regarded as so important.

Bunyan was an uneducated man. He had no formal training whatsoever. And yet his lack of education, combined with his genius, meant that he wrote about and for the people he knew with great conviction. His passion came from within and was the better for it.

Richard Burton (1821-1890)

Richard Francis Burton, one of the world's greatest explorers and adventurers, was born in Torquay, the son of an English colonel. He started life with an erratic and irregular education which ended with him being expelled from Oxford University.

By the time he'd finished with life he had been an explorer, writer, translator, secret agent, orientalist, soldier, linguist, poet, fencer, diplomat, hypnotist, ethnologist and publisher of some of the world's most famous erotic books.

Describing himself as 'fit for nothing but to be shot at for six pence a day' he joined the East India Company army and in 1842, at the age of 21, he served in Sind (Southeastern Pakistan). Unlike most of his contemporaries, he quickly mastered Arabic, Hindustani and Persian as well as Gujarati, Marathi and Panjabi. His reward from his fellow soldiers for this effort was to be accused of 'going native'. They called him 'the White Nigger'.

Burton was already turning into quite a character. He earned the nickname 'Ruffian Dick' for his ferocity as a fighter and was believed to have fought more single combat battles than any other man in the army. He kept a large menagerie of tame monkeys in the hope that he could learn their language. He learned to use measuring equipment and took part in a number of undercover investigations. During one undercover expedition he investigated a brothel in Karachi which was frequented by English soldiers and found that the prostitutes were young boys.

In 1849, he returned to England on sick leave. While recuperating in Europe he wrote his first book, learned fencing in Boulogne and met his future wife Isabel Arundell.

In 1853, though it was forbidden for non-believers to visit the most holy shrine of Islam, Burton made a pilgrimage to Mecca. He made the whole journey disguised as an Arab and wrote a fascinating account of this extremely dangerous pilgrimage.

Three years later he set out with another English explorer, John Hanning Speke on a journey which, in 1858, led to the discovery of Lake Tanganyika. The exploration was in many ways a disaster. Equipment was stolen or lost and both men had serious health problems. The two men were very different in character: Burton was a linguist who was able to talk to and fit in well with the native bearers but Speke was an old-fashioned imperialist.

After Burton was taken too ill to travel, Speke went on to discover Lake Victoria. Burton, the expedition's leader, was unhappy with Speke's work, claiming that his measurements were inaccurate, and he and Speke had a magnificent quarrel about it.

In 1861, Burton was British consul at Fernando Po and went on a mission to Dahomey. Over the next few years he worked as consul at Santos in Brazil, at Damascus and, in 1872, in Trieste. He never stopped criticising colonial policies, in both books and letters, and his courage in doing so undoubtedly damaged his professional career as a diplomat.

Burton wrote many books and scholarly articles on a wide variety of subjects, including ethnography, sexual practices, human behaviour, travel and fencing. He never held back his views or his information and his books are famous for their honesty and openness. In 1863 he co-founded the Anthropological Society of London.

During his travels and adventures he collected a huge library of notes and records dealing with the anthropological and sociological material he had collected. Much of the material he collected was frankly erotic and he published this material (as the *Kama Sutra, The*

Perfumed Garden and his annotated 16 volume edition of the *Arabian Nights*) privately in order to avoid prosecution. He managed to make a fortune in his later years from the sale of these privately published books. His work describes sexual techniques common in the regions he visited and an analysis of the measurements of the lengths of the sexual organs of male inhabitants of various regions.

Burton loved shocking people and often told stories against himself. He frequently seemed to authenticate rumours about him that had no foundation in fact. He was, for example, accused of murdering a boy who saw him urinating in European fashion when he was on his famous trip to Mecca. This accusation was taken seriously by many but it almost certainly had no basis in fact. As a result of his reputation, he was officially regarded as rather unpredictable and he was feared not so much for what he was known to have done but for what it was feared he might do. He was, nevertheless, knighted by Queen Victoria in 1886.

His wife, Lady Burton, shared in much of his travelling and his writing. She was a devoted wife and never recovered from his death. Sadly, she burnt many of his papers, including the manuscript of his final book *The Scented Garden Men's Hearts to Gladden* after his death. She had been offered six thousand guineas for the manuscript and she regarded the book as his 'magnum opus' but she imagined she was instructed to burn the manuscript by his spirit in order to protect his reputation.

Burton died of a heart attack in Trieste but his body was brought back to England to be buried. He and Isobel are buried in a tomb in the shape of a Bedouin tent in Mortlake in London.

Burton has appeared in numerous novels, as himself or as characters based on himself. He appeared as Mr Murthwaite in Wilkie Collins's detective novel *The Moonstone* and is mentioned in Arthur Conan Doyle's novel *The Lost World*.

William Byrd (1543-1623)

Byrd was England's first great composer and a fine professional musician. He was almost certainly born in Lincoln or thereabouts and was appointed organist of Lincoln Cathedral at the age of 20.

Nine years later he was made joint organist of the Chapel Royal, sharing the position with Thomas Tallis. In 1575, Elizabeth I gave the two men, Byrd and Tallis, the exclusive licence for printing and selling music in England.

Byrd was a staunch catholic and throughout his life he was repeatedly arrested and prosecuted for this, but the quality of his music, and the fact that he wrote equally beautiful music for his own church and for the newly established Church of England, meant that he remained in favour with the Queen.

He wrote music of great power and beauty and was (and still is) regarded as the greatest composer of sacred choral music. He is also remembered today for his songs and his keyboard music. He wrote three masses, over 200 short pieces of sacred choral music in Latin (known as motets), four Anglican services and 60 anthems. He also wrote four madrigals (part songs for small choirs, usually designed to be sung unaccompanied and arranged in elaborate counterpoint) and composed around 100 virginal pieces (music for an early spinet; an instrument which had strings parallel to the keyboard and which was popular in homes in the 16th and 17th century).

George Gordon Noel Byron (1788-1824)

Famously described by one of his many mistresses as 'mad, bad and dangerous to know', Lord Byron was a poet and philanderer and is remembered as much for his life as for his work. He was a leading poet of the 19th century English Romantic movement and his poetry has been expertly described as irreverent, ironic, impudent, high-spirited, satirical, elegant, contemptuous, humorous, burlesque, unconventional, generous, humane and reckless. The same adjectives apply, equally accurately, to his life.

Born with a deformed right foot which made him the butt of school-boy jokes, his mother had mood swings which made him distrust women in later life. His father had died when he was just three years old, but not before managing to spend Byron's mother's entire, considerable fortune. A female servant didn't help Byron's attitude towards women. She took a succession of male lovers with the nine-year-old Byron as a spectator.

At the age of 10 the young Byron became the 6th Baron and

with the title he inherited considerable estates. He attended Harrow School and discovered homosexuality. His mother began an affair with a 23-year-old rake, Lord Grey de Ruthyn who had also, and perhaps inevitably, made advances to the young Byron.

When he went to Cambridge in 1805, Byron patronised prostitutes with steadfast enthusiasm and fell in love with a choirboy called Edleston. When he put on weight he played cricket wearing six waistcoats so that he would sweat and lose some unwanted fat. While at the university he published his first poems (*Hours of Idleness*) and took his first mistress, a girl called Caroline whom he dressed as, and passed off as, a boy. The reviews of his first book were poor and so in 1809 he published *English Bards and Scotch Reviewers*, a satirical poem attacking the major literary figures of the time. He then left London and started a tour of Greece, Albania, Turkey and Spain with a friend called Hobhouse who was writing a book called *Sodomy Simplified* (which, perhaps not surprisingly, never found a publisher). When Hobhouse abandoned him in Greece, Byron acquired a 15-year-old Greek boy called Nicolo and spent a good deal of money on prostitutes. He returned to England in 1812 and John Murray published *Childe Harold's Pilgrimage*.

The poem, inspired by his journey, describes the exploits of a world-weary young lord who tries everything so young in life that he finds his later years boring. Byron became an overnight celebrity. It was as though he had won a television talent show and scored a hat trick for England on the same night.

Young men imitated Byron's brooding manner and his limp. Young women, attracted by his passion and his pleas for liberty and justice, threw themselves at him (quite possibly literally). Byron's new lovers included Lady Caroline Lamb and her mother-in-law Lady Melbourne. When he returned to Cambridge, Byron began an incestuous affair with his half-sister Augusta. He was seduced by a promiscuous woman called Lady Oxford.

Byron and his half-sister Augusta then moved to Newstead Abbey where she became pregnant. To silence the gossips Byron, by now aged 26, married Lady Melbourne's niece, a prim heiress called Annabelle. The marriage wasn't much of a success, possibly because Byron continued to 'flirt' with his half-sister and possibly because he was nearly always drunk. When his wife became pregnant he sodomised her late into her pregnancy. Exhausted by Byron's demands, by quarrels and by giving birth, Annabelle went home. When her parents found out what had been going on they would not let her return to the wicked lord. Suddenly the great poet was unfashionable and unwanted. Byron quit England in 1816. Having sold Newstead Abbey for the then fabulous sum of £94,500 he rented a palazzo in Venice where he initiated orgies which shocked even the previously unshockable Venetians. Byron's home soon became pretty much a brothel. The man himself was now fat and balding though still in his early thirties. While in Italy he wrote *Don Juan*, a long, witty poem about a handsome young man's adventures with women. A tempestuous affair with a married women caused some problems and Byron left Italy in rather a rush. He became an enthusiastic supporter of Italian and Greek freedom fighters and joined a secret Italian nationalist society.

He was a freedom fighter in Greece, leading troops against the Turks, when he caught a fever and, in proper poetic fashion, died young at the age of 36. It was a short but a full life. His family requested that he be buried in Westminster Abbey. Perhaps not entirely surprisingly, the request was refused.

Edith Cavell (1865-1915)

How many of the thousands of people who walk past Edith Cavell's statue in St Martin's Place, London, know who this woman was or what she did to deserve her monument? It's a tragedy that she should be just another largely forgotten hero; just another one of London's many statues.

The truth is that Edith Cavell was an extraordinarily courageous, patriotic woman. Well aware that the penalty for being caught was death, she helped around 200 Allied soldiers to escape from German-occupied Belgium during World War I. She was executed for this.

The daughter of a Norfolk vicar and the eldest of four children, Edith Louisa Cavell was born in 1865 in a village called Swardeston. She received her early education at home from her father, Frederick Cavell. Her upbringing was reputed to have been rather stern and certainly doesn't sound to have been a lot of fun; with the exception of *The Bible*, no books were allowed inside the house.

During her teenage years, Edith attended Laurel Court school, Peterborough, where she was taught French. It was soon discovered that Edith had a talent for the language. Edith's French was so good, in fact, that she was recommended for a governess post in Brussels in 1890. She worked there for five years before returning home to nurse her seriously ill father. It was nursing her sick father that helped Edith realise that she wanted to follow a career in nursing, and when she was 30 she began her formal training at the London Hospital. While there, and still a student nurse, Edith Cavell found herself looking after typhoid fever victims. She received the Maidstone Medal for her work. Following her training at the London Hospital, Edith Cavell worked at St Pancras Infirmary for a while and later worked as an Assistant Matron at Shoreditch Infirmary, where she pioneered the idea of visiting patients at home after they had been discharged from hospital. Edith believed that this would help reduce the number of re-admissions.

In 1907, because of her efficiency and the fact that she could speak French, Edith was recruited as head of nursing staff for a pioneer training school for nurses in Belgium. Edith became a very influential pioneer of modern nursing in Belgium. She was soon providing top-quality nurses for hospitals and schools.

Edith happened to be visiting her mother in England when the Great War started. She immediately insisted on going back to her clinic in Brussels, which was now being used as a Red Cross hospital.

Once back in Brussels, Edith helped nurse wounded soldiers. She hid a couple of fugitive British soldiers, and subsequently helped them to escape from German-occupied Belgium to neutral Holland. But Edith didn't stop there, with an underground organisation she managed to help many Allied soldiers escape to safety; saving the lives of around 200 soldiers.

In August 1915, Edith Cavell was arrested. The German occupation authorities had suspected for some time that she was hiding soldiers in her hospital. At her trial, Edith confessed to harbouring and aiding Allied soldiers and was sentenced to death by firing squad.

On the early morning of 12 October 1915, Edith Louisa Cavell, wearing her nurse's uniform, was taken out and shot dead. Her body was buried nearby. Her last words were reported to be: 'Standing as I do in the view of God and Eternity, I realise that patriotism is not enough. I must have no hatred or bitterness towards anyone.'

Just what sort of men could pull the trigger to shoot a nurse who had been accused only of saving lives isn't known.

There was, quite rightly, a worldwide outcry following her execution; the press coverage was phenomenal. Edith was seen as a martyr as well as a heroine. The Government used the media coverage of her death as a propaganda tool in order to enlist British men for the War. (There was no conscription at that time.) The following year, Edith's body was exhumed and returned to England. Her coffin was taken to Westminster Abbey for a spectacular memorial service; one of the people who attended was King George V. Edith Cavell's body was subsequently taken to her home county of Norfolk to be buried outside Norwich Cathedral.

Robert Cawdrey (1538-1604)

Robert Cawdrey was a schoolteacher who became country priest in Rutland more than 400 years ago. In 1565, he was ordained a deacon and in 1571 he was made rector of South Luffenham. However, Cawdrey's enthusiasm for the principles of Puritanism got him into considerable trouble. In 1576, he was in trouble for not reading the approved texts in his church and in 1578 he performed a marriage ceremony, despite the fact that he was not authorised to do so by the church. He was suspended for this for a while. In 1587, he was in trouble again. He was taken to the Court of High Commission where he stood trial for 10 weeks for objecting to the episcopal hierarchy. When he was deprived of his living and suspended, Cawdrey took the church to court and challenged the authority of the ecclesiastical commissioners and the legal right of the Queen to empower them. In the end, the judges decided that 'by the ancient laws of this realm, the kingdom of England is an absolute empire and monarchy'. The judges also upheld the divine right of the Crown. A few years later Charles I would rely on this ruling and lose his head as a result. Cawdrey, with a family to feed, had to go back to teaching to make a living.

Many new words were appearing in the English language towards the end of the 16th century and Cawdrey decided that there was a need (and, perhaps, a market) for an instructional textbook to help ease the confusion. His main concern was that the upper classes were using too many foreign words and phrases and were forgetting many of the available English words. '(Far journied gentlemen learn new words while in foreign lands, and then powder their talke with over-sea language,' he complained.)

It was Cawdrey and not Dr Samuel Johnson who compiled the first English dictionary. Cawdrey's was called *A Table Alphabeticall*, and appeared in 1604. (Dr Samuel Johnson's dictionary first appeared in 1755).

Cawdrey's *Table*, listing 2,500 words was, he explained, designed to 'contayne' and teach the 'true writing and understanding of hard...English words borrowed from the Hebrew, Greeke, Latine or French'. Cawdrey's book was sold at the publisher's shop at the great north door of 'Paules Church'.

Cawdrey stated that his book was designed 'for the benefit and helpe of Ladies, Gentlewomen, or any other unskilful persons'. Cawdrey had time to write his dictionary (and probably needed the royalties) because he was thrown out of the church and so we should, perhaps, be grateful to the authorities for their actions.

Cawdrie wrote several other books. While he was a rector he wrote *A Short and Fruitefull Treatise of the Profit of Catechising* and during his final schoolteacher phase he published *A Treasurie or Store-House of Similes*.

William Caxton (1422-1491)

William Caxton didn't invent printing from moveable type (that was a German called Joseph Gutenberg who designed an entire manufacturing process which enabled him to produce a completed printed edition of *The Bible* in Latin 1456) but he can reasonably be credited with having invented publishing as we know it today.

Caxton, who was born in Kent, was a cloth merchant who travelled around Europe on business. It was on one of his trips that he heard of a new process of printing from moveable type. The invention meant that books no longer had to be copied out by hand but could be printed time and time again from the same blocks of type.

Caxton immediately saw the commercial possibility of this invention and in 1474 he set up a press in Bruges where he printed *Recuyell of the Historyes of Troyes*, the first book in the English language. (It was a long poem which he had himself translated from the original French.) One of his next publications was *The Game and Playe of the Chesse*.

Two years afterwards he returned to London and opened a print shop near Westminster Abbey in London. The first book he published, and the first book printed in England, was *The Dictes or Sayengis of the Philosophres*, which was printed in 1477.

By the time he died, just fifteen years later, Caxton had published around 100 printed books, including an edition of Chaucer's *The Canterbury Tales*, Malory's *Morte d'Arthur* and Gower's *Confessio Amantics*.

Gutenberg, the man who invented modern printing and from whose ideas are derived many of the inventions and developments which have so influenced our lives, was a poor businessman. Although his invention changed the world he failed to take much advantage of it. He never managed to make money out of printing and he lost his printing equipment to a partner as a result of a lawsuit. He was first and foremost a printer, rather than a publisher.

Caxton's great achievement was to spot the significance of Gutenberg's invention and to be the first publisher. He used eight founts of type and began to use woodcut illustrations in 1480. As well as being a printer and publisher, Caxton was also the author or translator of many of the books he produced, and his work contributed enormously to the development of the English prose style.

The twin processes of printing and publishing, as first practised by Caxton, changed the world. During the next century, publishers in England and elsewhere around Europe produced a vast number of books. And those books truly changed the world in every conceivable way. Caxton started that revolution.

The mechanical invention of the printing press was, at first, little more than a novelty. It was Caxton (and those who came after him) who realised that the printing press was going to liberate thinkers and writers everywhere.

It took some time for the craft of printing to develop but, as printers learned their skills, so it became possible to use those skills, and the arts they acquired, to help spread the new ideas, the inventions, the discoveries which were springing up throughout Europe during the Renaissance.

Publishers like Caxton, and those who came after him, enabled inventors, adventurers, authors and artists to spread their work to a far wider audience than had been possible before the printing press was invented. Printing presses helped spread genius far and wide, and far more speedily than would have been possible if the only books available had been those laboriously written out by hand by patient monks.

Caxton, the first publisher, was at the forefront of the Renaissance. His speciality was (in the jargon of the 20th century media guru Marshall McLuhan) the medium, rather than the message, but nevertheless he truly helped change the world. The printing press was to the 16th century what the invention of the steam locomotive was to the 19th century. But the steam locomotive would not have made much of an impact without railway lines and railway stations. And the printing press would not have changed our lives without publishers and authors.

George Cayley (1773-1857)

He was born in Brompton-by-Sawdon, near Scarborough in Yorkshire and he died in Yorkshire. He was thoroughly English. And he was the founder of the science of aerodynamics, the pioneer of aerial navigation and the designer of the first modern aeroplane. He was the first person to understand the principles of flight and worked over half a century before people now often credited with inventing the aeroplane. (The Wright Brothers, often described by American writers as the first men to fly, did not get into the air with a heavier-than-air machine until 1903 – nearly half a century after Cayley's death).

Cayley started developing his ideas about the theory of flight and his plans for an aeroplane when he was still at school. In 1799, he invented the concept of the modern aeroplane as a fixed wing flying machine with separate systems for propulsion, lift and control.

In 1804, he built his first model glider, which had a pair of large monoplane wings near the front and a small tailplane at the rear. The tailplane consisted of a vertical fin and horizontal stabilisers. In other words his aeroplane design in 1804 was pretty much the design we are accustomed to.

Five years later, in 1809, he published ground-breaking aerodynamic research in his treatise *On Aerial Navigation* which was published in the *Journal of Natural Philosophy, Chemistry and the Arts*. He studied wing design, designing cambered wings and studied streamlining and stability in the air. He also investigated the aerodynamic forces of drag, lift and thrust. Sometime in the 1840's he designed and built a triplane powered with flappers. An unknown ten-year-old boy, chosen for his light weight, flew this aeroplane.

In 1853, Cayley constructed the world's first full-size flying machine, a glider, which was flown across Brompton Dale. It had a wing area of 300 square feet and was the world's first 'heavier-than-air' machine to fly. There is some confusion about the identity of the pilot, though it is generally believed that the first aviator was either Cayley's coachman, footman or butler, though it may have been his grandson who made the first flight. The flight, the first ever made, was described in the *Encyclopaedia Britannica* of 1855.

On the death of his father, Cayley inherited Brompton Hall and the associated estates, and the title of 6th baronet. He was a remarkable engineer and inventor and although he is now remembered as the inventor of the aeroplane and manned flight he did much, much more. He also invented the caterpillar tractor (the first example of which he built in 1825, calling it the 'Universal Railway'), invented a new type of telescope, developed artificial limbs, created the first tension wheel, helped to found the Regent Street Polytechnic in London, and was involved in railway engineering, land reclamation methods and allotment agriculture. He developed self-righting lifeboats, automatic signals for railway crossing, helicopters, a type of internal combustion engine fuelled by gunpowder, and seat belts. He worked on air engines, ballistics and theatre architecture. He was also an MP from 1832 to 1835. This extraordinary Englishman, now too often ignored by historians, died at the age of 83.

Edwin Chadwick (1800-1890)

A civil servant, lawyer and journalist, Chadwick was also a dedicated reformer whose work led to massive improvements in sanitation around the world – including America and the rest of Europe. His publications include *A Report of an Inquiry into the Sanitary Condition of the Labouring Population of Great Britain*, which he published in 1842 at his own expense. He was the first president of the Association of Public Sanitary Inspectors (later transformed into the Chartered Institute of Environmental Health).

Dismayed by the number of people killed by the cholera epidemic of 1831, Chadwick, who had been invited by the Government to help with Poor Law Reform, argued that proper sanitation facilities would improve the quality of life for ordinary people and would also be of massive value in economic terms. This deliberate mixing of health improvement and financial motive had been attempted (sadly, with little success) by the great economist Sir William Petty in the 17th century but Chadwick succeeded where Petty had failed.

The changing political climate in the early part of the 19th century meant that England was ready for change. Since working people were earning more, and becoming better educated, the politicians were under more pressure to do something about the foul conditions in which town dwellers usually lived.

Chadwick prepared maps showing where the worst death rates were in English cities. His figures showed that (including infant mortality) the average age at death was 43 for gentlemen, 30 for tradesmen and 22 for labourers crowded together in unsanitary conditions. These figures were, of course, kept desperately low by the high incidence of death among babies and children.

On the basis of these statistics, Chadwick concluded that disease was spread by overcrowding, poor water supplies, bad drainage and dirty towns. Richer people tended to live longer because they were protected from the problems inherent in the crowded parts of towns and cities.

Chadwick's 1842 report suggested that a circulatory system be used in towns and cities to supply clean water and to remove waste products. Most importantly, he showed that the authorities would actually save money by building proper facilities.

Chadwick filled his report with vital technical information, designed to make things easy for the politicians. He obtained evidence showing that although water supplied at high pressure tended to burst the traditional bored elm trunks, it did not damage iron pipes and he also showed that narrow-bore drains which had smooth inside walls would clean themselves when water closets were used.

Chadwick recommended building pumps to supply fresh water and sewer pipes to take away the wastes. He even suggested that sewage be processed and sold to farms as a valuable fertiliser.

Chadwick's recommendations were incorporated into a Public Health Act in 1848 and although not all his ideas were used (it was cheaper to import guano from Chile as a fertiliser than to use treated human sewage) there is no doubt that Chadwick made a massive contribution to the quality of life in England and the rest of the world. Almost alone, Chadwick provided the stimulus which eventually gave towns and cities everywhere clean streets, clean water supplies and efficient sewers.

Charles Spencer 'Charlie' Chaplin (1889-1977)

Since the cinema was invented by an Englishman (Eadweard Muybridge) it is appropriate that the world's first major screen star should also be an Englishman: Charles Chaplin.

Chaplin, who was born in Walworth, London, started appearing on the stage and in music halls from the age of five. His father was a singer and his mother was a singer and actress. They separated before he was three. Charlie then lived with his mother, staying with his alcoholic father only when his mother was in a mental asylum.

Chaplin's first stage appearance took place after his mother was badly injured by objects thrown at her when she was appearing at a music hall theatre. While his mother was crying offstage, Charles went on stage to quiet the crowd by singing a popular tune of the day.

He then joined Fred Karno's travelling circus (Arthur Stanley Jefferson, better known as Stan Laurel of Laurel Hardy fame was another member of the circus; he and Chaplin shared a room together) and, since it was a travelling circus, Chaplin travelled to America; first in 1910 and then in 1912.

By 1914, the young Chaplin had joined Mack Sennett's studios, which specialised in slapstick comedy, and that same year Chaplin created the character of the Tramp: the slight man in the baggy trousers and tight jacket, large shoes, small Derby hat and carrying a walking cane; the underdog who is pushed around by everyone but who always manages to survive; the little man who triumphs without ever quite succeeding. Officials, bumbling and cruel, are always made comical in Chaplin's films (which are more subversive than they appear to be).

The clothes Chaplin used for his character the Tramp were all borrowed. (The trousers came from Fatty Arbuckle.) The moustache was added to give the young Chaplin age without hiding his expression. The contradictions in the clothing (tight jacket and baggy trousers) were all deliberate. Chaplin's genius was to create a character who could make people laugh but also touch their hearts and who could, moreover, appear in an almost endless number of situations. The character, a gentleman vagabond, faced endless failure but remained ever hopeful; he was constantly falling in love but forever being disappointed.

The movies starring the Tramp were all silent movies and Chaplin was indisputably the most creative and influential personality of the silent movie era. He entertained millions throughout the First World War and it is doubtful if any individual has ever given more entertainment, pleasure and relief to so many human beings when they needed it most. (Chaplin was criticised for not joining the army during World War I but he had in fact tried to join up. He had been turned down as being too small and underweight. In addition to helping cheer up the world, Chaplin raised vast amounts of money through public speaking in aid of war-bond drives.)

George Bernard Shaw, the playwright, described Chaplin as 'the only genius to come out of the movie industry'. Chaplin's films were so successful that he was paid huge sums of money and given total creative control.

When the movie studios started making films with sound, Chaplin, unlike many of his contemporaries, survived and thrived, though he refused to make sound movies with the Tramp character. The movie Modern Times, released in 1936 is often described as the last 'silent era' film. Chaplin, as the Tramp, sings a gibberish song right at the end of the film as he disappears down an endless road, heading for the horizon.

Chaplin became an increasingly versatile and gifted screenwriter, actor and director. He produced his own movies and even wrote his own soundtrack music. (He wrote the original score for his film Limelight and it won an Oscar.) In 1919, together with D. W. Griffith, Douglas Fairbanks and Mary Pickford, Chaplin co-founded the film studio United Artists.

Charlie Chaplin continued performing almost until his death at the age of 88. In the early 1950's the American witchhunt for 'left' leaning talent in Hollywood resulted in him moving back to Europe, but Chaplin received three Oscars in his lifetime, though he had famously annoyed the Academy by using his first Oscar as a doorstop. When he was given a special Oscar in 1972 he received the longest standing ovation in Academy Award history – lasting five minutes.

There have, of course, been many cinema stars since Chaplin. But Chaplin was the first truly great international star and he set the pattern for successful actors for generations to come. He made many films (such as *City Lights*, *Modern Times* and *The Great Dictator*) which regularly appear on lists of the greatest films of all time.

Charlie Chaplin was knighted in 1975. His character, the Tramp, is still probably the most imitated created character in the world. Chaplin himself once entered a Chaplin-look-alike competition. He came third.

Unlike many lesser stars Chaplin always tried to keep his private life discreet and out of the public eye. He was not always successful. Over his long life he was involved with a good many women – often teenagers. At least one of his divorces led to a record-breaking financial settlement. He had eleven children by three different women and married his last wife, Oona O'Neill, in 1943 when he was 54 years old. She was 18. They had eight children, the last being born when Chaplin was 73.

Chaplin set the bar for screen stars. It is doubtful whether a single entertainer will ever again reach such heights, enjoy such success and have such complete control over his work, in what has become an increasingly collaborative industry.

Geoffrey Chaucer (approx. 1345-1400)

The son of a London wine merchant, Geoffrey Chaucer was extremely well-connected and lived as full a life as a man can live if he's not Lord Byron. In 1357, he was employed by the future Duke of Clarence and in 1357 he was in at the start of the Hundred Years War, though, not surprisingly, he didn't live to see the end of it. As a young man he served in the army alongside Edward III when the king invaded Flanders to assert his claim to the French crown. Chaucer was taken prisoner but ransomed. When he returned to England he married Philippa, the sister of John of Gaunt's third wife, and never looked back professionally; subsequently being given various positions at court.

He went on a mission for the King to Genoa and Florence in 1372-3 and was an early secret service agent in Flanders in 1376 and 1377. In 1378, he was attached to embassies in France and Lombardy, possibly again as a spy, and he appears to have roved Europe as a royal ambassador. During his travels he met Alighieri Dante, and Giovanni Boccaccio, the Italian poets.

In 1374, he was appointed controller of customs in the port of London and in 1386 he was made knight for Kent. He was clerk of the King's work at various places, including Westminster Abbey, and was obviously popular with royalty because he received pensions from Edward III, John of Gaunt, Richard II and Henry IV. Chaucer wrote much throughout his life. Most of his work was written to be read out loud at court and in the homes of rich noblemen. He was an early celebrity.

He is remembered today for *The Canterbury Tales*. He started work on this epic work in 1387, when he was in his 40's, though the stories weren't available in a printed version until William Caxton printed them in around 1478.

The Canterbury Tales is a collection of stories supposedly told among a band of merry pilgrims who are entertaining themselves as they make their way to the shrine of Thomas à Becket in Canterbury.

In the prologue, Chaucer describes the character of pilgrims such as the Wife of Bath, the Pardoner, the Knight and so on. He planned 120 separate tales but had finished only 22 (and started two more) when he died.

The stories (difficult to read in the original Olde Englishe) vary enormously in style and content – according to which of the pilgrims is telling them. Some of the stories are serious, religious and filled with philosophical thoughts. Some are romantic. And some are comic, rude and, on occasion, downright dirty. Some are gloomy, some are uplifting and some are merely entertaining.

The Canterbury Tales marked the beginning of English literature.

Winston Churchill (1874-1965)

English politician and author, Sir Winston Churchill, was born two months premature on 30 November 1874 at Blenheim Palace, Oxfordshire. He was the elder of two sons. His full name was Winston Leonard Spencer Churchill.

Winston Churchill's father (the third son of the 7th Duke of Marlborough) was Lord Randolph Churchill. At the age of 37, he was leader of the House of Commons and Chancellor of the Exchequer. Churchill's mother was the beautiful Jennie Jerome, the daughter of a rich American speculator. Churchill's ancestor, the first Duke of Marlborough, was Queen Anne's Captain General. Queen Anne had created him the first Duke of Marlborough in recognition for his military victories. In gratitude, Queen Anne also rewarded the Duke with the Royal Manor of Woodstock, and funded the building of Blenheim Palace (which was named after the Duke's victorious battle). The Duke of Marlborough was considered to be one of England's greatest generals.

Churchill experienced a lonely childhood and would often write begging letters to his parents asking them to visit him during his stay at boarding school. Most of the time, his pitiful requests went ignored.

Although he admired and respected him enormously, Churchill did not enjoy a close relationship with his father. Churchill's early memories of his mother were of a 'fairy princess'. Churchill wrote: 'I loved her dearly – but at a distance.' Instead, the young Churchill was closest to his nanny and friend, Mrs Everest, to whom he was devoted. After Mrs Everest's death in 1895 Churchill described her as the 'dearest and most intimate friend during the whole of the 20 years I had lived'.

The red-haired Churchill was described as a somewhat troublesome child; he was bumptious, wilful, restless and mischievous – personality traits which never left him.

At thirteen, Churchill attended public school at Harrow, and did not do as badly there as he later led many to believe. It is true that he was considered a dunce in some of his subjects, more notably Latin, but in truth he was only poor in the subjects that he did not care for. Winston was brilliant at subjects that interested him, especially English and History.

Churchill's father, disappointed and concerned at his son's relative lack of scholarly success, wondered what route his boy's life should take. One day, whilst watching his son at play with his toy soldiers, the idea of a military career for the young Churchill was born. This was good news for Churchill because it was a dream that he had coveted since he was a small boy. Churchill sat his Army preliminary examination at Harrow. The examination involved drawing a map. The evening before the examination, he wrote names of countries on pieces of paper and put them into a hat. He then picked out one to study. The country he blindly chose was New Zealand. In the examination paper the following day, he was asked to draw a map of New Zealand. This was an example of the luck that was to follow him throughout his life.

Two popular misconceptions about Churchill are that he was dyslexic and that he suffered from a stutter. Churchill was not dyslexic and he did not have a stutter, though he did have a slight lisp. However, his speech impediment did not deter him from becoming one of the greatest orators the world has ever seen.

In 1893, Churchill left school and attended the Royal Military Academy, Sandhurst. He graduated from Sandhurst in 1895, having done extremely well, and joined the Fourth Hussars. Nevertheless, the year 1895 was a tragic one for Churchill. It was the year his father died from a brain tumour at the age of 46 and the year his beloved friend Mrs Everest passed away.

Impatient with peacetime soldiering and desperate for action, the young Churchill, while on leave, travelled to Cuba, where the fighting between the indigenous rebels and the Spanish Government was reaching a conclusive phase. Before he left for Cuba, Churchill arranged a contract with the *Daily Graphic* to write articles about his experiences over there. This was the start of his career in journalism. He was paid £5 for each article. When he left Cuba Churchill was awarded the Spanish Military Medal (1st Class).

In 1896, Churchill was stationed with the Fourth Hussars in Bangalore, India and, the following year, when he had three months' leave, he got himself a job as a war correspondent (for the *Daily Telegraph* and the Indian newspaper, *Allahabad Pioneer*) in the north-west frontier of India where General Sir Bindon Blood was in command of an expedition to quell the tribal uprising in the Malakand Pass. Initially, Churchill wanted General Blood to appoint him as staff but there were no vacancies.

Churchill's experiences in north-west India inspired him to write his first book, *The Malakand Field Force*. Winston Churchill went on to become an eminent and prolific author, writing over 40 books. In 1953, he was awarded the Nobel Prize for literature. He started his writing career for financial reasons, and continued writing for financial reasons throughout his life.

During his time on leave, while still officially stationed in India, Churchill heard about a pending war to clean up the Sudan. Churchill tried to persuade Lord Kitchener to assign him to his army, but for various reasons Lord Kitchener refused. Never a man to give in, the young Churchill enlisted the support of the Prime Minister, Lord Salisbury, and successfully persuaded the Adjutant General to give him a post in the 21st Lancers. Before setting off for the Sudan, Churchill also managed to get a contract as war correspondent for the *Morning Post*. It was on the field of Omdurman on 2 September 1898, that the last classic cavalry charge in the history of British warfare was fought.

The war to liberate the Sudan from the Dervishes was successful despite the fact that a quarter of Kitchener's men were killed or wounded. Churchill wrote about the history of the campaign in his next book, *The River War*. In this book, Churchill criticised General Lord Kitchener's policies. The War Office responded by introducing a law restraining the literary freedom of serving soldiers in the British Army. It's a law that still exists. Winston Churchill was one of the very few modern political leaders to have real personal experience of war. He knew what it was like to be shot at and what it was like to be a prisoner of war.

In 1899, Churchill gave up his military career and decided to go into politics. Churchill always believed that he was destined for great things, and told a fellow officer while in Bangalore that he would one day be Prime Minister. His political career did not start well. He failed to win his first political contest – the by-election at Oldham. So when the *Morning Post*, impressed by his journalistic work during the Sudan, asked him to be chief war correspondent to report on the war with the Boers which was about to break out in South Africa, Churchill jumped at the chance.

While in South Africa, he was travelling on a British army armoured train when it was ambushed and partly derailed by the Boers. Unfazed by the bullets firing all around him, Churchill gallantly took charge of the situation and managed to direct the engine (fortunately, the engine was still on the line, it was the three trucks in front of the engine that were derailed) to safety, having first loaded the train with wounded men.

When Churchill returned on foot to help the remaining men, he was captured and taken to a prisoner of war camp in Pretoria. Churchill's courage in rescuing the armoured train was undoubtedly aided by his feeling of invulnerability. He felt that he was being preserved for a higher purpose. His thoughts on this are reflected when he wrote to his mother and said: 'Bullets are not worth considering. Besides I am so conceited I do not think the gods would create so potent a being for so prosaic an ending'.

A little less than a month later, Churchill managed to escape from the camp by climbing the enclosure. He travelled just under 300 miles to safety. When his escape was discovered, a 'Dead or Alive' price was put on Churchill's head with a £25 reward. Churchill's escapades made him a hero for a while in Britain.

After his escape from Pretoria, Churchill did not return to London but, instead, he went to Durban to rejoin the army commanded by General Sir Redvers Buller. At Durban, Churchill received a hero's welcome. General Buller wanted to enrol Churchill into the forces, but Winston didn't want to lose his job with the *Morning Post* so instead he accepted an offer of a commission in The South African Light Horse. This meant that he could be a soldier and continue as war correspondent for the *Morning Post*, for which he was the highest paid journalist of the day. Churchill was present at the battle of Spion

Kop (where he intervened and took over the role of commanding officer) and was among the first to arrive in Ladysmith and Pretoria, before resigning his commission and returning to Britain in July 1900. He was just 24 years old.

In 1900, Churchill again stood as a Conservative Party candidate for Oldham during the general election. This time, he was successful. His victory was no doubt helped by his fame as a military hero.

As a politician Churchill quickly proved himself to be a champion of the underdog. He spoke out about poverty in Britain and on the 31 May 1904, dissatisfied with the policies of the Conservatives (especially their proposed protective tariffs on foreign trade which he was against) and believing that the policies of the Liberals were more like his own he caused quite a stir when he crossed the floor of the House of Commons to join the Liberals.

In 1905, Churchill was appointed Under-Secretary of State for the Colonies when the Liberals came into power, with Sir Henry Campbell-Bannerman as Prime Minister. Churchill was appointed President of the Board of Trade when Liberal leader, Campbell-Bannerman was succeeded by Herbert Henry Asquith in 1908. As President of the Board of Trade, Churchill helped introduce legislation which transformed society. He set up Labour exchanges and established minimum wages for several hundred thousand workers. He also proposed unemployment insurance.

On 12 September 1908, Winston Churchill married Clementine Hozier, whom he had met at a dinner party six months previous. They had five children together: one son and four daughters. They named their son, Randolph, after Sir Winston's father. In contrast to his father, Churchill was an affectionate and attentive father to all of his children.

In 1910, Churchill was promoted to Home Secretary, becoming the youngest Home Secretary since Robert Peel. One of his first actions was to introduce the Coal Mines Bill, which made it illegal for children under 14 to work underground. During his time as Home Secretary, Churchill caused much criticism when he famously took charge of the Sidney Street siege in London's East End, and forced the criminals to surrender or burn by denying the fire brigade access when the house they were in caught fire.

After a year as Home Secretary, Churchill became the political head of the navy: First Lord of the Admiralty, where he helped to strengthen the British fleet in order to deter Germany's aggression. One of the many things he did was introduce aircraft into the Royal Navy.

During the First World War in 1915, Churchill unfairly received the lion's share of the blame for the ill-fated Gallipoli landings on the Dardenelles. Many felt that he lacked judgement. As a result, he was demoted to the post of Chancellor of the Duchy of Lancaster. The Conservatives had refused to form a coalition government with the Liberals unless Churchill was demoted.

Soon after, Churchill resigned from the Government (although he remained an MP) and rejoined the army. He served in the trenches on the Western Front for several months, first with the Grenadier Guards and then as Commanding Officer of the 6th Battalion Royal Scots Fusiliers.

In 1916, Prime Minister Asquith resigned from the coalition Government and was replaced by the English-born professional Welshman, David Lloyd George. In 1917, Lloyd George appointed Churchill his Minister of Munitions and in 1919 Churchill was made Secretary of State for War. Two years later, in 1921, Churchill set up a conference in Cairo to settle Mesopotamia's future.

Lloyd George resigned as Prime Minister in 1922, and the Conservatives withdrew from the coalition government. The Conservatives returned to power in the 1922 general election after an interval of 17 years. Churchill, recovering from an appendicectomy, found that he was without a parliamentary seat. He responded by saying he was, 'without an office, without a seat, without a party and without an appendix'.

In the first month of 1924, the Conservatives were defeated in Parliament, and Ramsay MacDonald became the first Labour Party Prime Minister of Britain. In the same year, the Conservatives offered Churchill the safe seat of Epping – a constituency that he represented for 40 years. In October, the Conservatives won the General Election and Stanley Baldwin appointed Churchill as Chancellor of the Exchequer, a position that his father had held almost 40 years earlier. As Chancellor of the Exchequer one of the many things Churchill did was introduce pensions for everyone at 65. He also reduced income tax for the lowest income groups.

In 1929, the Conservatives were defeated in the General Election, and Labour came back into power with Ramsay MacDonald as Prime Minister. Churchill was relegated to the back benches. During the next few years, which he described as his 'wilderness years', Churchill concentrated on his writing, after having resigned from the Shadow Cabinet because of his strong stance against Indian Home Rule. During his time out of office, Churchill called on Britain to strengthen itself against Germany as he saw the rise of Adolf Hitler as a threat. His warnings were ignored.

In September 1939, on the day the Second World War started, the Prime Minister Neville Chamberlain appointed Churchill First Lord of the Admiralty and in May 1940, when Chamberlain resigned after having been blamed for a number of defeats during the beginning of the war, Churchill was made Prime Minister. He was 65 years old. In his first speech as Prime Minister of the coalition government Churchill famously said: 'I have nothing to offer but blood, toil, tears and sweat'.

Churchill's impassioned famous speeches were a great inspiration to many during the war and helped to raise the nation's morale.

On the 8 May 1945, Churchill brought Britain to victory against Germany. Despite Churchill's leadership during World War II, he was heavily defeated in the 1945 election by Clement Attlee and the Labour Party.

Churchill, now 76, returned as Prime Minister of the Conservative Party after Labour's defeat in the 1951 General Election. In 1953, Churchill was made Knight of the Garter.

Churchill stepped down as Prime Minister on 5 April 1955, but he continued as a member of parliament until six months before his death.

Sir Winston Churchill, the famous Havana cigar-smoking British statesman and author, died on 24 January 1965. He was given a state funeral and was buried in St Martin's Churchyard, Bladon. When Churchill's coffin passed down the Thames, the cranes of London's docklands bowed in salute.

Churchill had two famous hobbies. First, he painted. And he did it very successfully. He exhibited and sold his works at public exhibitions in Britain and France under the pseudonym of 'Charles Morin'. Churchill saw several of his works exhibited in the Royal

Academy under the name of 'Charles Winter', and, later, had several more in the Royal Academy under his own name. Second, he was also an accomplished bricklayer. He took it up as a hobby during his time as Chancellor of the Exchequer. Churchill even built some of the buildings on his estate at Chartwell.

Americans often say, with that scandalous disregard for history that typifies the American view of the world, that without America we would all be speaking German. The truth is that without Churchill we would all be speaking German. He saved England, Scotland, Wales, America and the rest of the world.

Churchill was archetypically English and although he had his faults (arrogance and vanity to name but two) it was his good fortune (and ours) that he was able to turn his faults into virtues and to use his self-confidence to enhance his qualities as a leader. He was a lucky leader and a lucky man; a born survivor.

Not many people change the course of history single-handedly. Churchill did. Churchill, the ultimate egoist and self-publicist changed history. If it hadn't been for World War II he would be no more than a political blip. But if it hadn't been for Churchill, Hitler would have won World War II.

I don't think Churchill was a great statesman or a great politician. He was too opinionated, too pugnacious and too obviously self-centred (other politicians are equally driven by self-interest but they hide it more effectively). But he was a great warrior, the greatest war time leader any country has ever produced and, quite possibly, the greatest orator. That's quite enough for one man.

William Cobbett (1763-1835)

Author, journalist, publisher, campaigner, social historian, politician and rebel – it's difficult to sum up William Cobbett who was, without a doubt, one of the most determined, bloody-minded and brave Englishmen who ever lived. He wrote what he believed and didn't give a hang for the consequences. He believed that England had a personality and that it needed and deserved a genuine 'England' policy. He believed it was important to preserve the personal peculiar characteristics of England and to respect the special individual liberties enshrined in the nation's history and culture. He believed that a popularly elected Parliament, representing an informed democracy, would end the borough mongering and the sinecures which, in his day, still disgraced public life.

Naturally, Cobbett wasn't popular with the boys with the moats and the duck houses. He was imprisoned for defending freedom and the rights of ordinary working men.

William Hazlitt, a contemporary of Cobbett and probably the most famous of all English essayists, described him as 'a kind of fourth estate in the politics of the country' and said that he was 'not only unquestionably the most powerful political writer of the present day, but one of the best writers in the language. He speaks and thinks plain, broad, downright English'.

'His knowledge grows out of the subject,' wrote Hazlitt. 'And his style is that of a man who has an absolute intuition of what he is talking about, and never thinks of anything else.'

'His egotism is delightful, for there is no affectation in it. He does not talk of himself for lack of something to write about, but because some circumstance that has happened to himself is the best possible illustration of the subject; and he is not the man to shrink from giving the best possible illustration of the subject from a squeamish delicacy...He writes himself plain William Cobbett, strips himself quite as naked as anybody could wish: in a word, his egotism is full of individuality and has room for very little vanity in it. We feel delighted, rub our hands, and draw our chair to the fire, when we come to a passage of this sort: we know it will be something new and good, manly and simple, not the same insipid story of self over again. We sit down at table with the writer, but it is of a course of rich viands – flesh, fish and wild fowl – and not to a nominal entertainment, like that given by the Barmecide in the *Arabian Nights*, who put off his visitor with calling for a number of exquisite things that never appeared.'

'As a political partisan, no one can stand against him. With his brandished club, like Giant Despair in the *The Pilgrim's Progress*, he knocks out their brains: and not only no individual, but no corrupt system, could hold out against his powerful and repeated attacks... wherever power is, there is he against it: he naturally butts at all obstacles, as unicorns are attracted to oak-trees, and feels his own strength only by resistance to the opinions and wishes of the rest of the world.'

Cobbett was blisteringly honest, forever shrewd and wrote without fear or favour. He had a singular talent for arousing passion among his readers. It was, and could have only been, Cobbett who, protesting about the social costs and consequences of the Industrial Revolution, claimed that England was building her industrial dominance on the backs of thirty thousand little girls.

Writing in 1838, shortly after Cobbett's death, Thomas Carlyle, the historian, described him 'as the pattern John Bull of his century, strong as the rhinoceros, and with singular humanities and genialities shining through his thick skin'. He was, said Carlyle, 'a most brave phenomenon'.

Self educated, and born the son of a farmer and innkeeper, the young Cobbett left home without telling his parents and took a job at Kew Gardens. On the way to Kew he bought a copy of Swift's *Tale of a Tub* with his very last threepence. It was a book he always treasured.

On taking a day out from his new job to visit Portsmouth to see his uncle he fell in love with the sea and decided to join the navy. He bribed someone with sixpence and somehow managed to talk himself aboard a man-o-war where the captain persuaded him to return home.

After numerous adventures Cobbett found himself a job as a lawyer's clerk in London. He was 21 and hated it. 'No part of my life has been totally unattended with pleasure,' he wrote, 'except the eight or nine months I passed in Gray's Inn.' He complained that he had merely assisted in the foment and perpetuation of quarrels between John Doe and Richard Roe. Bored and despairing he went to Chatham and joined the marines. He taught himself grammar and became clerk to the garrison commandment. 'I learned grammar when I was a private soldier on the pay of sixpence a day,' he wrote. 'The edge of my berth, or that of my guard bed was my seat to study in; my knapsack was my bookcase; a bit of board lying on my lap was my writing table; and the task did not demand anything like a year of my life. I had no money to purchase candle or oil; in winter time it was rarely that I could get any evening light but that of the fire, and only my turn even of that. And if I, under such circumstances, and without parent or friend to advise or encourage me, accomplished this undertaking, what excuse can there be for any youth, however poor, however pressed with business, or however circumstanced as to room or other conveniences?'

In 1785, he travelled to Nova Scotia and New Brunswick with his regiment the 54th Foot, quickly rising through the ranks to become a sergeant major. He served as a soldier in Florida until 1791. (Florida had been a British possession from 1763 until 1783 and then returned to Spanish control. But the British continued to use Florida as a base.) In 1791, he returned to England, married, and blotted his copybook as a soldier by accusing officers from the 54th Foot of embezzlement. He quickly realised that the authorities were on the side of the officers and so he fled to France. From there he went to Philadelphia. He stayed in America for eight years, teaching English to French refugees and while there he wrote and published an English grammar for French students. He also wrote pamphlets denouncing the French Revolution.

It was while in America that Cobbett started publishing pro-English pamphlets. In 1795, he started to use the pseudonym Peter Porcupine and issued *The Political Censor*, a report of proceedings in Congress together with a commentary. He also opened a bookseller's shop. When threatened with physical violence he wrote *Life and Adventures of Peter Porcupine* as a defence of his views. He published *Porcupine's Gazette* and *Daily Advertiser* to denounce the French and advocate an English Alliance.

He hadn't been living in America long before he once again got into trouble, this time for describing the American Government as: 'the most profligately dishonest that I have ever seen or heard described...the most corrupt and tyrannical that the world ever knew.' He was heavily fined for a libel on Benjamin Rush and so left America in dudgeon.

When he got back to London in 1800, Cobbett was offered the editorship of an official government paper. He refused and started his own newspaper *The Porcupine*. He campaigned against the weaknesses of the proposed peace with the French.

In 1802, he launched a weekly newspaper called *Cobbett's Political Register*, which he continued to write, edit and publish until his death in 1835. The *Register*, which started off with Tory views and gradually drifted towards more radical opinions, grew to achieve a massive circulation. Wherever there was Cobbett, there was always trouble. He was fined for attacking a Ministry for its conduct of

Irish affairs and his house was attacked by a mob. In the same year he founded *Cobbett's Parliamentary Debates* (a publication which was later taken over by *Hansard*).

By 1805, Cobbett had enough money to buy a farm. But he continued to write and published constantly; taking an active part in national politics and campaigning against bribery and on behalf of ordinary citizens who were, he felt, getting a pretty raw deal from the politicians. He campaigned vociferously for parliamentary reform and, inevitably, continued to get into trouble. In 1810, he was sentenced to a fine of £1,000 (an enormous sum at the time) and two years imprisonment for an article reporting the flogging of mutinous militiamen. Sent to Newgate prison he continued to write his weekly newspaper and also wrote *Paper against Gold*, condemning paper money and calling for the National Debt to be abolished and gold to be reintroduced as the nation's only currency.

Upon his release from prison, in 1812, he began to attack the system of tithes. He also wrote *Letter to the Luddites* in an attempt to dissuade labouring men from violence. He reduced the price of his newspaper from one shilling and a halfpenny to twopence. The circulation and authority soared. Cobbett wrote scathing comments about 'pocket boroughs' and 'rotten boroughs'; complaining viciously about the way that parliamentary seats could be bought or handed over to 'favourites'. He also attacked the way that corruption and bribery affected the decisions of MPs. He raged about the 'sinecurists, placemen and taxeaters' who took from the country but never gave anything back in return. He complained bitterly about fiat money. He pointed out that 'it is the Government's job to help keep us safe, healthy and happy'.

'It is,' he wrote, 'the chief business of a government to take care that one part of the people do not cause the other part to lead miserable lives.'

None of this went down any better with the 19th century establishment than it would have gone down with the present day establishment, and in 1817 the Government suspended the Habeas Corpus Act so that it could imprison, without trial, anyone whom it regarded as undesirable. Everyone knew that the suspension of the Habeas Corpus Act was done specifically to get at author (and self-publisher) William Cobbett. His enemies even started a journal entitled *Anti-Cobbett*. Rightly fearing the Government's intentions Cobbett absconded and fled first to France and then to America where he took a farm on Long Island. He didn't return to England until things had quietened down a little. He continued to direct the *Political Register* and wrote and published *A Year's Residence in the United States of America* and *A Grammar of the English Language*. While in the USA he dug up the body of Thomas Paine, taking the bones back to England to bury them there. (The bones remained in Cobbett's possession until his death when they were mislaid. He had never got round to reburying them.)

In 1820, Cobbett was back in England. The Government introduced a stamp duty on periodicals in an attempt to close down his publications. He stood for Parliament at Coventry but was defeated. He became bankrupt.

At this point Cobbett really started to work hard. He wrote and published a number of books including *Cobbett's Monthly Sermons* and *Cottage Economy*. In 1830 he reprinted portions of his Register under the title *Cobbett's Twopenny Trash*. In 1831 he was indicted on a charge of encouraging disorder. He conducted his own defence and the prosecution failed. This was the last attempt by the Government to coerce the press by legal action. Cobbett's victory was a real victory for journalism and for the people.

He published *State Trials* and wrote several other books on economics and other subjects. Somehow he managed to find time to run farms too; first in Hampshire and then in Surrey.

In 1829, he published his book *Advice to Young Men* and in 1830 Cobbett published the book for which he is now probably best known, *Rural Rides*, an astonishing and revealing social document which also happens to be an immensely readable account of his horseback adventures around the country. Both were first published as part of his *Register*.

In 1832, he became member of parliament for Oldham. He spoke frequently. He continued to write and publish and to represent Oldham as an MP until his death in 1835.

William Cobbett, author, editor and publisher, made many enemies throughout his life. But he also made many people think. Cobbett was one of the greatest Englishmen of all time. 'He is always a hearty Englishman,' wrote the diplomat Sir Henry Lytton

Bulwer in his book *Historical Characters* in 1868. 'He may vary in his opinions as to doctrines and as to men, but he is ever for making England great, powerful and prosperous – her people healthy, brave and free.'

Cobbett was an original; he fought for journalism against authority and, with John Wilkes, was the originator of the modern concept of the 'free press'. During the early 19th century writers were transported, imprisoned and fined without limit. Around 500 publishers were imprisoned in one six year period when Cobbett was operating. Cobbett forced the Government to allow writers and publishers more freedom.

It was Hazlitt who pointed out that a really great and original writer is like nobody but himself. 'It is easy to describe second-rate talents,' Hazlitt wrote, 'because they fall into a class and enlist under a standard: but first-rate powers defy calculation or comparison, and can be defined only by themselves. They are sui generis, and make the class to which they belong'. In this respect Hazlitt put Cobbett into the same category as Defoe and Shakespeare.

Cobbett's work was read by millions during his life. Thousands followed his coffin when he died.

Cobbett himself said that his popularity was 'owing to giving the truth in clear language'.

No writer can, or should, aim higher.

Richard Cobden (1804-1865)

Richard Cobden was the father of international trade; he is sometimes known as 'the Apostle of Free Trade'.

Born in Heyshott, near Midhurst in Sussex, the young Cobden was sent for five years to one of the terrible boarding schools which were later so hated by Charles Dickens. The school was in Yorkshire and the young Cobden's father sent him there when he had to sell his farm. The family, a large one, had become relatively poor.

In 1819, after leaving school, Cobden was sent to a warehouse in London which belonged to an uncle. There he quickly showed skills both as a commercial traveller and a clerk.

Nine years after starting work in his uncle's warehouse Cobden formed a partnership with two friends in order to sell wholesale calico in London. In 1831, they set up a calico printing business in Lancashire and the year afterwards Cobden moved to Manchester. In 1835, he visited the USA for the first time and in 1836 he travelled in the Levant.

As a result of his two trips he wrote two pamphlets England, Ireland and America and Russia. In the first he wrote about the importance of free trade, explaining why governments should not interfere in trade between countries. In the second he warned against what he called 'Russophobia'. Even after the start of the Crimean War, he continued to argue in favour of friendly relations with Russia.

In 1838, he and a group of other merchants from Manchester formed the Anti-Corn-Law League to fight against the corn laws (which kept the price of corn artificially high in England, for the benefit of large landowners). He travelled the country speaking out against trade restrictions and in 1841 was elected as the member of parliament for Stockport. The Prime Minister, Robert Peel, acknowledged that it was Cobden's campaigning which was largely responsible for the abolition of the Corn Laws.

For Cobden personally all this campaigning had a downside. He had failed to give attention to his private business and he went bankrupt. He also became ill; exhausted by his efforts. The public recognised his sacrifice and in 1847 the enormous sum of £80,000 was raised in recognition of his services to the people. With the money he now had Cobden bought Dunford, the farmhouse in Heyshott where he had been born. He also took just over a year off and travelled throughout Europe to convalesce.

When he got back to England, Cobden found that he had been elected as MP for both Stockport and the West Riding. He chose the latter constituency. In 1859, he visited America again and when he came back found that he had been elected MP for Rochdale. He was offered the job of President of the Board of Trade but declined. He did, however, arrange a treaty of commerce with France in 1860. The treaty he negotiated included material that was later duplicated in a number of other treaties between countries. He was a strong supporter of the North during America's Civil War.

Richard Cobden died in 1865 and was buried in Sussex, the county of his birth.

John Cockcroft (1897-1967)

In 1932, an Englishman was the first person to split the atom. His name was John Cockcroft. He received the Nobel Prize in Physics for splitting the atomic nucleus and his work was instrumental in the development of nuclear power.

John Cockcroft was born in Todmorden, the son of a mill owner. During the First World War he was a signaller in the Royal Artillery. He then studied electrotechnical engineering and maths in Manchester and Cambridge.

In 1928, Cockcroft began work on the acceleration of protons with Ernest Walton. Four years later the two men succeeded in transmuting lithium into helium by bombarding it with high energy protons. It was this achievement which was widely known as 'splitting the atom'.

In 1946, Cockcroft set up the Atomic Energy Research Establishment to develop England's atomic power programme. He is famous for having insisted on extra safety procedures being installed on nuclear power stations. At the time these were considered unnecessary. Cockcroft was awarded a knighthood in 1948.

John Constable (1776-1837)

It's a piece of England that has been skilfully captured onto canvas and there is no doubt that John Constable's oil painting depicting a hay wain on the River Stour in Suffolk, is one of England's best-known works of art. But sadly, it took the French to alert our Royal Academy to the talent of one of England's greatest landscape painters.

Baptised on the day of his birth because he wasn't expected to live, John Constable was born 11 June 1776 in East Bergholt, Suffolk. His father, Golding Constable, was a mill owner, grain merchant and farmer. Owing to the fact that John's older brother was mentally impaired, John was the heir to his father's business and was expected to work for his father after he left school.

One of six children, John had a fairly happy childhood with parents who weren't overly strict with him. For example, when John told his parents how miserable he was being made by the incredibly brutish discipline meted out by one of the schoolmasters at his boarding school in Lavenham, they withdrew him from the school and moved him to Dedham Grammar School – a school which he loved, although he was considered something of a daydreamer and did not show much academic promise. However, he did show artistic talent, especially for penmanship, which endeared him to his schoolmaster, Dr Thomas Grimwood.

When John Constable was 16 years of age he did as was expected of him, and began working for his father in the mill. It wasn't until several years later that John Constable was to realise his true ambition to become a painter.

It was John Constable's friendship with John Dunthorne, who was six years his senior, that led him on the path to becoming a painter. Dunthorne wanted to be an artist, which Constable found fascinating. Together, Constable and Dunthorne would go off on local painting expeditions, taking their easels and paints with them to paint a piece of landscape.

John Constable once famously said: 'The sound of water escaping from mill dams, willows, old rotten planks, slimy posts and brickwork... those scenes made me a painter and I am grateful'.

When his younger brother Abram agreed to take over John's place in the family business, the way was clear for John Constable to pursue his dream as a painter. He was coming up to 23 years old when he entered the Royal Academy Schools in London as a probationer. Whilst there, he drew models and plaster casts, attended anatomy classes and studied the Old Masters. Constable studied at the Royal Academy around the same time as another great artist, J. M. W. Turner. (Constable's less than pleasant encounters with Turner on several occasions later on in his life, led Constable to believe that Turner detested him.)

In 1802, Constable exhibited at the Royal Academy for the first time. In the same year, he was offered a job of drawing master at Great Marlow Military College but he declined the offer. His dream was to be a landscape painter no matter what financial sacrifices he had to make. Later on, to make ends meet, he worked for a while as a portrait artist.

Like a lot of great artists, John Constable often struggled financially and only managed to sell around 20 paintings in England. However, in 1828, he came into an inheritance, which enabled him to give up the portraits and to devote himself entirely to landscape painting. John Constable's greatest love was painting the English landscape, especially around his native home: the valley of the River Stour around Dedham East Bergholt, which is now known as Constable Country. He adored the countryside: the fields, the trees and the sky with its formation of clouds. His love of painting nature as it truly is was reflected in a sentence that he wrote in one of his letters to his dear friend Archdeacon John Fisher: 'A gentleman's park is my aversion. It is not beauty because it is not nature'.

Despite strong opposition from her father, Constable married Maria Bicknell in 1816. It was a happy marriage which resulted in seven children. But sadly, her health was poor and the couple moved from central London to Hampstead Heath because Constable believed the air would be better for her. After just 12 years of marriage, Maria died in 1829 from tuberculosis, leaving Constable utterly heartbroken and sending him into a deep depression.

Melancholy was no stranger to Constable as he often suffered from bouts of depression throughout his life, although not to the extent of the melancholia he suffered after Maria's death. The intense sorrow he felt over the death of his beloved wife is revealed in his dark and bleak painting, Hadleigh Castle.

A year after his wife died, Constable, who was then 52, was finally awarded full membership of the Royal Academy, though the membership was awarded rather grudgingly. Tragically, he never gained the level of fame he ought to have done in England.

It was in France where Constable was most famous. In 1824, several of his paintings, including The Hay Wain, received instant acclaim at the Paris Salon where they were exhibited. (Constable's other notable works include, Dedham Vale, View on the Stour, Salisbury Cathedral, The Cornfield and Salisbury Cathedral from the Meadows). Constable was awarded gold medals from the King of France for several of his paintings. His paintings were said to have had a profound influence on the French artist Delacroix and, later on, the Barbizon school. His fascination with the effects of shadow and light are believed to have inspired artists of the impressionist movement.

The great English landscape artist who once said that his art could be 'found under every hedge and in every lane' and that that was why 'nobody thinks it worth picking up', died in 1837, probably from a heart attack. He was 60 years old. He was buried beside his wife in St John's, Church Row, Hampstead, London.

Since his death, Constable's work has gone in and out of fashion with art dealers and collectors. But for Englishmen and Englishwomen everywhere John Constable, the greatest painter of the English countryside, will always be in fashion.

James Cook (1728-1779)

The man who discovered Australia and New Zealand started his maritime life as an ordinary deck hand on a collier taking coal from Whitby to London. By the end of his professional life he had commanded not one but three great voyages of discovery. Captain James Cook was one of the greatest sailors and explorers the world has ever seen.

Born in Marton, in Cleveland, Yorkshire, the son of an agricultural labourer, Cook began his working life in a haberdasher's shop at Staithes. He then became an apprentice to a Whitby ship-owner and spent some years in the coasting and Baltic trade. He joined the Royal Navy in 1755 and in 1759 he obtained his master's certificate. In 1763-1767 he surveyed the St Lawrence River and the Coast of Newfoundland.

The success of this surveying venture meant that in 1768 he was appointed commander of the first scientific expedition to the Pacific Ocean. Sailing on HMS Endeavour, he carried with him a scientific expedition intending to observe the transit of the planet Venus. After the completion of this mission, and on the way back home, he discovered and charted the two main islands of New Zealand and discovered and explored the eastern coast of Australia. He claimed the lands he had discovered for England. During the trip he landed at Botany Bay, not far from the current city of Sydney.

The voyage lasted three years and Cook came back with a mass of scientific material. He sailed through the strait between Australia and New Guinea and completed the voyage by way of Java and the Cape of Good Hope. Just as important as the discoveries he had made was the fact that Cook had managed to command such a long sea voyage without losing any of his crew members to scurvy. Up until then scurvy had been a significant problem for long-distance sailors and navies around the world had often lost more men to the disease than to enemy action. Cook discovered that a diet of fresh fruit and vegetables prevented scurvy.

When he returned to England Cook was promoted to commander and was then sent with two ships, the Resolution and Adventure, to make the first circumnavigation of the earth. He was expected to sail into the Antarctic and find out how far the lands of the Antarctic stretched northwards. That expedition also took three years (from 1772 to 1775) and is generally regarded as the greatest of all sailing-ship voyages. Cook sailed further south than any man before him. He sailed around the edge of the ice and made meticulous measurements. Cook also visited Tahiti and the New Hebrides and discovered New Caledonia and other groups of islands. Thanks again to his precautions against scurvy, Cook lost only one crew member during the three years.

Cook died on his third major voyage, which set off in 1776 with the ships Discovery and Resolution. Searching for a Northwest Passage around Canada and Alaska, Cook took the scenic route and sailed via the Cape, Tasmania, New Zealand, the Pacific Islands, the Sandwich islands and the north west coast of North America. He surveyed the coast as far as Icy Cape in Bering Strait but was forced to turn back. He sailed to Hawaii and reached there in January 1779. At first the natives were friendly but they suddenly changed their attitude. On the 14 February, when Cook landed with a party of sailors to recover a stolen boat, he was attacked and killed. He was just 51 years old.

James Cook did more than any other navigator to enhance our knowledge of the Pacific Ocean and the Southern Ocean. By the time he died, the labourer's son from Yorkshire had become the world's greatest sailor and explorer. He would, in time, sit alongside Drake and Ralegh, as one of the world's three greatest and best-known sailors.

Thomas Cook (1808-1892)

Born in Derbyshire, Thomas Cook started work as an assistant to a local market gardener when he was 10 years old. When he was 14 he became an apprentice cabinetmaker. Brought up as a strict Baptist he joined the local Temperance Society and in 1826 became a preacher, touring the area as an evangelist and publishing and distributing temperance pamphlets. He became a minister in 1828. Cook had the idea that was to change the world of travel while waiting for a stagecoach on the road to London. On 5 July 1842 he arranged to take 570 temperance campaigners from a railway station in Leicester to a rally in Loughborough, just eleven miles away. He did a deal with the rail company and they agreed to charge one shilling a person for return rail tickets and food for the journey. The rail tickets were legal contracts between the company and the passengers, and Cook wasn't allowed to sell tickets himself but he received a share of the money received by the train company. He made similar arrangements for three consecutive summers and in 1844 the Midland Counties Railway Company made the deal permanent. He then started a business running rail excursions for pleasure – and taking a percentage of the money taken by the rail company.

In 1846, he overstretched himself and went bankrupt after taking 350 people from Leicester on a tour of Scotland. He bounced back, took 165,000 people to the Great Exhibition in London and made money. In 1850, he arranged his first excursion abroad and took a group from Leicester to Calais to visit the Paris Exhibition.

From then on he didn't look back. He started arranging 'grand circular tours' of Europe and by the 1860's he was taking parties to Switzerland, Italy, Egypt and even to the United States of America. He introduced the idea whereby tourists could travel independently while his agency arranged all the travel, food and accommodation over any route. As usual he took his percentage from railway companies, shipping lines and hotels.

He formed a partnership with his son and founded a travel agency called Thomas Cook and Son with offices in Fleet Street in London. His shop sold luggage, footwear, telescopes and guidebooks. Cook and his wife ran a small temperance hotel above the shop and office.

In 1872, Cook started a round-the-world tour. For 200 guineas, travellers were taken across the Atlantic on a steamship, across America by stage coach, across the Pacific to Japan by paddle steamer, and overland across China and India. The journey lasted 222 days. Two years later he introduced travellers' cheques.

It is no exaggeration to say that Thomas Cook created the modern tourist industry.

Oliver Cromwell (1599-1658)

Oliver Cromwell, the father of British Parliament, was born on 25 April 1599 in Huntingdon, Cambridgeshire; the son of Robert Cromwell and Elizabeth Steward and a descendant of Thomas Cromwell, who was Henry VIII's chief minister. The young boy was named after his rich uncle, Sir Oliver Cromwell. The young Oliver would become a brilliant and inspirational leader, a man of action, and a military mastermind. He would lead the Parliamentary forces to victory in the English Civil War and be the man most responsible for establishing modern parliamentary democracy, first in England and later throughout the rest of the world. Many great men have ideas, or institute changes, which would have probably surfaced without them – they just happened to be the first to think of them or to be the men in the right position at the right time. But if Oliver Cromwell had never lived it is likely that the parliamentary forces would have lost the English Civil War. Would there have been another revolution?

It is reasonable to assert that the world would not be the same place today if Oliver Cromwell had not existed. The parliamentary forces had been badly battered before Cromwell took control. It is likely that without him they would have lost, and democratic government would not have been maintained in England.

Cromwell's victory was a trigger which led to the French Enlightenment and the French Revolution, and to the establishment of democratic governments throughout western Europe and in English colonies such as Australia, Canada and the United States of America.

Oliver Cromwell grew up on his father's farm in Huntingdon and was one of ten children: 3 boys and 7 girls. Sadly, Oliver Cromwell's two brothers died in infancy, effectively making Oliver the only son of Robert and Elizabeth.

Very little is known about Cromwell's childhood except that he attended the grammar school at Huntingdon where he was taught by the clergyman and schoolmaster Dr Thomas Beard.

In 1616, when he was 17, Cromwell went to Cambridge University but after just a year there his father died, and he was obliged to return to the farm to help look after his widowed mother and his 7 unmarried sisters.

On 22 August 1620, at the age of 21, Cromwell married Elizabeth Bourchier the daughter of a retired, rich fur trader. Together, they had nine children: four girls and five boys. Oliver Cromwell was a great family man who cared deeply for his wife and children.

With nine cousins already sitting in Parliament, Cromwell wanted to follow family tradition and in 1628 he was elected as one of two MPs for Huntingdon. Then, in 1629, after the young Cromwell had been an MP for only one year, King Charles I dissolved Parliament after he had been refused money to pay for another attack on France.

Charles I then ruled for 11 years without a Parliament, a period which became known as the 'Eleven Years Tyranny'. King James I, believed in 'the divine right of kings' and once told his parliament, 'Kings are God's lieutenants upon earth and sit upon God's throne'. He instilled this absurd belief into his son Prince Charles and it was this teaching, which would, during Charles's reign as king, cause a conflict between him and Parliament and, consequently, bring about his death.

In 1631, Cromwell was involved in a local feud, which led him to sell his family's properties in and around Huntingdon and move with his family to a farmstead (where he leased the land) in St Ives. Cromwell, no longer a country gentleman, was now a yeoman. But five years later, childless Sir Thomas Steward died leaving an inheritance to his nephew, Oliver Cromwell. Oliver's financial circumstances had gone up again. In 1640, Charles I recalled Parliament because he needed financial help with his campaign against the Scots. Once more, Cromwell (who had undergone a powerful religious conversion during his time out of Parliament and was now a Puritan) was back in Parliament.

From this time on Cromwell's religious beliefs influenced every decision he ever made; like all Puritans he believed the purpose of life was to work hard and to serve God and he was convinced that he was being guided to carry out God's will. Many laws were brought in to rid society of what the Puritans deemed as evil; things which distracted people from worshipping God. Some of the long list of restrictive laws included: no Christmas festivities (for example, mince pies were banned), no travelling on Sundays, no dancing, all theatres to be closed down, no football and so on. It wasn't exactly a fun time.

In 1640, after three weeks of Parliament, King Charles again dissolved Parliament after he was refused money for his campaign against the rebelling Scots. Parliament's three-week period after a decade's closure was, not surprisingly, known as the Short Parliament.

However, Cromwell wasn't without a Parliamentary seat for long as Parliament was recalled later that year (this one was known as the Long Parliament because it lasted in various forms for 20 years).

At the end of 1641, the Grand Remonstrance – which Oliver Cromwell supported – was drafted by the Long Parliament. This listed a mass of grievances about King Charles's government of both Church and State, and a number of recommended reforms. A copy of the document was given to the King who wasn't much taken with it. In January 1642, goaded by his wife Queen Henrietta, the King stormed into the Chamber of the House of Commons with his swordsmen and attempted to arrest the five main MPs who were involved in the drafting of the Grand Remonstrance. Fortunately, the five MPs had been tipped off that the King was coming and had quickly escaped through another door. However, the MPs were furious that Charles I should dare barge into the House of Commons.

(King Charles' storming into the House of Commons is the reason why Black Rod (senior official of the House of Lords) performs his ceremonial duty on the annual State Opening of Parliament today. When the monarch is ready to deliver his or her speech in the House of Lords, Black Rod is dispatched to the chamber to the House of Commons to summon MPs to hear the speech. As he approaches the entrance to the Commons chamber, the door is slammed in

Black Rod's face to show the independence of the Commons from the Sovereign. With his rod, Black Rod bangs three times on the door. The door to the Commons chamber is then opened, Black Rod enters, bows respectfully and informs the MPs that they are needed at the House of Lords. The MPs then follow Black Rod to the House of Lords to hear the monarch's speech.)

Shortly after King Charles's failed attempt to arrest five of his biggest critics, he left London to raise an army to fight Parliament. And in August 1642, the King raised his standard at Nottingham: marking the beginning of the First English Civil War. The war was fought between the Cavaliers and the Roundheads (the Roundheads were so-called because of their pudding basin haircuts). The Cavaliers, or royalists were mostly Anglican and Catholics, and the Roundheads, the supporters of Parliament were mostly Puritans.

In 1642, at 43 years of age, Cromwell was appointed captain in charge of a small group of cavalry (which he raised) in Parliament's army, which was led by Lord General Essex. On the 23 October 1642, the first major battle was fought at Edgehill in Warwickshire where both sides claimed victory. A year later Cromwell, who had no previous military experience, was commissioned as a colonel to raise a cavalry regiment in the Eastern Association. Cromwell's regiment was later famously known as the Ironsides. With his regiment, Cromwell managed to suppress a royalist uprising at Lowestoft and recapture Stamford.

In 1644, Cromwell was appointed Lieutenant General of the Eastern Association. As Lieutenant General he was able to put his brilliant military ideas into practice and go on to win many notable victories such as the famous great battle at Marston Moor on 2 July 1644. Not only did Cromwell's success increase his military reputation but it also helped to increase his influence in politics.

Cromwell then became Lieutenant General of the New Model Army – England's first national army. Sir Thomas Fairfax, known as Black Tom because of his dark hair and eyes, was Commander-in-Chief. Cromwell went on to win the last major battle of the First Civil War against the Royalist army at the battle of Naseby in 1645. The year 1646 marked the end of the First Civil War.

In the June of 1646, King Charles handed himself over to the mercy of the Scots even though they had fought against him during the war and in February 1647, the Scots aware that their attempts to persuade King Charles to renounce his Anglican faith and convert to Presbyterianism were unsuccessful, sold the King to Parliament.

Around this time, Parliament demanded that most of the New Model Army should be disbanded but the soldiers mutinied. Oliver Cromwell was sent by Parliament to army headquarters to discuss how the grievances could be addressed but, unfortunately for Parliament, Cromwell's sympathies lay with the army. At the end of May in 1647, the army kidnapped King Charles and held him in Newmarket under their control. He was then taken to Hampton Court where Parliament and the army (the army had more or less taken over Parliament) had debates – known as the 'Putney Debates' because they were in and around Putney church – on what next to do with the King.

In November 1647, the king escaped from Hampton Court to the Isle of Wight where he was re-captured and held in Carisbrooke Castle. While he was there King Charles was involved in secret negotiations with the Scots, promising them much if they would side with him against Parliament.

In 1648, the Second Civil War began, and Parliament appealed to Cromwell for help. Cromwell, along with the army, then managed to crush the Royalist Scots at Preston.

While the King was still imprisoned on the Isle of Wight, Parliament, fearing a military take over, implored him to agree to peace talks, but the King wanted time to make a decision. Exasperated by the King's indecisiveness, Cromwell and Parliament ordered Charles to be taken to Windsor Castle and put on trial for treason. Cromwell, whose name appeared third on the list of signatories, was one of the people who signed King Charles' death warrant.

On an icy cold day in January 1649, King Charles was sentenced to death. For his beheading, King Charles wore two vests just in case anyone mistook his shivering of the cold for fear. King Charles faced his death with great dignity and courage. It is reputed that Cromwell went to see King Charles's corpse while it lay in its coffin at Whitehall, and on seeing the dead king he was reputed to have murmured, 'cruel necessity'.

In 1648, very shortly before the regicide, the army replaced

Parliament with the Rump Parliament, which consisted mostly of Independents like Cromwell, and the following year the monarchy and the House of Lords were abolished by an Act of Parliament, and England was declared a Commonwealth.

The biggest threat to the new Commonwealth was the uprising in Ireland and in the same year, Cromwell was appointed Lord Lieutenant of Ireland and Commander in Chief of the army in Ireland. In 1649, Cromwell defeated the Irish at Drogheda in a gruesome massacre. He then went on to defeat the Irish at Wexford. To this day, Oliver Cromwell is still reviled in Ireland for his actions at Drogheda and Wexford.

Cromwell was recalled from Ireland and appointed Commander in Chief of the New Model Army for the war against the Scots. The Scots wanted to restore Charles II to the English throne but were defeated at the battle of Dunbar in 1650 (even though they had twice as many men). The battle at Dunbar is thought to be Cromwell's greatest victory. Cromwell regularly credited his military victories to God's will – firmly believing that he was fighting God's cause.

On 1 January 1651 at Scone, the Scots crowned King Charles's son – Charles II – King of Scotland. Charles II, along with the Scots, was determined that he should regain the throne that his father once had. Realising that his army was greatly outnumbered by Cromwell's, Charles II made his way to the old royalist strongholds on the borders of Wales in an attempt to gather more troops on the way before heading to London. But Cromwell managed to catch up with Charles II and his army at Worcester, and went on to fight a victorious battle against Charles II and his Scottish supporters on 3 September 1651. Cromwell described the battle as his 'crowning mercy'. It was the final battle of the English Civil War.

After the battle of Worcester, Charles II fled to France but, before escaping, he hid from the pursuing army up an oak tree. After his restoration to the throne years later, many pubs in England were re-named the Royal Oak in honour of the tree that had saved Charles II from being captured.

In 1653, Cromwell became exasperated with the Rump Parliament and forcibly dissolved it, marching into the House of Commons and shouting: 'You have sat too long here for any good you have been doing. Depart, I say, and let us have done with you. In the name of God, go!' He called in six musketeers from his regiment, dragged the speaker out by his hair and emptied the House of Commons. Cromwell replaced the Rump with the Barebones Parliament (a Parliament of carefully nominated honest men who were known as the Parliament of Saints). The Barebones Parliament collapsed within a year and in 1653, Cromwell became Lord Protector of England, Scotland and Ireland. As Lord Protector, Cromwell was addressed as His Highness Lord Protector and moved into the King's former palace at Whitehall. At Whitehall Palace, Cromwell lived like a King, employing many of King Charles' old servants. Cromwell was now leading the life that he had loathed and fought hard against when King Charles I and King Charles II were on the throne.

Cromwell had great ambitions to make England great again and he succeeded. His navy defeated the Spanish at the battle of Santa Cruz in the Canary Islands, he gained a foothold in the West Indies, made peace with the French and ended a trade war with the Dutch.

In 1657, despite the House of Commons urging him to accept the crown in a document called the Humble Petition and Advice, Cromwell declined the offer of becoming King of England, Scotland and Ireland.

Finally, on 3 September 1658, at the age of 59, Oliver Cromwell, Lord Protector of the Commonwealth of England, Scotland and Ireland passed away, possibly from a malarial-type disease that had recurred. It is believed that the death of his beloved daughter, Elizabeth, less than a month earlier had not only weakened his spirit but had weakened his body too. Contrary to everything he believed in when he was alive, Cromwell was given a state funeral with no expense spared. His body was laid to rest at Westminster Abbey.

After Oliver Cromwell's death, he was succeeded by his eldest son Richard Cromwell but in 1659, Richard Cromwell, derogatorily known as 'Tumble-down-Dick', was forced to abdicate. Less than a year later, Charles II was restored to the throne after being invited back by Parliament. In a typically vindictive gesture, the remains of Oliver Cromwell were dug up and hung from the gibbett. But King Charles II realised that the battle for royal absolutism had been lost. He did not contest the supremacy of Parliament. When the foolish James II tried to restore royal absolutism he was thrown out in a bloodless revolution in 1688. The changes made by Cromwell were not, and would never be, reversed.

Books and films have traditionally made the more colourful cavaliers the heroes of English history. Cromwell's Roundheads are invariably portrayed as boring dullards – the bad guys. The truth is the opposite. The Cavaliers, all curly wigs, thigh-length boots and fancy jackets, were the oppressors, the bad guys, the new sheriffs of Nottingham of their day. The Roundheads were the 17th century descendants of Robin Hood and his band of outlaws.

Critics have accused Cromwell of being hypocritical, and have pointed out that although he always argued in favour of democracy he did establish a military dictatorship. This is unfair. Cromwell was devoted to the principles of parliamentary democracy and when circumstances beyond his power forced him to take on power that he did not want to take he insisted that he did so temporarily. When offered the throne of England he refused it. And he refused the offer of a permanent dictatorship.

Cromwell, plainly dressed, rather scruffy even, had a 'swollen and reddish' face that was cursed with warts. He was quite an unattractive man but he was never ashamed of his lack of good looks. For example, when Cromwell had his portrait painted, he insisted that Mr Lely, the Court painter, include his warts in the painting. (This is the origin of the saying 'warts and all'.)

Cromwell was a moderate and tolerant and passionate man; a sincere campaigner for the people, for religious tolerance and for an England combining a constitutional monarchy with a parliamentary democracy. He was the achetypal English hero: tough and uncompromising but driven by strong ideals and honourable and honest beliefs. Everyone in the world who now lives in a democratic country owes Oliver Cromwell a huge debt.

John Dalton 1766-1844

Remembered and revered around the world as one of the fathers of modern physical science, John Dalton was born in Eaglesfield, Cumberland and died, 78 years later just a little further south, in Manchester.

Dalton's formal schooling ended when he was 11 years old. He taught himself science and was such a brilliant young man that he became a teacher at the age of 12. He moved to Kendal, in the Lake District at the age of 15 and when he was 26 he moved to Manchester where he lived until he died. He became a chemist and physicist and was the scientist who introduced fundamental atomic theory into the mainstream of science.

The idea that all material objects are made up of very small, indestructible particles called atoms was probably first suggested by the Greek philosopher Deomocritus in around 400 BC. The hypothesis was adopted by Epicurus and Lucretius and, much later, by Isaac Newton. But the idea remained just that – a philosophical notion. There had been no attempt to express atomic theories quantitatively, or to use them in any sort of scientific research, until John Dalton presented a distinctive, precise quantitative theory which could be tested in the laboratory and used to interpret chemical experiments.

Dalton created the concept of the existence of atoms, molecules, elements and chemical compounds and in 1808 he argued, in a book entitled *A New System of Chemical Philosophy*, which listed twenty specific elements, that although there is a huge number of atoms in the world, there is a relatively small number of types of atom. Today, we know that there are more elements than Dalton thought existed, but his work was crucial to our understanding of our world. Although his book was not published until 1808, Dalton had created his atomic theory in 1804.

Dalton created a table listing the relative weights of different types of atom and argued that atoms of the same species are identical in all their properties, including their mass. He even gave the elements specific symbols to help identify them. (Scientists later showed that there are exceptions to Dalton's rule and that a single chemical element may exist in different isotopes – having the same chemical properties but slightly different mass.)

Moreover, Dalton realised that any two molecules of a single chemical compound will be made up of the same combination of atoms; in other words, including the same elements in the same proportions.

Within two decades Dalton's theory had been widely adopted by scientists around the world, and chemists everywhere had learned to follow the blueprint he had suggested for defining atomic weights and the combination of atoms within each species of molecule. Dalton's atomic hypothesis is fundamental to our understanding of chemistry and modern physics.

Like many great scientists, Dalton did a great deal more than the work that made him famous. In 1787 he became interested in meteorology and published a book on the subject in 1793. The meteorological journal he kept all his life contains more than 200,000 observations. He performed important experiments which enabled him to formulate vital laws governing the behaviour of gases. And, his curiosity aroused because he himself suffered from the condition, he also published the first scientific paper on colour blindness.

Abraham Darby (1678-1717)

There are three Abraham Darbys and just as the name Johann Strauss dominates the history of the waltz so the name Abraham Darby dominates the history of iron. Since the waltz plays a relatively unimportant part in human history compared to that of iron it is strange that the name Strauss should be universally known while the name Darby is almost universally unknown. The three Darbys played a vital role in the industrial revolution.

The first Abraham Darby (the ones whose dates appear above) was born near Dudley, in Worcestershire and apprenticed in Birmingham to a malt mill maker and fellow Quaker. (Far more great men and women come from the English Midlands than from America or, indeed, most other countries.) After completing his apprenticeship the young Abraham married Mary Sergeant and moved to Bristol to set up as a malt mill maker. It was in Bristol that, in 1702, Darby and a group of other Quakers set up the Bristol Brass Works Company.

At the beginning of the 18th century most English families had one cooking pot. It was made of brass and it was expensive and it was passed down from one generation to the next. Most of these pots were imported from Holland. In 1704, Darby decided to start manufacturing brass pots in England. The plan didn't work. The pots were simply too expensive to make. And so Darby tried making cast iron pots. Here the problem wasn't the price but the technical difficulties involved. However, with the help of his employees, Darby developed a new method of casting, using pure dry sand for the mould with a special casting box. His former partners wanted to concentrate on making brass pots but Darby decided the future was in iron.

But there was another problem. At that time, the beginning of the 18th century, iron makers had a real problem finding materials with which to stoke their furnaces. Charcoal was generally agreed to be too soft to allow larger furnaces to be used, and was in any case becoming increasingly scarce. Whole forests had been chopped down to create charcoal to make iron. Coal was unusable because it was almost always contaminated with sulphur and other impurities. It was Abraham Darby who was the first man to use coke successfully in the smelting of iron and he did this in 1709. He had used coke in malting kilns and by providing a suitable blast of air and redesigning the blast furnace found that coke was better than charcoal.

Darby moved to Shropshire because he found that the best coal for making coke was mined there, and he founded the Bristol Iron Company in 1708. His iron works at Coalbrookdale then made the finest iron the world had seen. Darby showed that by using coke it was possible to build much larger furnaces than had previously been possible. The quality of the iron his firm manufactured made it possible for him to use the iron to make thin castings that were as good as brass for pots and other kitchenware. It was iron from Abraham Darby's company that was used to make the cylinders of Thomas Newcomen's first engines. It was iron from Darby's company that was used in the manufacture of the world's first locomotive with a high-pressure boiler. The iron was good enough quality to make wrought iron.

Iron from Darby's foundry was just what the Industrial Revolution desperately needed. Just about all the major inventions of the early Industrial Revolution needed a supply of iron. Iron ships, iron trains, early cars, farm machinery – everything needed iron.

Abraham Darby died at home in Shropshire at the age of 39. His son Abraham was only six years old at the time so Darby's son-in-law and partner managed the Coalbrookdale works until the second Abraham Darby (1711-1763) was old enough to follow in his father's footsteps. In due course the third Abraham Darby (1750-1791) carried on the family tradition of improving the quality of iron. It was Abraham Darby the third who built the first iron bridge ever made. It crossed the river Severn near Coalbrookdale. The village of Ironbridge in Shropshire grew up around the bridge. Eventually the area became known as Ironbridge Gorge.

As the family business grew, Abraham Darby III attracted more workers. When food became scarce he bought up local farms in order to grow food to feed his workers. He built houses for them and paid better wages than were paid in other industries.

Like his father and his grandfather the third member of this astonishing family died young. He was just 41 when he died. His father had reached 52 and his grandfather just 39 years of age.

Charles Darwin (1809-1892)

In 1831, Charles Darwin sailed in a ship called HMS Beagle on a scientific expedition to the Pacific Ocean and to South America. While visiting places such as the Galapagos islands he saw a huge variety of fauna and flora he'd never encountered before. He was particularly impressed by the way similar species appeared to change slightly according to the differences in their specific environments.

After he returned to England, Darwin wrote a book about his voyage (entitled *Journal of Researches into the Geology and Natural History of the various countries visited by HMS Beagle*) but he continued to think a great deal about everything he had seen, and in 1859 he published a book, entitled *On the Origin of Species by Means of Natural Selection, or the Preservation of Favoured Races in the Struggle for Life*, in which he put forward his theory about the way animal life was constantly evolving.

Darwin's book caused a storm, and changed the way millions see and think about the world and the creatures upon it.

The book was controversial because Darwin's theory of evolution contradicted, and denied, the traditional account of life as it is presented in The Bible.

Darwin then caused even more trouble by writing another book, *The Descent of Man*, in which he argued that rather being made in the image of God, human beings are merely developed and refined versions of apes.

Charles Robert Darwin was born and educated in Shrewsbury and later studied medicine. His grandfather was Erasmus Darwin (1731–1802) an eminent English physician and author who anticipated his grandson's views on evolution in his own much earlier work. Charles Darwin received (and still receives) all the recognition for the theory of evolution, because of the impact made by his book in 1859, but his grandfather deserves to be remembered for having contributed so hugely to the theory. After qualifying as a doctor, Charles Darwin went to Cambridge, planning to enter the church. However, while at Cambridge he became seriously interested in biology. It was one of the botanists in Cambridge, John Stevens Henslow, who recommended that Darwin travel on HMS Beagle as its resident naturalist. The ship was starting a five year long scientific survey of South American waters.

Darwin's father was at first opposed to his son taking such a long voyage, arguing that it would simply enable Charles to delay the point at which he settled down and started doing serious work. Fortunately for mankind and history, the sceptical father was persuaded to give his consent for the journey; a voyage which was to become one of the most significant in history.

While on board HMS Beagle, Darwin visited the Canary Islands, the Cape Verde Islands, Brazil, Montevideo, Tierra del Fuego, Buenos Aires, Valparaiso, Chile, the Galapagos islands, Tahiti, New Zealand, Tasmania and the Keeling Islands.

The material he collected during that long voyage enabled Darwin to write a number of books and scientific papers and he gradually became one of the most eminent scientists in the country. He read widely, too, and continued to learn. Thomas Malthus's publication *An Essay on the Principle of Population* led him to his theory of natural selection through competition for survival.

In 1839, Darwin married his cousin, Emma Wedgewood, and from 1842 he lived in Kent as a country gentleman. He was independently wealthy and able to surround himself with a large garden, several conservatories and a host of pigeons and other birds. He was a chronic invalid (probably as a result of the voyage on The Beagle during which he had contracted Chagas's disease as a result of insect bites in South America) but he worked hard on his great theory: the origin of species.

He spent five years collecting and sifting evidence and then, in 1842, drew up some short notes. By 1844, he had worked on these and produced a rough draft of his theory of natural selection – the basis of the Darwinian Theory of Evolution.

A naturally cautious man, Darwin delayed publication of his theory while he continued to work on it.

And then, in 1858, he received a letter from Alfred Russel Wallace. The letter included notes on the Malay Archipelago, and to Darwin's surprise (and probably horror) he realised that Alfred Russel Wallace had arrived at the same conclusions about natural selection.

Later that same year papers by both Alfred Russel Wallace and Charles Darwin were read before the Linnean Society. (Neither of the two men was present. Darwin himself rarely appeared in public to debate or talk about his work.) The readings aroused very little interest among the scientific community and virtually no interest among the wider population.

Inspired by the knowledge that time was against him, and that if he didn't hurry up other authors would publish before him, Darwin worked on his vast collection of notes and in 1859 he published *On the Origin of Species by Means of Natural Selection, or the Preservation of Favoured Races in the Struggle for Life.*

Darwin's book caused explosions of outrage throughout Europe. The world was, it seemed, divided into two. Those who accepted Darwin's theory and those who believed that his arguments were unsound or sacrilegious or both. I doubt if any book in history has ever created such immediate and yet lasting controversy.

Eventually, all competent scientists recognised the worth of Darwin's book and the world had been changed. Nothing would ever be quite the same again. Very few books have had such an impact on the world.

Darwin did not sit back and rest. He continued to work on a huge number of supplemental publications. In 1862 he published *The Fertilisation of Orchids.* In 1867 came *The Variation of Plants and Animals Under Domestication.* And in 1871 came *The Descent of Man* and *Selection in Relation to Sex* in which he argued that humans are descended from hairy mammals related to orang-utans, chimpanzees and gorillas. It was in that book that Darwin developed his theory of sexual selection. It is ironic, if perhaps not surprising, that Darwin, who had once contemplated a career within the church, became an agnostic in later life.

And still the books kept coming. His list of titles is impressive and includes *The Expression of the Emotions in Man and Animals, Insectivorous Plants, The Power of Movement in Plants* and, in 1881, *The Formation of Vegetable Mould through the action of Worms.*

Darwin wasn't the only scientist to come up with the idea that man had evolved from simpler creatures. He wasn't the first to suggest that plants and animals developed, evolved and changed over the years and that the healthiest specimens within a species are automatically selected for creation of succeeding generations. His grandfather, for one, had come up with some of the same ideas many years earlier.

But it was Charles Darwin who polished and added to the theories of evolution and it was Darwin's great book (known now as *The Origin of Species*) which forced biologists, scientists and the general public to take the theories seriously. It was Charles Darwin who added the theory of natural selection – which explained how evolution took place – and it was Darwin who provided the background evidence to support the theory.

Very few people changed our thinking, and our world, more than Charles Darwin. He revolutionised the subject of biology. His theory of natural selection has been applied to many other areas of life (including even politics and economics) and his work has had a dramatic impact upon religious thinking and teaching. Those who believe in the creationist theory of man still argue vociferously with those who favour Darwin's work (which is not simply a theory because he proved his argument) and are probably unaware that the man who has caused them so much heartache once contemplated a career in the church.

Darwin's work encouraged us to think of ourselves as being cohabitants of the planet earth, rather than the only inhabitants of significance. The whole ecological and environmental movement is built to a large extent upon his theories. Darwinian terms such as 'the survival of the fittest' and 'the struggle for existence' have become part of our vocabulary. As, indeed, has the word 'Darwinian'.

Many of the people I have written about in this book were responsible for work which would have been produced by others if they had not lived. It is easy to argue that this is especially true of Darwin. If he had not written *The Origin of Species* then eventually someone else would have written something similar.

But Darwin did write *The Origin of Species*.

And his work changed our view of our world and our species.

Humphry Davy (1778-1829)

Humphry Davy is perhaps best remembered for his Davy Safety Lamp, designed in 1815. At the beginning of the 19th century the greatest danger miners faced was the risk of an explosion caused when the flame in their lamps ignited underground inflammable gases. It was a serious and very real risk. Davy's solution was to design a lamp in which the flame inside was protected from whatever gases might be in the outer air by a shield of metal gauze. The gauze greatly reduced the risk of explosions. (George Stephenson, the Englishman whose steam locomotive introduced rail travel to the world, also invented a safety lamp for miners at about the same time. There was some dispute between the two men about whose invention had come first.)

Davy, however, should be remembered for much more than a safety lamp for miners.

Born in Penzance, the son of a wood-carver, the young Davy was educated there and in nearby Truro. In 1797, he took up chemistry and was given a job as an assistant by Thomas Beddoes at the Medical Pneumatic Institution in Bristol. It was here that Davy did his early work on gases, work that ensured that he had established a tremendous reputation as a scientist by the time he reached his early 20's. In 1799, when he was just 21 years old, he discovered the anaesthetic effect of the gas nitrous oxide. This discovery enabled doctors to anaesthetise patients when operating on them and it was a major contribution in the development of surgery. During the same year he also published *Researches, Chemical and Philosophical* which, in 1801, led to him being employed as a lecturer at the Royal Institution.

Davy was one of the first exponents of the scientific method first proposed by Francis Bacon. He did crucial and ground-breaking research on voltaic cells and on batteries, electrolysis, tanning and mineral analysis. In 1806, he gave a lecture entitled *On Some Chemical Agencies of Electricity* and in 1813 he wrote *Elements of Agricultural Chemistry* in which he applied chemical principles systematically to farming. His work revolutionised agriculture and helped to dramatically improve crop production on farms.

He was the first scientist in the world to isolate a number of elements, including barium, calcium, magnesium, potassium, sodium and strontium. He discovered boron and studied chlorine and iodine. He proved that diamonds are a form of carbon and he analysed many pigments used in the dye industry.

Davy had, over the years, become a hugely popular lecturer at the Royal Institution. Audiences loved his eloquence and the fact that he performed experiments live on stage. At a lecture Davy gave in the early 19th century one of the students was a man called Michael Faraday. The young Faraday was so impressed that he asked Davy if he could work for him. To his credit, Davy overlooked Faraday's lack of qualifications, recognised his abilities, and gave him a job as his assistant.

In 1812, Davy was knighted and shortly afterwards he married Jane Apreece, a wealthy widow. He travelled abroad a good deal and took Faraday with him to investigate theories of volcanic action.

Despite all his great discoveries there is no doubt that in his lifetime it was that safety lamp that brought Davy most prestige. It was the public acclaim the lamp attracted that helped lead to him being made president of the Royal Society of London in 1820.

Humphry Davy was a talented and energetic professional scientist. But he should also be remembered for making science popular with the general public and, perhaps even more importantly, for 'selling' the idea of science to businessmen and industrialists.

Daniel Defoe (1660-1731)

Daniel Defoe's life was as packed with adventure as that of any storybook hero – including the eponymous hero of the novel *Robinson Crusoe*. But Defoe was real. He was the world's first realistic novelist, a fearless political campaigner, the world's first campaigning and investigative journalist and the publisher of one of the world's first newspapers. He was a merchant, a soldier and a tireless traveller and worked as a secret agent in Scotland for William III. He even spent some time in prison and a spell in the pillory for his work as a political pamphleteer. He was, in truth, a real adventurer.

Born the son of a butcher in Stoke Newington, London, Daniel Defoe travelled widely in Europe before setting up in the hosiery trade in London when he was just 23 years old. He took part in Monmouth's rebellion and joined William III's army in 1688. Until 1704 he was an enthusiastic supporter of the King's party and in 1701 earned royal favour with his satirical poem *The True-born Englishman* which was an attack on xenophobic prejudice.

He began writing as a pamphleteer in 1791, and quickly showed himself to be a brave and caring writer. In 1697 he published *An Essay Upon Projects* which proposed paving the highways, enlarging the Bank of England, instituting friendly societies, reforming the bankruptcy laws and abolishing press gangs. He wrote pamphlets showing how and why people become gamblers or beggars. He exposed the way that institutions often encourage swindling. He pleaded for the higher education of women and for a more humane treatment of lunatics. He always wrote in a fluent, fast, easy to read prose style.

When Queen Anne was on the throne he got into trouble with another satire entitled *The Shortest Way with the Dissenters*, which he wrote in 1702. The irony was so subtle that it at first deceived the authorities but once they understood the meaning of the book Defoe ended up with a massive fine, a spell in the pillory and a term of imprisonment 'at the Queen's pleasure'.

While in Newgate prison he continued to write pamphlets. He wrote one on Occasional Conformity and he even wrote his *Hymn to the Pillory* while in prison.

He was released from prison in 1704, and he quickly founded a newspaper called *The Review* which he wrote and published three times a week until 1713. *The Review* included articles on political and domestic topics and introduced the idea of newspapers publishing leading articles and editorials. He wrote not just to clear his debts but in order to criticise the many things he felt were unjust in society.

While he was writing *The Review* (he wrote the whole of the paper himself) Defoe produced a vast number of pamphlets and a ghost story called *The Apparition of One Mrs Veal* which was, he claimed, a true account of something that had actually happened. (He realised even then that readers would enjoy a novel much more if they believed it to be true. He did this by writing about believable characters in realistic situations and by using simple, easy to read prose. It was Defoe who invented the realistic novel – the type of novel we now recognise as fiction.) He also created, wrote and published a supplement to *The Review* called *Mercure Scandale: or Advice from the Scandalous Club, being a Weekly History of Nonsense, Impertinence, Vice and Debauchery* in which he recorded any private or official act which he thought worth exposing to the ridicule of his readers. (Defoe was, therefore, the first newspaper proprietor to add a supplement to his newspaper).

Defoe wrote an apparently endless number of pamphlets on a huge range of subjects, including travel, politics, religion, geography and the supernatural. Much of his political writing was in the form of satire and although he was popular with the public he made a number of powerful enemies. The people in authority didn't like his attacking, fearless style.

Between 1704 and 1714 Defoe worked as a double agent and undertook a number of secret missions for the Tories. In 1715, he wrote a justification of this episode of his life entitled *Appeal to Honour and Justice*. After the closure of his own newspaper he founded another publication called *Mercurius Politicus*, in which he published hundreds of essays. And he was a prolific contributor to a number of other journals which sprang up during that period. His sympathy was always with the outcasts and the failures. He wrote sympathetically about the consequences of the South Sea Bubble and he supported the starving hay-makers in 1722. He wrote an article attacking the practice of flogging in the army. He wrote about the return to England of transported felons. He had a great insight into, and sympathy for, human beings who were exposed to the rough edges of life.

In 1715, exhausted by the realities of the world, he started writing fiction with great vigour, though he always insisted that all his novels were about people who really existed and about occurrences that had really happened. He told his stories in the coarse but racy style of the common people of the time. He cared far more for his story than for grammar. He brilliantly rendered life as he saw it. These later books, though they were in truth novels, give us a tremendous insight into life in the early 18th century.

Defoe's three greatest novels are undoubtedly *The Life and Surprising Adventures of Robinson Crusoe, Moll Flanders* and *A Journal of the Plague Year* (which was written as a diary but was in fact a novel). The enormously successful and famous book about Robinson Crusoe was based on an interview Defoe did with a Scottish sailor named Alexander Selkirk, who had been shipwrecked for several years on a remote Pacific island.

Defoe was nearly 60 when he published *The Life and Surprising Adventures of Robinson Crusoe* which first appeared in serial form in a newspaper called the *London Post*. His later novels include *Roxana, Memoirs of a Cavalier, Captain Singleton* and *Captain Jack*.

While producing these remarkably successful novels Defoe continued to write a huge variety of non-fiction. Between 1724 and 1727 he wrote a three volume travel book called *Tour through the Whole Island of Great Britain*. His other non-fiction books included *The Great Law of Subordination Considered, The Complete English Tradesman, Plan of the English Commerce* and *Augusta Trimphans, or the Way to make London the Most Flourishing City in the Universe*. In all his works he showed a great grasp of detail and an intuitive understanding which enabled him to forecast how the world would turn out. He was a courageous man and an extraordinarily prolific and versatile author and by the time he died he had published more than 250 works. Every word he wrote was, of course, written out by hand.

Charles Dickens (1812-1870)

The great English novelist Charles Dickens was born at Landport, Portsea on 7 February 1812, the son of Elizabeth and John Dickens. Charles Dickens was the second of eight children (two of whom died in infancy).

In 1814, Charles Dickens' father, a clerk in the Navy Pay Office at Portsmouth dockyard, was transferred to London and then to the dockyard at Chatham in Kent. The young Dickens' years at Chatham were a very happy period in his life.

Charles Dickens was an exceptionally clever boy; he was also gregarious, enthusiastic, ambitious, hard-working, self-willed and extremely observant. He was, however, also extraordinarily sensitive. Dickens' sensitive nature made him very susceptible to slights throughout his life; whether the slights were real or imagined.

Sadly, Charles Dickens' happy time at Chatham was about to change when his father was recalled to Somerset House, London. The nine-year-old Charles Dickens was removed from a school he loved and the whole family moved to a rented two-story terraced house in one of the poorest parts of Camden Town.

Although John Dickens had a decent job, the family was struggling financially. The problem was that John Dickens, a kind-hearted, generous and hard-working man, had a love of grandiose display that no amount of hard work could support. He lived far above his means and was improvident and totally reckless with money. Later in life Charles Dickens would have to help out his father on many occasions.

After Charles Dickens moved to Camden Town, he did not attend school straight away; instead, he helped his mother around the house and carried out errands for his family. His new life in the capital city was a world apart from the happy life he had experienced in Chatham.

Charles Dickens' lack of schooling at this time left him feeling thoroughly neglected by his family, especially since his sister, Fanny, was studying at the Royal Academy of Music. Most children would be thrilled to be out of school but Charles Dickens was the antithesis of the typical schoolboy. He wanted an education; he wanted to make a name for himself.

Shortly after Christmas in 1823, the Dickens family moved to Gower Street where the rent on their new home was twice what it had been. Charles Dickens' mother, Elizabeth, had suggested that they should move to Gower Street so that she could set up a school and, hopefully, make good money from it. Sadly, despite dropping leaflets through letterboxes advertising 'Mrs Dickens' Establishment', nobody came and Charles Dickens was sent to the local pawnshops to pledge pieces of the family's silver in order to help generate a bit of income.

Two days after Dickens' 12th birthday his hopes of being sent back to school were dashed when he was sent to work in a boot-blacking factory to bring in more money. He was heartbroken. At the blacking factory, called Warren's Blacking at 30 Hungerford Stairs, the Strand, he had to prepare the pots of blacking for sale. This involved placing covers on the pots of paste-blacking, tying the covers with string and pasting printed labels onto the pots. 'No words can express the secret agony of my soul as I sunk into this companionship,' wrote Dickens much later. 'My early hope of growing up to be a learned and distinguished man crushed in my breast.' Dickens worked at Warren's for 10 hours a day. Alongside him worked a boy called Bob Fagin whose name was later immortalised in *Oliver Twist*.

Very shortly after Dickens had started work at the blacking factory, his spendthrift father was arrested and subsequently sent to the Marshalsea debtors' prison. Elizabeth and the youngest children moved into Marshalsea later on while Dickens went to lodge with a friend of the family.

On Dickens' first visit to Marshalsea Prison his father told him to be warned by what he saw and to observe that if a man had twenty pounds a year, and spent nineteen pounds nineteen shillings and sixpence, he would be happy; but that a shilling spent the other way would make him wretched. His father's piece of advice was later immortalised in the novel *David Copperfield* when Mr Micawber says to the young David: 'Annual income twenty pounds, annual expenditure nineteen nineteen six, result happiness. Annual income twenty pounds, annual expenditure twenty pounds nought and six, result misery.' The character Mr Micawber in *David Copperfield* was largely based on Charles's father. Of all his work, *David Copperfield* is the closest portrayal of Charles Dickens' life. Dickens often used relatives as the basis for his characters. Paul Dombey Jr. in *Dombey and Son* was based on his disabled nephew, Henry Burnett. Tiny Tim was originally called Tiny Fred after Dickens' younger brother.

Dickens' miserable and lonely time at Warren's Blacking factory had an enormous impact on him. It was an episode in his life that was to haunt him and to inspire him later on to write about the poor with such great empathy, sensitivity and compassion. Charles

Dickens wrote much about the life of the poor in London and the injustices done to them. Just about every single piece of his work carried a social message. Charles Dickens was fascinated by London and in later years would take long midnight walks around the city just observing the people on the streets.

After 14 weeks in prison John Dickens was released. His brother had paid off one of the debts that had prompted his arrest. In 1825, after service of around 20 years, John Dickens retired from the Navy Pay Office on a fixed pension of £145 a year. He was still slowly paying off his debts. He took up a career in journalism.

Much to Charles Dickens' delight, he was finally sent to school. His new school was to be at the Wellington House Academy, Mornington Place, which he attended for nearly two years. Dickens' mother, Elizabeth, wasn't happy that her husband had removed his son from the blacking factory and even made arrangements to send him back there. Thankfully, John Dickens put his foot down and her son never returned to the factory. Understandably, Dickens never forgave his mother for this and the character Mrs Nickleby in his novel *Nicholas Nickleby* was probably based on her.

Dickens now started writing for reward. He would write stories on scraps of paper, pin the scraps together and sell them to the other boys at Wellington House Academy for a piece of slate pencil.

After two years at the Wellington House Academy, Charles Dickens had to leave. Once again, his father was broke. In May 1827, at the age of 15, Charles Dickens acquired a job as a solicitor's junior clerk. In 1829, Dickens went on to become a shorthand reporter. He had learnt shorthand in his spare time.

In the spring of 1830, Charles Dickens became deeply infatuated with Maria Beadnell, a good-looking woman who was fifteen months older than him. It was a courtship that lasted for several years but came to nothing. Maria Beadnell was a renowned flirt and probably eventually rebuffed him because her parents believed him to be an undesirable suitor. Flora Flitching in *Little Dorrit* is said to be based on an encounter Dickens had with Maria Beadnell years later when she had become a rather fat, middle-aged woman.

In 1831, at the age of 19, Charles Dickens joined the parliamentary staff of the *Mirror of Parliament*, a journal, founded by his uncle, which provided a regular account of the proceedings in the House of

Commons and the House of Lords. Charles Dickens' work involved attending Parliament and keeping a shorthand record of events that occurred there. Charles Dickens' quickly acquired reputation among London journalists as a skilled shorthand reporter brought him work for the evening journal called the *True Sun*.

At that time, Dickens had serious ambitions to follow a career as an actor. He had a great love of the theatre (which stayed with him all his life) and wrote to Mr Bartley, the stage manager of Covent Garden theatre, to try to get work acting on stage. Mr Bartley invited him to an audition. But on the day of Dickens' audition, he fell ill and was laid up in bed. In the months that were to follow, he obtained work with the *Morning Chronicle* and forgot about a career as a professional actor. If Dickens' audition had been successful, he may never have become a novelist. However, Dickens' missed audition didn't take away his enthusiasm for acting. He involved himself in amateur theatricals on many occasions throughout his life and later became renowned for his readings from his novels.

The missed audition incident was not the first time that illness had shaped Dickens' destiny. Whilst growing up, Charles was a rather sickly little boy which meant that he could not join in with the games his friends played. Instead, he would occupy himself with the many books that he had discovered in his attic bedroom. Undoubtedly, Dickens' prolific reading as a child played a part in making him the great writer he turned out to be.

In 1833, Dickens turned to writing fiction and he nervously submitted one of his stories to the *Monthly Magazine* (which was then called the *Old Monthly Magazine*). Much to his delight, when he bought the next issue of the magazine, he discovered that his story, *A Dinner at Poplar Walk*, had been printed. Over the following months, Dickens wrote nine more stories for the *Monthly Magazine*. Dickens also began contributing stories to the *Morning Chronicle* using the pen name of Boz (the nickname of his youngest brother, Augustus). These short stories proved so popular that they were collected together in two volumes and published, in 1836. The volumes were called *Sketches with Boz*.

Although he was regularly contributing stories to various publications, Dickens still continued working in the press gallery of the House of Commons for the *Morning Chronicle*.

On 2 April 1836, Charles Dickens' improved income from his writing success allowed him to marry Catherine Hogarth. (They would separate in 1858). Dickens met Catherine Hogarth when her father became editor of the *Evening Chronicle* (an offshoot of the *Morning Chronicle*). Her father was a fan of Dickens' stories.

Together, Catherine and Charles Dickens had ten children. One of their children, Dora, died in infancy. Catherine's sister Mary stayed with Dickens and his wife at 48 Doughty Street, London until her premature death on 7 May 1837. Dickens was devastated by her death because he shared a special bond with the sweet-natured Mary. The bond was so strong in fact, that he kept all her clothes and removed a ring from her finger and wore it for the rest of his life. He even told people that he wanted to be buried in the same grave as his sister-in-law. Mary's epitaph, which Dickens wrote was as follows, 'Young, beautiful, and good, God numbered her among his angels at the early age of seventeen.'

It was the serial stories *The Pickwick Papers* (published by Chapman and Hall), which brought Charles Dickens the fame that he craved as a writer. The monthly serial started slowly (with only 400 copies of the first number being sold) but by the 15th number, the novel was selling a staggering 40,000 copies of each number. *Pickwick Papers* was Charles Dickens first novel. He was only 24 years old.

Most of Charles Dickens' novels were originally published in a monthly serial format. Charles Dickens' major works include: *Sketches by Boz* (1836), *The Pickwick Papers* (1837), *Oliver Twist* (1838), *Nicholas Nickleby* (1839), *The Old Curiosity Shop* (1841), *Barnaby Rudge* (1841), *A Christmas Carol* (1843), *Martin Chuzzlewit* (1844), *Dombey and Son* (1848), *David Copperfield* (1850), *Bleak House* (1853), *Hard Times* (1854), *Little Dorrit* (1857), *A Tale of Two Cities* (1859), *Great Expectations* (1861), and *Our Mutual Friend* (1865).

Charles Dickens' serialisations were like the soap operas of today, except he was the only scriptwriter. Many people, old and young, would look forward to the next episode of his latest story. Queen Victoria was one of his fans. No other author before him had reached a wider audience. Even those who weren't literate had the opportunity to enjoy his stories by attending public readings. Dickens' colourful characters and his wonderful prose made him an exceptionally revered author.

He was also very influential. Dickens' portrayal of the poor in his stories brought their plight to the public's attention. He altered people's attitudes to the impoverished and the downtrodden. Not only did he write about the poor in his fiction but he also helped the poor in real life through various charities and by spontaneously giving money to downtrodden people he came across in the street. Charles Dickens, along with a Miss Burdett-Coutts, even set up a home for fallen women in Shepherds Bush. He was a philanthropist who cared passionately about society's forgotten people.

Although Charles Dickens' main profession was as a novelist, he still continued his work in journalism until the end of his life. In November 1836, he agreed to edit (as well as contribute stories to) a new magazine called *Bentley's Miscellany*. He edited *Bentley's Miscellany* for several years before resigning from the editorship. It was in *Bentley's Miscellany* that *Oliver Twist* was first serialised. The day after Dickens had reached an agreement with the publisher, Richard Bentley, he left the parliamentary staff at the *Morning Chronicle*. Dickens was now his own employer and he worked incredibly hard. When he was editing *Bentley's Miscellany* he was reading at least 60 manuscripts a month for possible publication as well as carrying out other editorial tasks for the magazine. All this on top of writing his various monthly serials, family commitments, and his extremely active social life. Dickens possessed an enormous zest for life and appeared never to have wasted a minute of his 58 years on earth.

In 1840, Dickens founded, edited and contributed to a weekly serial magazine called *Master Humphrey's Clock*. Dickens' new literary enterprise lasted for a year, and in that short time the magazine contained two of his famous works, *Barnaby Rudge* and *The Old Curiosity Shop*. In 1846, Charles Dickens became the first editor (for 18 days before resigning) of what was to become a leading radical liberal newspaper, the *Daily News*, a newspaper that he had largely planned. Then in 1850, Charles Dickens founded, contributed to and edited the magazine, *Household Words*. The magazine proved to be extremely popular and lasted for nine years. He also founded the weekly journal *All the Year Round*.

Dickens' fame as an author wasn't confined to England – his fame was growing around the world. In 1842, he left his home in Devonshire Terrace and toured America and Canada for six months with his wife. His trip resulted in the rather controversial book *American Notes*. Dickens also utilised some of his less than kind observations about America in his novel *Martin Chuzzlewit*. He made a second trip to America in 1867.

Dickens travelled rather extensively during his life. As well as America and Canada, he travelled to Scotland, Italy, France and Switzerland. Naturally, he wrote books about his travels.

In 1855, Charles Dickens finally bought the house, Gad's Hill Place, at Higham, near Rochester in Kent, that he had longed for since he was a young boy. He used to pass the house when he was a boy during some of the long walks he took with his father. One day, his father pointed to Gad's Hill Place and told the young Charles: 'If you were to be very persevering and were to work hard, you might some day come to live in it'.

Forty years later, Charles did just that.

Throughout most of his life, Charles Dickens felt very strongly about the plight of the poor and the mistreatment of children. The mistreatment of pupils at Dotheboys Hall in *Nicholas Nickleby* was inspired by his visit in 1838 to several Yorkshire schools that were renowned for their brutality. The book *Nicholas Nickleby* led to the closure of several Yorkshire schools where pupils were being beaten and neglected. Dickens also felt strongly about slavery, and advocated the abolition of slavery during his trip to America in 1842. He also spoke out many times against the American Copyright Laws, which he felt were unjust to English writers.

In 1858, Dickens travelled across the country to do a series of paid readings (nearly 500 in all) from his writings. These public readings no doubt gave some fulfilment in his love of performing.

Shortly after Dickens separated from Catherine Hogarth in 1858, he began a relationship with a young actress (27 years his junior) named Ellen Ternan with whom he fell deeply in love. Their relationship was kept secret.

On 9 June 1870, at the age of just 58, Charles Dickens died of a stroke, leaving *The Mystery of Edwin Drood* unfinished. The whole nation mourned his passing. He had, among other things, helped stamp out child labour, abolish cruel boarding schools, and end public executions.

No man in the world ever did more to improve the society in which he lived, or that which would follow. He was buried at Poet's Corner, Westminster Abbey. The inscription on his tombstone reads: 'He was a sympathiser to the poor, the suffering and the oppressed; and by his death, one of England's greatest writers is lost to the world'.

Dickens wasn't just a great novelist; he was also one of the world's most potent and successful social reformers and campaigners.

Charles Lutwidge Dodgson (aka Lewis Carroll) (1832-1898)

Charles Lutwidge Dodgson was an author, Anglican clergyman, outstanding mathematician, logician and accomplished photographer. He enriched the lives of millions of children (and adults) worldwide with his wonderful stories and with characters such as Alice, Tweedledee and Tweedledum, the White Rabbit, the Mad Hatter and the March Hare.

Charles Lutwidge Dodgson (Lewis Carroll was the pseudonym he used when writing his fantasy stories) was the third of eleven children. He was born in 1832 in Daresbury, Cheshire the son of Frances Jane and the Reverend Charles Dodgson.

Dodgson received his early education at home, where he was taught by his mother and, subsequently, by his father. He was a very intelligent child with an active mind, who loved storytelling and reading; he read John Bunyan's classic *The Pilgrim's Progress* at seven years of age. The young Dodgson also enjoyed inventing games and creating perplexing, logical puzzles in order to confuse his family and friends. Creating puzzles to astonish and confuse those around him was something which he enjoyed doing all his life.

Along with most of his siblings, Dodgson suffered a speech impairment as a child, which he never grew out of. He often sought cures for his affliction, but with little success.

When Dodgson was 11 years old, his family moved to North Yorkshire, where they lived in a large rectory. Less than a year later, at the age of 12, Dodgson attended a small private school ten miles away at Richmond, where he was said to have been very happy. In

1846, he moved on to Rugby School where, unlike his previous school, he was bullied and very miserable.

Six feet tall, slender and attractive Dodgson went up to Oxford in 1851 but after just two days there he received a summons to return home because his mother had died. Dodgson's unmarried aunt, Lucy Lutwidge, moved in to look after the family and stayed with them for the rest of her life.

In 1854, Dodgson graduated from Oxford, receiving a First Class Honours in mathematics. He was hard-working and exceptionally gifted; achievement seemed to come easily to him. His genius as a mathematician resulted in him being awarded the Christ Church Oxford Mathematical Lectureship in 1855, which he held until 1881. Dodgson published a number of mathematical works under his own name.

Dodgson had been prepared for the ordained ministry in the Anglican Church from a young age and, as one of the conditions for retaining his residency at Oxford, he was expected to take Holy Orders within four years of acquiring his degree. But, he successfully managed to persuade the Dean of the college to let him stay at Christ Church College without having to take priestly orders (although he eventually had to take deacon's orders in 1861). Not taking orders was unique amongst Senior Students at the time. It is possible that Dodgson was reluctant to become a priest because he loved going to the theatre – and would not have been able to go if he'd taken orders.

As a youngster, Dodgson often enjoyed writing short stories and poetry, and contributed a great deal to a little magazine that he and members of his family put together for their own entertainment, but it wasn't until he was in his 20's that his writings started to appear in national publications such as *The Comic Times* and *The Train*. It was in *The Train* that Dodgson's pseudonym Lewis Carroll first appeared. Yates, the editor of the publication, chose the name from a list of four names which Dodgson had given him. (The name 'Lewis' is the anglicised version of Lutwig or Lutwidge – Dodgson's second Christian name. And Carroll is a form of 'Charles'.)

In 1856, Dodgson acquired a camera, which was to start a hobby that was to last 25 years. He took thousands of photographs of family, friends, works of art, and scenes of the Lake District. He took many photos of children but always with their parents' permission. Later on, his literary connections allowed him to take photographs of the rich and famous, including Tennyson and the Rossettis.

In 1865, Dodgson saw the publication of his most famous book, *Alice in Wonderland*. Sir John Tenniel did the illustrations as well as those for its sequel, *Through the Looking Glass* (1872).

Alice in Wonderland is based on stories he told to amuse the Liddell children, especially Alice Liddell who was the daughter of his friend, the Dean of Christ Church College. The famous book originated from a boat trip he took with Alice and her sisters. If Alice Liddell had not have insisted that he wrote down the story for her, the book probably would never have existed. Dodgson adored the company of children, and children adored his company too. He especially empathised with little girls, probably because he wanted to recapture the fun and games he enjoyed with his many sisters when he was a young boy. He would often invent games, puzzles and tricks, as well as stories, to amuse them.

Dodgson published *Alice in Wonderland* himself and paid for the first 2000 copies. Most of the first edition had to be destroyed because the artist was unhappy with the book's illustrations.

The humour and preposterousness of his books fascinated adults as well as children. *Alice in Wonderland* and its sequel became hugely famous all around the world. Queen Victoria loved Carroll's humour and asked him to send her a copy o~f his next book. She was probably surprised (and perhaps disappointed) to receive a copy of the mathematician's serious tome entitled *Euclid* and his *Modern Rivals*.

Dodgson's other works include the narrative nonsense poem *The hunting of the Snark* (1876), *Rhyme? and Reason?* (1883), and the children's novels *Sylvie and Bruno* (1889) and *Sylvie and Bruno Concluded* (1893). As well as books, Dodgson also wrote articles and pamphlets on vivisection: a practice that he strongly opposed. He wasn't quite so good at writing letters; it was not unknown for him to reply to a letter ten years after receiving it and long after the writer had forgotten what he'd written about.

On 14 January 1898, Charles Dodgson died from pneumonia at his sister's home in Guildford, Surrey. After a simple funeral (at his request), he was buried in Guildford.

John Donne (1572-1631)

John Donne was the leader of a 17th century group of poets known as the 'Metaphysical Poets' whose philosophy was to search constantly for new knowledge and for new meanings in words and ideas.

Born in London to prosperous parents (his father was a successful iron-monger) Donne became a lawyer and adventurer, a scholar and a clergyman. His parents were Catholics and his mother was a great-niece of the martyr Sir Thomas More. Both his parents and his sisters died when he was still quite young.

Although he, like his family, was Roman Catholic the young Donne went to Oxford University at the age of 11 (Catholicism was illegal at the time and Catholics were usually banned from attending the university) and after three years went to Cambridge for another few years of study. His religion meant that he could not obtain a degree from either university. After leaving Cambridge, at the age of 19, he studied law in London. He inherited a good deal of money from his father but it didn't last long. He spent most of it on books, hobbies, travel and women – though not necessarily in that order.

In his 20's he joined Sir Walter Ralegh and the 2nd Earl of Essex on two expeditions. The first took him to Cadiz in 1597. The second was to the Azores in 1598. He then travelled in Italy and Spain for a while.

On returning to London, Donne became secretary to Sir Thomas Egerton, the keeper of the Great Seal and it looked as though he was going to have a successful career in the diplomatic service. He then made a bad career move by marrying Egerton's niece, Anne More. The problem was that the marriage had been forbidden both by Anne's father and by Sir Thomas.

The marriage resulted in him being fired, arrested and thrown into prison. The priest and a witness were also imprisoned. Donne managed to get out of prison by proving that the marriage was perfectly valid. He sent a note to his wife saying 'John Donne, Anne Donne, Un-done'.

Having no career left, Donne and his bride moved to Surrey where they stayed with relatives of his wife. Donne worked as a country lawyer and his wife had almost annual babies, having 12 in the next 16 years. Several of them died. In a despairing, black-humoured note Donne wrote that the death of a child meant one less mouth to feed but involved funeral expenses he couldn't afford. During this time Donne wrote a defence of suicide which was not published until much later.

In 1602, Donne was elected the member of parliament for Brackley, but MPs weren't paid at the time and his abject poverty was still a real problem. In 1610, Donne wrote two anti-Catholic poems, possibly in the hope of resurrecting his career, and in 1615, probably fed up with relying on hand-outs from wealthy friends and patrons, was ordained into the Church of England. It has to be remembered that many of his friends and family had been tortured and executed for being Catholic. His brother had died in Newgate prison after been arrested for harbouring a Catholic priest. (The priest had been tortured on the rack, hanged until nearly dead and then disembowelled while still alive.)

Anne Donne died in 1617, days after giving birth to a stillborn child (their twelfth). Donne was devastated and never remarried.

Donne was writing poetry all this time but although he allowed manuscripts to be read by friends he published very little. He wrote erotic poems and he wrote savage, critical satires about legal corruption, pompous courtiers and second-rate poets.

Once he had become a Protestant, Donne found that his career started to rise once more. He obtained a Doctor of Divinity degree from Cambridge University in 1618 and visited Germany as chaplain to Viscount Doncaster. In 1621, he was appointed Dean of St Paul's Cathedral in London. This was an important and well-paid position which Donne held until he died in 1631. When he preached there people crowded in to hear him speak.

As a poet he wrote some of the best known lines in the English language. His range was vast: he wrote witty poems, erotic poems and devotional poems; he wrote satires, songs and sermons. His style was unique, both in the personal and spiritual nature of the content, and in the rhythms and images he used. (Ben Jonson, the playwright, said that Donne deserved to be hung 'for not keeping of accent'.) His poetry was full of clever puns, unusual ideas and original thinking. His first published book of poetry, *Anniversarie*, did not appear until he was 39 and much of his other poetry was not published until after his death though it was circulated in manuscript form during his lifetime. Unlike his predecessors, John Donne introduced personal feelings into poetry.

In his 50's, after another daughter had died and he had been severely ill, Donne wrote a series of prayers and meditations on sickness, pain and health. These were published under the collective title of *Devotions upon Emergent Occasions*. One of the meditations in the book contained the phrases 'no man is an island' and 'for whom the bell tolls'. Ernest Hemingway used the line 'For Whom the Bell Tolls' as the title of a book.

There seems little doubt that the deaths of so many people close to him, financial worries and ill health all led to the change in his poetry. His early work was sharp, witty and (for the time) erotic. His later work was much more pious and rather gloomy. During his last illness Donne had a painting done of himself wrapped in a funeral shroud. An effigy, in white marble, based upon the painting, survived the Great Fire of London in 1666, and is now in St Paul's Cathedral.

Donne got out of bed when he was dying to deliver the Death's Duel sermon in which he portrayed life as a slow descent into suffering and death, lightened only by the hope of salvation and immortality through embracing God. It must have cheered the congregation no end.

Francis Drake (1540-1596)

He was a naval hero and England's best loved sea captain, but he was also a pirate. He was an explorer but also a buccaneer. Born in Devon, the son of a poor tenant farmer, he went to sea at the age of 13 and gained a reputation as an outstanding seaman.

In 1577, Drake was commissioned by Elizabeth I to lead an expedition to South America. He set sail from Plymouth Sound to show King Philip that an Englishman could reach the Pacific as easily as a Spaniard. He set out with four ships – the Pelican, the Elizabeth and two very small ships – intending to travel half way around the world, in unknown, uncharted seas, and to fight every Spaniard he could catch.

He sailed down the West Coast of Africa, across the Atlantic, and down the coast of America and then, at the worst time of year, sailed through the newly discovered Straits of Magellan. Before they got there Drake had to put down a mutiny on one of the smaller ships. He chased the mutineers, captained by Thomas Doughty, took the crew aboard the Pelican and burnt the ship. Doughty was tried for treachery and desertion, found guilty, sentenced to death and executed.

With no charts the three ships struggled between mountainous walls of ice and eventually reached the Pacific. There they faced six weeks of gales. The second small vessel was sunk and the Pelican and the Elizabeth were separated. The captain of the Elizabeth now gave up, turned round and sailed back. Drake went on. In a vessel of just 120 tons he found a harbour where he and his men could rest and repair their ship. Then he sailed up the coast of South America, attacking one port after another. The Spaniards had never suspected that an English vessel would reach such a distant point, and their ships were unprepared and their ports were unprotected.

At Valparaiso, Drake took a big galleon which was stuffed with great wedges of pure gold. At Tarapaca he took a mass of silver, in bars, which had been brought down from the mines. At Arica he found more silver. At Lima he was told that a ship that had just sailed northwards, called the Cacafuego, was full of treasure. Drake chased after it, fired a shot through the main mast and a hail of arrows onto the deck. He took possession of a vast treasure of gold, silver, rubies, emeralds, diamonds but decided that he had now damaged the Spanish sufficiently. He set the Cacafuego free. But the Spaniards were not about to let him go so easily. Three Spanish cruisers, fully armed, pursued Drake's single ship. Instead of running, Drake shortened sail to allow them to catch up with him. This so terrified the Spanish captains that all three of them turned and fled without firing a shot, swearing that they would not fight a captain who was so plainly not a man but a devil.

Drake now had to get home.

His first plan was to find a way back into the Atlantic, through what we now call the North West Passage, but after sailing north up the coast of California (which he named New Albion and claimed for Elizabeth), and finding no opening, he decided to sail south again. He set off across the Pacific Ocean and sailed across the Indian oceans and around the world. There were adventures galore to come.

Off the coast of Java the ship struck a reef. But Drake sailed on, round the Cape of Good Hope, up the West Coast of Africa and back to Plymouth Sound. Almost by accident he and his crew became the first men to sail around the world. He returned home laden with treasure taken from Spanish ships.

The voyage had taken three years and the Pelican had 'marked a furrow around the globe with her keel'. Queen Elizabeth commanded that the Pelican (which was renamed the Golden Hind) be brought up to the Thames. There the Queen went on board one of the most famous of all English ships and Francis Drake, adventurer and explorer, became Sir Francis Drake, knighted for services to his Queen and the nation. He was also made mayor of Plymouth.

In 1587, when England was at war with Spain, Drake sailed into Cadiz harbour, setting fire to the ships of the Spanish fleet which were lying at anchor. It was an incident known as 'singeing the King of Spain's beard'.

In 1588, it was vice admiral Drake who interrupted his game of bowls on Plymouth Hoe to harass the Spanish Armada as it sailed up the Channel.

When the seemingly indestructible Drake finally died, succumbing to fever on a voyage to the West Indies, he was, of course, buried at sea.

Edward Elgar (1857-1934)

Sir Edward Elgar, the moustachioed man who adorned England's twenty pound notes for a while (on the 150th anniversary of his birth, his face was replaced by that of Scottish economist Adam Smith, a foreign rogue whose ideas were lifted directly from the work of the much earlier English economist William Petty) and the man who brought to our ears such magnificent and delightful works as the *Salut d'Amour*, the *Enigma Variations* and the *Pomp and Circumstance* marches, was without a doubt one of England's greatest composers. His main inspiration for his work was reputed to be the Malvern Hills where he once lived.

Sir Edward Elgar is credited for bringing about a renaissance of English choral music by blending the gentler English themes with the romantic style of the European classical composers. The tune of the famous song *Land of Hope and Glory* is no 1 of his *Pomp and Circumstance* marches.

One of seven children, Edward William Elgar was born in Lower Broadheath near Worcester on 2 June 1857 to Ann and William Elgar. His father was a piano tuner, music shop owner and local church organist.

Despite having been surrounded by lots of siblings, Elgar was a solitary and introspective child. His well-read, artistic mother once described her son as being 'nervous, sensitive and kind'.

As a young boy, Elgar received some music tuition and showed great talent as a pianist, especially in improvisation. His father would often take him to his rich clients to show off his talents. Elgar also became very proficient on the organ and, his favourite instrument, the violin – an instrument on which he was largely self-taught.

In 1863, at the age of six, Elgar attended the Roman Catholic 'dame school' in Britannia Square Worcester. There, he received pianoforte lessons and music theory tuition. He left school at the age of 15 in 1872. The family didn't have enough money for him to follow his dream of going to Leipzig to study music and so he went to work in a solicitor's office, which he found rather dreary.

A year later he left his job to give violin lessons to students and to work in his father's shop in Worcester's High Street. Although he had received some music tuition, Elgar mainly taught himself music theory by studying books and by experimenting with the instruments in his father's shop.

Along with his father, Elgar was a member of the Worcester Glee Club where he composed, played the violin and even conducted. He also played the violin at the Worcester Festival and in the Birmingham orchestra.

In 1879, he was appointed conductor for the County of Worcester Lunatic Asylum at Powick Orchestra. It was whilst working as conductor there that he composed some of his earliest pieces. Elgar also worked as organist in the local St George's Roman Catholic Church, succeeding his father in the post.

Through his teaching, Elgar met his future wife, Caroline Alice Roberts, who was 8 years his senior and the daughter of a late Major General. They married in 1889 despite opposition from her aunts (both of her parents were dead) who disapproved because of Elgar's lack of wealth. Together, they had one daughter whom they named Carice (a contraction of Caroline Alice). With the encouragement of his wife, who believed it would help advance his musical career, they moved to London. The move to London proved unsuccessful, so they moved back home to Great Malvern for a while before moving to London again. Elgar's wife possessed an unshakeable belief in her husband's genius, and her love and encouragement gave an enormous boost to his musical career.

Although Elgar was gaining a reputation in the 1890's as a composer, mainly for the works he did for the great choral festivals of the English Midlands, he still wasn't getting much national or international recognition.

However, finally, in 1899, Elgar's first major orchestral work, his *Enigma Variations* followed a year later by the oratorio, *The Dream of Gerontius*, brought Elgar the fame he rightly deserved and established his position as one of the world's leading composers.

Less than five years after his success with *Enigma Variations* and *The Dream of Gerontius*, Elgar was knighted. In 1924, Elgar was appointed Master of the King's Musick.

In the same year that he was knighted, Elgar moved with his family to a large house overlooking the River Wye on the outskirts of Hereford. In 1912, for the sake of his music, he once again left the countryside he loved so much (Elgar's love of the countryside shows through a great deal of his music) to return to London.

The First World War had a great impact on the highly sensitive Elgar and affected him enormously. Unsurprisingly, he didn't produce many great works during that period.

Elgar's beloved wife and biggest supporter, Caroline Alice, died in 1920. After her death, the broken-hearted Elgar, whose music fell out of fashion after the War, composed very little. His last masterpiece, the *Cello Concerto in E minor* was composed shortly before his wife's death.

On 23 February 1934, Elgar died from cancer in Worcester. He left a symphony and an opera uncompleted. He was buried next to his wife in the graveyard of St Wulstan's Church, Little Malvern.

Elizabeth I (1533-1603)

When Queen Elizabeth first sat on the throne of England in 1558, her country was in ruin and virtually bankrupt. England was despised abroad and confused at home.

In 1603, when she died, it was the end of an era of heroes. It was, for England, a golden time. Elizabeth was the most outstanding queen the world has ever seen. Only Queen Victoria comes close.

Elizabeth, Queen of England and Ireland, and the fifth and last monarch of the Tudor dynasty, was born on 7 September 1533 at Greenwich Palace, Kent, to King Henry VIII and his second wife, Anne Boleyn. It was confidently predicted by physicians and astrologers that King Henry and Anne Boleyn would have a boy and so when Elizabeth was born there was much disappointment all round. King Henry now had two legitimate children, the 17-year-old Princess Mary Tudor by his first wife, Catherine of Aragon, and the red-haired Princess Elizabeth. But both were girls.

Less than six months after her birth, Elizabeth went to live in Hatfield, north of London. It was the custom in Tudor times for children of royalty to live in separate households from their parents.

In 1534, Henry VIII managed to persuade Parliament to pass a new Act of Succession that allowed Elizabeth and any more children her mother should have to be the only legitimate heirs to the throne. Mary Tudor, who was still only a teenager, was thus declared illegitimate and demoted from princess to lady-in-waiting to her half sister, Elizabeth. Mary Tudor was also banished from ever seeing her mother again.

Wanting a reason that would free him of his wife because he had grown to despise her and believed that his marriage to her was cursed because she had failed to produce a male heir, King Henry VIII had Protestant Queen Anne Boleyn beheaded at the Tower of London on 19 May 1536 for alleged multiple adultery and for incest with her own brother. No doubt King Henry's determination to dispose of his wife was strengthened even further when he fell in love with the rather retiring Jane Seymour. Elizabeth was not yet three years of age when her mother was executed.

A few days before Anne Boleyn's beheading in 1536, Elizabeth, like her half sister Mary Tudor before her, was declared illegitimate and excluded from the line of succession. King Henry VIII married Jane Seymour less than a fortnight after Anne's execution. Ironically, just as Anne Boleyn was Catherine of Aragon's maid of honour, so Jane Seymour was Anne Boleyn's maid of honour.

On the 12 October 1537, King Henry finally had his much-awaited son, Edward VI, with his third wife, Jane Seymour. Since his half sisters had been decreed illegitimate, Edward VI was now first in line to the throne. Sadly, Jane Seymour died less than a fortnight after the birth of her son. Henry VIII was said to have been devastated and heartbroken, and made arrangements to be buried next to his beloved Jane after his death. The death of Jane Seymour did not, however, prevent him from marrying three more times; first to Anne of Cleves, then to Catherine Howard and finally to Catherine Parr.

Although Elizabeth lived in a separate household from her father, nevertheless, one can only imagine how confusing it must have been for the growing Elizabeth to have had so many stepmothers.

As well as inheriting her father's red hair, Elizabeth inherited her father's intellect. Elizabeth, who was brought up in the Protestant faith, was a natural scholar and loved to study; she was very well educated and learnt a number of languages. She could speak French fluently by the time she was 14 and also learnt Italian, Latin, Greek, Flemish and Spanish. Elizabeth also knew some Welsh. She was also a competent horsewoman with a love of riding at great speeds. In addition, Elizabeth could dance, compose music, play the lyre, lute and virginals skilfully.

In 1544, King Henry VIII's third Act of Succession reinstated Elizabeth and her half sister Mary to the line of the throne – although it did not officially recognise them as legitimate. Their half brother, Prince Edward VI (by King Henry and his third wife, Jane Seymour) was still first in line to the throne, Mary Tudor was second in line and Elizabeth was third in line to the throne.

On 29 January 1547, Henry VIII died after a short illness and, as requested when he was alive, was buried next to his third wife, Jane Seymour. Elizabeth was residing at Enfield when she learnt of her father's death, and was reported to have been very upset by the news. Although she had never shared a close relationship with her father, Elizabeth did admire and respect him. Throughout her life, Elizabeth would often proudly refer to herself in public as the daughter of King Henry VIII.

On Henry VIII's death, Elizabeth's half brother, Edward VI, became King but because he was only nine years old his uncle, Edward Seymour, was appointed Lord Protector and head of the Council of Regency. In 1550, the Earl of Warwick (who named himself the Duke of Northumberland in 1551) assumed power of the regency after masterminding the fall of Edward Seymour. Edward VI became the first Protestant to sit on the English throne.

After her father's death, Elizabeth lived for a while with her stepmother Catherine Parr (Henry VIII's last wife) at Chelsea Palace. Not long after the death of Henry VIII, Catherine Parr married Sir Thomas Seymour, the younger brother of Edward Seymour.

While living with Catherine Parr and Sir Thomas, the young Elizabeth is believed to have had a sexual relationship with Sir Thomas Seymour. Ill at ease with Elizabeth and Thomas's 'relationship', Catherine Parr made arrangements for her stepdaughter to live elsewhere and, as a result, by the end of 1548, 15-year-old Elizabeth had acquired a household of her own. After Catherine Parr died her husband Thomas Seymour, was executed at the Tower of London for treason.

On 6 July 1553, King Edward VI died, probably from tuberculosis. Worried about losing his powerful position, Edward's Chief Minister the now Duke of Northumberland had managed to persuade the devout Protestant King to contravene the 1544 Act of Succession, to exclude his half sisters from the succession and to make the Duke's daughter-in-law (also the King's cousin), Lady Jane Grey, as the next heir to the throne. The unwilling Lady Jane was proclaimed Queen on 10 July. Mary was furious, and raised an army to fight for the crown. Lady Jane very happily relinquished the crown when ordered to do so, and the 37-year-old Catholic Mary Tudor was proclaimed Queen on 19 July. Lady Jane and her husband, Guildford Dudley were sentenced to death at the Tower of London. The tragic, sweet teenager Lady Jane Grey, whose terrible end was caused by the power-hungry Duke of Northumberland, famously became known as the 'Nine-day Queen'.

As Queen, devout Roman Catholic Mary Tudor overturned the anti-Catholic laws that had been introduced by her father, King

Henry VIII. And she went to great lengths to restore Catholicism into England. Her persecution of Protestant rebels, and the execution of hundreds of heretics, earned her the nickname, 'Bloody Mary'.

On 18 March 1554, Elizabeth was taken to the Tower of London on the orders of her half-sister, Queen Mary. The exceedingly unpopular Queen Mary believed her very popular half-sister to be involved in a plot with Sir Thomas Wyatt to overthrow her. Despite Elizabeth's pleas to her half-sister, claiming her innocence, she was still sent to the Tower. Thomas Wyatt gave a speech minutes before he was executed, exonerating Elizabeth from all complicity in the rebellion. That speech helped gain Elizabeth her release and in the May of 1554, Elizabeth was freed from the Tower of London after two months' imprisonment. She was sent to the royal palace at Woodstock in Oxfordshire under house arrest. It was with the help of Queen Mary's new husband Philip II of Spain (who became King of Spain in 1556), that Elizabeth was finally freed from house arrest and allowed to return to Hatfield.

In November 1558, Queen Mary knew that she didn't have much longer to live and, with the encouragement of King Philip II, wrote to her half-sister, Elizabeth, telling her that she would allow her to succeed to the throne only if she agreed to certain conditions. One of the conditions was that she would retain the Roman Catholic faith in England.

Whilst in the grounds (the story goes that she was sitting underneath an oak tree) of Hatfield House, 25-year-old Elizabeth learnt the news of her half-sister's death and was informed that she was now Queen of England. On learning of her accession, she quoted in Latin from the *118th Psalm*: 'This is the Lord's doing; it is marvellous in our eyes.'

On the advice of astrologer, Dr John Dee, Elizabeth held her coronation on 15 January 1559 in Westminster Abbey. When Elizabeth came to the throne, the nation was divided by religion. And because there had been years of fighting wars, there was little money left in the Treasury.

In 1559, shortly after Elizabeth came to the throne, Mary Tudor's Catholic legislation was repealed, and Elizabeth became Supreme Governor (and not Supreme Head as her father had been) of the Church of England. She helped to restore England to Protestantism.

Unlike her unpopular Roman Catholic half-sister, Queen Elizabeth was religiously tolerant and wasn't overly concerned about what religion her people followed. She claimed that she 'would not open windows into men's souls'. Her only priority was to persuade the people to be loyal to the crown. She didn't like any sort of religious extremism.

But, in 1570, religious extremism in England escalated after Queen Elizabeth was excommunicated by Pope Pius V. The Queen's Catholic subjects were absolved from allegiance to her and as a result, Elizabeth was forced to bring in laws to keep Catholic extremism under control. Throughout most of Queen Elizabeth's reign there were death threats from Catholic plotters who didn't want a Protestant Queen on the throne.

After Elizabeth nearly died from smallpox in 1562, Parliament worried that civil war would erupt upon her death if she did not produce an heir to the throne. MPs urged her to marry, as did her advisers. The pressure was increased by the fact that nobody believed that a woman could rule by herself.

Elizabeth was seen as the best catch in the whole of Europe, and had many suitors competing for her hand in marriage, including Philip II of Spain who had been married to her half-sister, Mary Tudor. At one point, marriage negotiations were seriously planned to François the Duke of Anjou (youngest son of Henry II and Catherine de'Medici) whom she nicknamed her 'frog'.

However, of all her admirers, the man Elizabeth felt the greatest affection for was her Master of Horse, Robert Dudley (the Earl of Leicester). Elizabeth and Robert Dudley had known each other in childhood, and were even imprisoned in the Tower of London together early in Mary Tudor's reign, although it is widely claimed that they never saw each other during their imprisonment. The married Robert Dudley was derogatorily nicknamed 'the gypsy' because of his charm, cunning nature and dark looks.

It is possible that Elizabeth deliberately didn't marry so that she could use the possibility of marriage as a diplomatic tool. Elizabeth's life as a spinster earned her the nickname, the 'Virgin Queen', a nickname which she herself promoted.

Meanwhile, having been forced to abdicate as Queen of Scotland and hand over the crown to her young son, Elizabeth's cousin, the

Roman Catholic Mary Stuart, who was known as Mary Queen of Scots, sought refuge in England. This wasn't a good move. Elizabeth immediately had her placed under virtual house arrest for almost twenty years. Mary Queen of Scots, along with many other Roman Catholics, considered herself to be the true Queen of England.

Mary wasn't the only one to question Elizabeth's right to the throne. Much of Europe did not consider Elizabeth to be the true Queen of England because her father's divorce from Catherine of Aragon had never been sanctioned by the Pope. There were a number of plots by Roman Catholics to replace Elizabeth with Mary (who had become the figurehead for rebelling Roman Catholics everywhere) as Queen of England. It was Lord Walsingham, Queen Elizabeth's Spy Master, who helped unveil several of the plots against her. Lord Walsingham and his network of informers and spies were England's first organised secret intelligence service.

In 1587, Mary was condemned to death because she was accused of complicity in a plot (known as the Babington Plot) against the Queen. For a long time, Elizabeth refused to sign her cousin's death warrant because of Mary's royal status, fearing it would set a dangerous precedent. She also didn't want England to be attacked by angry Catholic countries. Eventually, the death warrant was signed, and Mary Queen of Scots was beheaded at Fotheringhay Castle in 1587. As Elizabeth had feared, many monarchs throughout Europe were furious. The beheading of the Roman Catholic Mary Queen of Scots was the final straw that motivated Philip II, the King of Spain, to send the Spanish Armada to attack England the following year. English piracies against Spanish possessions, and Elizabeth's aiding of Dutch rebels in the Netherlands against Spanish rule, hadn't helped. King Philip II was determined to restore Catholicism in England.

Over the early years of her reign, Elizabeth had dramatically improved her country's financial position through the efforts of officially approved pirates. Sir Francis Drake, for example, had enriched the nation considerably when he had been commissioned by the Queen as a privateer ('privateer' was Elizabeth's politically correct name for 'pirate'). Drake's raids against Spanish colonies had proved very lucrative.

Drake also played an important role in defeating the Spanish Armada in 1588. Francis Drake was playing bowls at the time when he was told about the sighting of the Spanish Armada. He is reported to have said: 'There is plenty of time to win this game and thrash the Spaniards too'.

Before the defeat of the Spanish Armada, which was won by a combination of violent storms, well-built ships and the brilliant tactics of the English fleet, Queen Elizabeth gave a now legendary speech to her troops at Tilbury as they awaited the arrival of the Spanish Armada in 1588.

'My loving people, we have been persuaded by some that are careful of our safety to take heed how we commit ourselves to armed multitudes for fear of treachery, but I assure you I do not desire to live to distrust my faithful and loving people. Let tyrants fear; I have always so behaved myself under God, I have placed my chiefest strength and safeguard in the loyal hearts and goodwill of my subjects. And therefore I am come amongst you, as you see, at this time not for my recreation and disport, but being resolved in the midst and heat of battle to live and die amongst you all. To lay down for God, my kingdom and for my people, my honour and my blood even in the dust. I know I have the body of a weak and feeble woman, but I have the heart and stomach of a King and a King of England too and think it foul scorn that Parma or Spain or any Prince of Europe should dare to invade the borders of my realm; to which, rather than any dishonour shall grow by me, I myself will take up arms, I myself will be your General, Judge and Rewarder of every one of your virtues in the field. I know already for your forwardness you have deserved rewards and crowns; and we do assure you, on the word of a Prince, they shall be duly paid you.'

This patriotic speech endeared her to the people of England. The defeat of the Spanish Armada firmly established England as the world's leading naval power and increased Queen Elizabeth's popularity tenfold. The defeat of the Spanish Armada proved to all those who were sceptical that a woman was just as capable as any man as a war time leader.

In 1599, Elizabeth sent the 2nd Earl of Essex to Ireland to defeat Catholic Irish rebels who were rebelling against the anti-Catholic laws that Elizabeth had imposed. Essex fell out of favour with Elizabeth when he made an unauthorised treaty with the Irish and returned to England without the Queen's consent. This led Elizabeth to dismiss him from all his offices and stop most of his income. As revenge, and encouraged by rebels, he tried to get the people of London to revolt against Elizabeth. In 1601, the Earl was executed for leading a rebellion against Elizabeth's government. The English courtier and soldier had been a favourite of Queen Elizabeth's, even though she had shared a rather tempestuous relationship with him.

On 24 March 1603, aged 69, Queen Elizabeth, the last of the Tudor Monarchs, died at Richmond Palace, Surrey. Her reign had lasted for nearly 45 years. Elizabeth was buried at Westminster Abbey. The King of Scotland, James VI (son of her cousin, Mary Queen of Scots) was her successor to the English throne. As King of England, James VI became James I of England and, for the first time, united the kingdoms of England and Scotland.

Queen Elizabeth was a proud, strong-willed, quick-witted and a highly intelligent woman who was a shrewd judge of character. She was determined, cautious and secretive, and kept her thoughts and feelings close to her heart, a trait which always kept even those around her guessing. With her red hair and pale skin, Queen Elizabeth was striking in appearance. She enjoyed wearing the latest fashions (owning over 2,000 dresses) and adorned herself ostentatiously with expensive jewels.

Although she had serious romances with several lovers during her reign, Queen Elizabeth I never married. She was, however, something of a flirt. She was a hugely popular queen and would often go on walkabout tours and talk to the young, the old, the rich and the poor alike. She was a Queen who was wedded to the English people, and the people loved her for it. They called her Good Queen Bess.

Queen Elizabeth reigned during a time when women were considered far from equal to men, but she was one of England's greatest sovereigns. She helped unify the country against foreign enemies and led the country to victory over the Spanish.

Elizabeth's reign was a time of great expansion and discovery. The adventurer, Sir Walter Ralegh named an American state 'Virginia' in the Queen's honour. And Sir Francis Drake became the first Englishman to circumnavigate the world. It was also a time of great poets and playwrights (most notably William Shakespeare, Ben Jonson and Christopher Marlowe).

By the end of Elizabeth's reign, however, the nation was not in a good state. Continuing troubles in Ireland, poor harvests, rising prices and increasing poverty had caused a huge dent in Elizabeth's popularity.

Nevertheless, the shortcomings of her successor, King James I, soon restored Elizabeth's reputation with the people as one of England's greatest rulers. They didn't like him, and missed her.

Her 45-year reign is considered to be England's 'Golden Age'. She had many faults: she was unscrupulous and often ready to lie if she thought it would be to her advantage; she was vain and easily influenced by flatterers; and she was rarely grateful to those around her. But she cared passionately for England and the English. She worked hard to govern wisely and well. And she has been described as the 'bravest woman who ever lived'. When she first addressed Parliament she said: 'Nothing, nothing, no worldly thing under the sun is so dear to me as the love and goodwill of my subjects.' During her life she proved that she meant it.

Michael Faraday 1791-1867

No single invention has changed our world, and the way we live, more than electricity. Without it we would have very few of the things we nowadays regard as essential. Many men have contributed to the development of electricity but the man who discovered the real value of electricity, and who can be said to have 'invented' electricity as a human tool, was Michael Faraday, an Englishman.

Born in Newlington, Faraday's parents were poor (his father was a blacksmith) and when he reached the age of 14 the young Faraday was apprenticed to a bookbinder and bookseller. He had received only a very basic education in a church Sunday school. He took advantage of his position in the bookshop to read extensively – far more widely than he would have been able to read had he taken a post in almost any other establishment.

At the age of 20, Faraday listened to a lecture given by Sir Humphry Davy, the famous English scientist and was so enthralled that he wrote asking for a job. Davy, recognising something in the young Faraday, ignored the fact that the young man had no formal qualifications and employed him as his assistant.

Within a few years Faraday showed that although he had no academic training he was a brilliant experimental physicist.

In 1819, a scientist called Hans Christian Oersted had found that the needle of an ordinary magnetic compass would be deflected if the compass was placed close to a wire in which an electric current was flowing.

Faraday decided to see what happened if the magnet was kept fixed in one position. His theory was that the wire might move instead. He constructed a brilliantly simple but ingenious device in which a wire, through which an electric current flowed, rotated continuously in the vicinity of a magnet. Faraday had invented the electric motor – the first device to use an electric current to move a material object. Every electric motor used today follows Faraday's simple design.

The problem was that the only way of generating an electric current was by using a chemical battery – and the chemical batteries available in the early 19th century were rather primitive. Faraday believed that there must be a way to use magnetism to generate electricity. In 1831, he discovered that if a magnet is passed through a closed loop of wire, a current will flow in the wire while the magnet is moving. Faraday had invented the basis of the first electric dynamo and had discovered electromagnetic induction – a way of generating continuous electric currents. The law describing this discovery is Faraday's Law. The electric generators which supply power to our homes, shops and factories are based on Faraday's discovery.

These discoveries alone would have made Faraday one of the most important men in history (he invariably appears near the top of lists of the most important individuals in world history) but Faraday hadn't finished. He also worked as a chemist and discovered a number of organic compounds, including benzene, and was the first man to devise a method for liquefying gases. His work in electrochemistry (the study of chemical effects of electric currents) was crucial and he established the two laws of electrolysis which bear his name. It was Faraday who made popular terms such as ion, electrode, cathode and anode. It was Faraday who introduced the idea of magnetic and electric lines of force. He discovered that if polarised light is passed through a magnetic field its polarisation will be altered – thereby establishing the existence of a relationship between magnetism and light. It was Faraday who discovered and named diamagnetism. It was Faraday's genius that paved the way for many advances in modern physics, and numerous other great inventors owe an enormous debt to the blacksmith's son.

A brilliant man who was also a marvellous teacher and lecturer (he was appointed professor at the Royal Institution in 1833), Faraday was indifferent to money, fame and honours. He lived, quite simply, for his work. He had a long, happy marriage. He declined the offer to become president of the British Royal Society and also declined a knighthood, though in 1855 he did retire to a house provided for him by Queen Victoria. He died in 1867.

Elizabeth Fry (1780-1845)

The Prison Governor was horrified at the prospect of the refined lady who stood before him visiting the female prison quarters at the notorious Newgate prison. He was anxious for her safety and was convinced that the female prisoners would rob her of the clothes on her back. But Elizabeth Fry insisted that she should be allowed to see the prisoners so that she could hand out the warm clothing she had brought for them. The Governor, realising that Elizabeth would not take 'no' for an answer, reluctantly let her into the female quarters of the prison.

Walking down the cold, damp stone corridors, the stench was overwhelming and the noise from the mayhem of the prisoners was ear-shattering. However, nothing prepared Elizabeth Fry for what she was about to see.

The room, which was originally planned to house a maximum of 60 prisoners, was crammed with over 300 female prisoners and their children. The living conditions, and the condition of the women and children, were truly shocking. Elizabeth Fry was aghast at the grotesque sight before her.

Suddenly, the deafening noise of sheer pandemonium descended into stillness. The women and children looked in awe as this refined, gentle angel flitted around the room handing out clothing and giving comfort to the frightened and the sick. The prisoners could see that this incongruous vision actually cared and didn't judge them; they could tell that she looked at them not critically or cruelly but with love and compassion.

Before Elizabeth Fry left the prison she prayed in front of the prisoners and, as if hypnotised into joining her, the 300 plus women and children fell to their knees in prayer. What an awesome sight this must have been, especially for the Prison Governor who had been so concerned for her safety.

A born philanthropist, English Quaker minister and prison reformer, Elizabeth Fry, was one of 12 children. She was born Elisabeth Gurney, on 21 May 1780, in Norfolk to a wealthy Quaker banking family.

Elizabeth – affectionately known as 'Betsy' by her family – was a very shy, nervous and sickly child. Sadly, her fragile health was to burden her for the rest of her life. However, Elizabeth's delicate health, did not thwart her innate kindness, which she showed to everybody she met – even to the household servants.

As children Elizabeth and her 11 siblings were encouraged to talk to and to show respect to the less fortunate. Elizabeth Fry would often adopt young waifs and strays in the street, and – with the help of her father's wealth – feed and clothe them and teach them basic schooling. These waifs and strays became known by the family as 'Betsy's imps'. At one point, Elizabeth had a flock of over 80 children being taught in one of the wings at the grand family home in Earlham, Norfolk.

Every week, Elizabeth had to attend the Quaker meetings with her family, although she and her siblings often found them rather tedious and hated going to them. Nevertheless, her attitude was to change when a Quaker called William Savery spoke at one of the meetings. His speech had a profound effect on the 17-year-old girl. It was Savery's speech that set Elizabeth on the path to doing great things; he was the trigger who resulted in her being immortalised as one of England's greatest female philanthropists; a woman whose virtuous, benevolent face has adorned England's five-pound notes.

In 1800, Elizabeth – no doubt she shed many tears of heartache at having to do so – said farewell to her dear family, and to her gang of waifs and strays, before embarking on the journey from Norfolk to London to live in her new marital home. Still only 20, she had married Joseph Fry, also a Quaker. The couple would themselves eventually have 11 children of their own.

Busy married life did not suppress Elizabeth Fry's inherent desire to look after the less fortunate; she often carried out acts of kindness to those who needed it. She ran schools for poor children and regularly attended Quaker meetings (she became a minister in 1811).

But it was her visit to Newgate prison in 1813 that was to make her famous. Her visit to Newgate prison, where she was appalled at the conditions she found, eventually resulted in the reform of prisons throughout Britain and Europe, and also led to a vast improvement in the conditions of prisoners being transported to Australia.

In 1818, accompanied by her brother, Joseph John Gurney, Mrs Fry visited prisons throughout the North of England and Scotland. The conditions they witnessed in the prisons were brought to the attention of the public and to the authorities, and this greatly helped Elizabeth Fry's campaign.

In addition, to her lifetime involvement with prison and asylum reform at home and abroad, Elizabeth Fry helped set up refuges for the homeless in London and in Brighton. In fact, every spare moment of her time was spent on helping others and on finding ways to improve the lives of the poor and underprivileged. She even helped to make hundreds of coastguards' jobs less miserable by organising books to be sent to them.

How this fragile lady, who must have been nearly always pregnant or nursing her own children, found the energy and the strength to do so much is a mystery.

But everything about Elizabeth Fry was extraordinary. In her 65 years on earth (she died on 25 October 1845), Elizabeth Fry achieved much and transformed the lives of millions of people.

W.G. Grace (1848-1915)

It may seem strange to include a cricketer in my list of the top 100. But William Gilbert Grace was far more than the world's greatest ever cricketer: he was the world's first sporting superstar; the man who created, virtually single-handedly, the celebrity sportsman. He was the most recognisable individual in Victorian England and, after Queen Victoria herself, the second most famous Victorian.

Although he played as an amateur, it is no exaggeration to say that he single-handedly created professional sport. He realised that professional sport is a branch of the entertainment business. (This is something that most modern sportsmen don't grasp. They are, too often, arrogant and self-satisfied and have a regrettable tendency to treat their fans with disdain.)

In his day, Grace (who worked as a general practitioner) was such a draw that cricket grounds used to double their prices if W.G. Grace was playing. A normal admission ticket would cost six pence, but one shilling if W.G. was on the ground. How many sporting stars are there today whose pulling power among the public is so huge that they could double the ticket price simply by appearing in a match?

Grace, a huge, powerful, bearded, man was, without a doubt, the greatest cricketer who ever lived. It is easier to argue than refute that he was also the most notable sportsmen who ever lived.

He came from a cricket-mad family. His father helped to develop the game in the west of England and his two brothers were among the finest players of his age.

When W.G. played cricket people left their offices and factories to watch him play. There has never been a sportsman, in any time or in any sport, who was such a popular figure and who has dominated sport, the media and public life as emphatically as W.G. Grace did.

Grace was an enormously gifted batsmen, who hit the ball vast distances, and a fierce and successful bowler but it was his personality, his determination and confidence and his character, which made him such a great entertainer and unyielding competitor. He was still playing top class cricket in his 50's, at an age when most of his contemporaries had retired to coach schoolboys or run public houses.

As a doctor he was a kind man, who did what he could to help poor people. He gave them money or presents and he helped them find work. When he was on his rounds he would put down his medical bag and join in an impromptu game of cricket with local boys. He once joined in a snowball fight. But, like all great men and women he had his faults. He had a violent temper and limited patience and could be easy to provoke.

And he wasn't faultless as a cricketer either.

In 1889 he caught a youth practising on the new county cricket ground at Bristol. He battered him with a cricket stump and had to apologise in order to avoid prosecution. In 1878, he kidnapped Billy Midwinter, an Australian player who also happened to be registered with his county side (Gloucestershire), and dragged him off to The Oval for a county match.

Although he played cricket as an amateur, he made more money out of cricket than any of the professionals with whom he played. He was so competitive that he bullied and questioned umpires in a way that would today be regarded as unsporting. He was a bounder, a man who would today be described as a 'character'.

And he wasn't over imbued with modesty.

After being given out (in a relatively unimportant match) he once stood his ground and told the umpire (with unerring but unsporting accuracy) that 'these people came here to watch me bat, not to watch you umpire.'

At another charity match, where a huge crowd had turned up to watch him bat, one of his bails was removed by the second ball of the match. W.G bent down and replaced the bail. 'Strong wind today,' he said to the wicket-keeper. No one objected and Grace went on to score 142. The crowd was delighted.

Despite these anecdotes, W.G. was no cheat. He was talented, disciplined and enthusiastic. He played the game to win. But in serious games he could accept defeat and believed in playing the game fairly.

Grace was an all rounder. As a batsman he created (what was then) a modern scientific method of batting. He turned cricket from a pastime beloved by gamblers and few others into a national institution. He imposed his personality and his will upon a sport and upon an age.

He played first class cricket from 1865 until 1908 and scored 54,211 runs at an average of 39.45. He scored 124 first class centuries on rough, poorly prepared grounds where the ball was likely to jump and bounce with alarming unpredictability. Most of his runs were scored on pitches which modern cricketers would describe as unplayable. As a fieldsman he took 875 catches and, as an occasional wicket keeper, he stumped 5 batsmen. As a bowler he took 2,808 wickets at an average of 18.15 per wicket. He was a round-arm seamer in his youth but in older age he bowled seductive leg breaks. Any modern professional cricketer would die for those career statistics. He played 22 test matches (all against Australia, the only available opponents at the time) and, as a batsman, averaged 32.29 runs. As a bowler the test match wickets he took cost 26.22 runs apiece. Between 1857 and 1914 he scored another 45,283 runs and took another 4,578 wickets in minor matches. He took another 656 catches too. Other cricketers, playing on the same pitches, were accustomed to scoring far fewer runs.

In 1871, he scored 2,739 first class runs in the season. The next most successful batsman scored just 1,068. In one month in 1876 he scored two triple-centuries. In the same year, playing in Grimsby, he scored 400 not out against a team consisting of 22 fielders. In 1895, he was the first player to score over 1,000 runs in the month of May – before the season had really got started. The statistics seem endless. But they are all remarkable.

His cricket career began at the age of 15 when he played for a Bristol twenty two against William Clarke's professional cricket circus. (The county championship had not been invented then.) When he was over 50 he was still opening the batting for England in test matches against Australia. He played with and against some of the sporting immortals; men such as C. B. Fry, John Lillywhite, F. R. Spofforth and Jack Hobbs.

He doesn't seem to have been too keen on life as a doctor. In his early fifties, just as his playing career was coming to an end, he gave up medicine and became full time secretary-captain of the London County Club. Even when he had officially retired, he never stopped doing things. He played golf and bowls and loved beagling. Whatever he did he was larger than life. A farmer once tried to stop Grace pursuing his beagles into the farmer's fields. Grace simply picked up the farmer and tucked him under his arm. He then strode across the fields and put the farmer down on the other side, threatening to smack his bottom if he interfered again.

W. G. Grace probably wouldn't have survived today. The politically correct would have had him tarred and feathered. But he lived his life as though every moment of it mattered. He lived his life as though he meant it.

Edmond Halley (1656-1742)

Born at Shoreditch, near London and educated at Oxford University, Edmond Halley was an astronomer, a meteorologist and a mathematician. He published scientific papers on the orbits of the planets, on the occultation of Mars and on a sunspot when he was still at university.

In 1676, when just 20 years old, he sailed for the South Atlantic, intending to compile an accurate catalogue of the stars of the Southern Hemisphere. Just two years later he produced a star catalogue which recorded the positions of 341 individual stars. In 1680, he went to Paris and started studying comets in detail.

In 1684, at the age of 28 he became friends with Isaac Newton, Robert Hooke and Christopher Wren. Halley, Hooke and Wren all helped Newton with his Law of Gravitation and Halley edited Newton's book *Philosophiae Naturalis Principa Mathematica*. Halley then paid for the book to be printed and published in 1687.

A year earlier, in 1686, Halley had produced the first meteorological chart (which showed the distribution of the prevailing winds in the world's oceans).

In addition to his astronomical studies, Halley was also a keen diver and underwater explorer. In 1690, he produced plans for the construction of a diving bell which would be capable of remaining submerged for long periods of time. Halley's bell was fitted with a window so that individuals inside could explore deep beneath the surface of the sea, and involved replacing air by sending weighted barrels of air down to the bell from the surface. The Halley design was the first practical design for a real underwater vessel – a proper submarine.

In 1701, Halley produced the first magnetic charts of the Atlantic and the Pacific oceans. He published valuable early work on the planets Mercury and Venus and established the mathematical law which connects barometric pressure with heights above sea-level. He published studies on trade winds, monsoons and magnetic variations. His *Breslau Table of Mortality*, which he published in 1703, laid the actuarial foundations for life insurance and annuities.

Despite all this important work, it is, however, as an astronomer that Halley is best remembered today. He described the parabolic orbits of 24 comets which had been observed in the years 1337 to

1698 and in 1705 he demonstrated that three of these (comets seen in 1531, 1607 and 1682) were so similar that they had to have been the same comet. He accurately predicted its return in 1758. This is now known as Halley's comet. It was the first comet whose return was predicted, proving that some comets, at least, are members of the solar system. Scientists later showed that Halley's comet was the large, bright comet seen during the Norman conquest (and shown in the Bayeux Tapestry) and sighted as far back as 240BC. Halley's comet, which has a nucleus approximately nine miles across, approached earth twice in the 20th century (in 1910 and 1986).

In the early 18th century, Halley built an observatory on the roof of his house and in 1720 he was appointed astronomer-royal of England.

John Harrison (1693-1776)

John Harrison was an inventor and horologist. Born in Foulby near Pontefract, and the son of a carpenter, he was fascinated by clocks and everything associated with them. Given a watch to amuse himself when in bed with smallpox as a boy he spent hours studying it and playing with it. Self-taught, he built his first longcase clock in 1713, when he was just 20 years old. He made a number of clocks with wooden movements and several are still working. He invented the gridiron pendulum, consisting of brass and iron rods so that the different expansions and contractions cancel each other out and he had, by 1726, built a timekeeper which had a fully-functioning compensating mechanism designed to correct errors due to variations in climate. He also invented the grasshopper escapement which, being virtually frictionless, needs no lubrication.

It was his invention of the first effective and reliable marine chronometer which makes Harrison a truly great Englishman.

Harrison invented the first practical marine chronometer in 1735. He then produced smaller and increasingly accurate improvements. After years of work, Harrison finally produced a marine chronometer which, on a voyage to Jamaica in 1761 and 1762, determined the longitude with remarkable accuracy. He was 68 years old and he sent it on its trial with his son William. His chronometer had to be highly accurate over long time intervals (and not require resetting

– since at sea that would be impossible) and able to tolerate huge variations in temperature and humidity. It had to be impervious to salt air corrosion and able to function on a pitching and yawing deck during a storm.

When the ship reached Jamaica the watch was just 5 seconds slow.

His invention, the chronometer, gave mariners the ability to fix their position at sea from celestial observations. It was the first time that this had been possible and the chronometer was a huge boon to sailors everywhere. It revolutionised long distance travel at sea.

The Government had been so aware of the need for an effective method of measuring longitude that it had offered a prize of £20,000 for an effective chronometer. Harrison won the prize (which would, today, be worth around £3,000,000) though not without having to badger the authorities (and perform a second trial by sending his chronometer on a trip to Barbados). The bureaucrats in charge of the prize money had claimed that the accuracy of the Harrison chronometer was down to luck. Eventually, Harrison received £8,750 from Parliament but only after King George threatened to appear in person in the House of Commons to complain on his behalf. Harrison never received the rest of the money he won.

His invention saved many lives. Before his marine chronometer existed shipwrecks were commonplace as sailors lost their way at sea.

William Harvey (1578-1657)

Theories about the circulation of the blood had been proposed, argued about and refuted by scientists and physicians for centuries. For many years doctors had accepted the theory put forward by the Roman doctor Galen, who had argued that the blood circulating in the arteries was different from the blood circulating in the veins, that both kinds of blood ebbed and flowed, rather than circulating around the body, and that blood permeated within the heart from the right side to the left. In this, as in so many other areas, Galen's mistaken theories misled doctors for many centuries.

It was William Harvey, an English physician who was educated in

Canterbury and then at Cambridge, who first proved and published the truth about how blood travels around the body. Harvey realised that, since the heart was pumping blood with every beat, it must be moving the blood somewhere. It seems obvious to us now that the blood had to be moving around the body in a closed circulatory system but Harvey's thinking was, at the time, original and revolutionary. He published his theory in a famous treatise entitled *Exercitatio Anatomica de Motu Cordis et Sanguinis.*

Harvey's explanation about how blood moves about the body led directly to many other vital discoveries about human anatomy and physiology. There was also an immediate practical advantage for Harvey's discovery led directly to the realisation that blood loss during operations could be fatal and that blood-letting, by cupping or applying leeches to the patient's body, was not always an entirely logical or beneficial procedure. Harvey's book also helped refute the theory that weakness could be remedied by drinking human blood – a belief which had survived until the 15th century, when the inappropriately named Pope Innocent VIII had been given fresh blood from three healthy young boys to drink.

William Harvey was royal physician to both James I and Charles I (his book was dedicated to Charles I) and as a member of the royal court he demonstrated his theory around Europe. He was present at the battle of Edgehill in 1642, as doctor to Charles I, and afterwards accompanied the King to Oxford. When Oxford was surrendered to the Parliamentary forces, Harvey returned to London. In 1651, he published a book on animal reproduction entitled *Exercitationes de Generatione Animalium.* Harvey was originally buried in Hempstead, but in 1833 he was dug up and re-buried in the Harvey Chapel in nearby Saffron Walden.

Rowland Hill (1795-1879)

By the early part of the 19th century there were enough literate people in England for the sending of letters, packets and parcels to be a regular business. But there was a problem: there was no organised way of moving such items around the country. There was no system or order for the delivery of mail. Much mail was moved around under the personal franks of Members of Parliament and peers. Postal rates were enormously complicated and it was often the people who received the letters who had to pay, rather than the people who sent them. Recipients who were too poor to pay could simply send the letter back. Crafty folk would put tiny messages on the outside of the envelope so that the recipient could receive a message without paying for it. Postal officials were often crooked and censorship was by no means unknown. The result was that the postal system in England was slow, expensive and inefficient. The situation was the same everywhere else in the world.

And then along came Rowland Hill.

Hill, born in Kidderminster, was a teacher until 1833. (He began teaching in his father's school at the age of 11, which may seem a little early to us but, hey, Mozart was composing music at the age of five). He taught astronomy and earned pocket money by mending scientific instruments. As he grew older Hill became a keen landscape painter, acquired a job at the Birmingham Assay Office and turned into an inventor and a social reformer. He was one of the founders of a wonderfully English-sounding organisation called the 'Society for the Diffusion of Useful Knowledge'.

In 1819, Hill moved the school his father had founded to Edgbaston. He designed the new school himself and included a science laboratory, a swimming pool and a form of central heating. In 1822, he published a report with the nifty title of *Plans for the Government and Liberal Instruction of Boys in Large Numbers Drawn from Experience* in which he argued that kindness got more out of boys than caning (which was then extremely popular) and that moral influence, rather than fear, should be the primary driving force behind school discipline.

The French education leader Marc Antoine Jullien (who had been Robespierre's secretary) was so impressed that he sent his son over to England to be educated at Hill's school.

Hill took an interest in many other things. He was, for example, secretary of the South Australian Colonization Commission, which successfully established a settlement without any convicts, in what is now Adelaide.

And, with all these varied interests it is perhaps not surprising that he also took an interest in the sending of letters.

In 1837, he privately published a booklet entitled *Post-office Reform* in which he advocated a low and uniform rate of postage for sending mail between any two places in the British Isles. His idea (his moment of genius) was that the cost of sending a letter should be prepaid with little labels, called stamps, which would be bought by the writer of the letter and stuck onto the letter (envelopes were not then in common use) as proof of payment. The story is that Hill became interested in postal reform after seeing a young woman turn away a letter from her fiancé – because she was too poor to pay for it.

Politicians denounced Hill's proposals. The Postmaster, Lord Lichfield dismissed his 'wild and visionary scheme' and the Secretary to the Post Office described the idea of post offices selling sheets of sticky stamps as 'preposterous'. But businessmen thought Hill's notion brilliant and in 1839 bankers and traders formed a Mercantile Committee to push for his ideas to be accepted. The businessmen won and in 1839 Rowland Hill was given a two year contract to run the new postal system according to his design.

Within three years of the publication of his original booklet, Hill's idea had become reality and the uniform penny rate for letters was introduced with, in May 1840, the penny black becoming the first and most famous stamp in the world. The stamp carried an engraving of the young Queen Victoria. Early stamps had to be cut from the sheet. It was only later that perforations were introduced.

Astonishingly, Hill was dismissed from the Post Office by Robert Peel's Conservative Government in 1842. Hill didn't sit quietly moping. He was chairman of the board of the London and Brighton Railway from 1843 to 1846, expanding routes, lowering fares, making commuting comfortable and introducing special excursion trains.

And then he returned to the Post Office.

In 1846, the Liberals made Hill secretary to the postmaster general and in 1854 he was made secretary to the Post Office, where he introduced the book-post. He also reformed the money order office and the packet service.

In a report he wrote in 1867, after having finally resigned from the Post Office, Hill advocated national ownership of the railways so that people could move themselves around the country as easily as their letters were travelling. That was not to happen for some time to come.

It is for the invention of the postage stamp, and a system of low and uniform postal rates, that Hill will always be best remembered. He effectively introduced postal services around the world and he created an environment which made commerce infinitely more efficient and profitable.

Today, England, as the originator of the postal system, is the only country in the world which does not have to have its name or flag or symbol on its stamps.

Thomas Hobbes (1588-1679)

Hobbes, author, philosopher and political theorist, was born in Malmesbury; coming into the world prematurely when his mother heard the news of the approaching Spanish armada. The excitement brought on her labour. Hobbes's father was a country vicar who abandoned his young family early on, leaving Thomas to be brought up by an uncle.

After graduating from Oxford University, Hobbes became a professional tutor and travelled around Europe with the family of the Earl of Devonshire. The Earls of Devonshire, the Cavendish family, remained his patrons for the rest of his life. He was tutor, companion and secretary to William Cavendish (who became the second Earl of Devonshire) for twenty years.

It was on those early travels, with a family of great wealth and influence, that Hobbes met many of the most important figures in Europe at the time. In England he met Francis Bacon (for whom he was for a time an amanuensis), Ben Jonson, the playwright and John Selden the historian, jurist and antiquary. In Florence he met Galileo, with whom he had philosophical discussions on the nature of motion, and in Paris he met Descartes and Gassendi. He travelled on the Continent three times in charge of pupils from the family.

In around 1628, Hobbes was introduced to Euclidean geometry and was deeply impressed. He had the idea of extending this sort of deductive certainty to an understanding of man and society. In his book *Elements of Law Natural and Politic* he attempted to describe in a mathematical fashion the rules of a new political science. However, as a political theorist his views were rather out of favour since he supported absolutism – an uncomfortable position to take in a country where antiroyalist feeling was rising rapidly. When the Long Parliament assembled in 1640 Hobbes fled immediately to Paris. While there, he turned to tutoring. This time he became tutor in mathematics to the exiled Prince of Wales, the future King Charles II of England. (Sadly, it seems that his knowledge of mathematics wasn't quite as good as those hiring him might have hoped.)

While living in Paris he wrote *Objections* (a reply to *Meditations* by Descartes), *De Cive* (a statement of his new science of the state philosophy) and his best-known book *Leviathan* (published in 1651) in which he tried to justify the absolute power of the monarch by arguing that having a king or queen who had total power enabled citizens to protect themselves from one another by agreeing to obey their sovereign in all matters. It is in this book that Hobbes draws together his thoughts on political philosophy, psychology and metaphysics. He had become a materialist who believed that only in a sovereign state could men be forced to surrender their natural rights of aggression to an absolute ruler. He believed that man is driven only by appetite or desire and that his one object is to attain happiness and satisfaction for himself. Since all men are the same, all driven by their own selfish pursuits of happiness, and altruism has no natural place in man's heart, the result, he argued, must be conflict, envy, dispute and war. He believed that if men agreed to submit to a stronger power, given to an individual who could impose laws and demand obedience, there would be much less fighting. His idea was for a social contract based on a monarchical society.

Unfortunately for Hobbes his book *Leviathan* offended his patrons, the exiled English royalists, and the French Government of the time, because in it he made it clear that he was hostile to the idea of the church having any real power. He believed that even the church should obey, and be subservient to, the sovereign state, and the monarch.

Hobbes returned to England after the death of Charles I, in the same year as *Leviathan* was published. In 1652, he made his peace with Cromwell and the Parliamentarians and settled first in London and then at Hardwick Hall, the seat of the Cavendish family. But he continued to write and to cause controversy. In 1655, he published *De Corpore* and in 1658 he published *De Homine.*

When Charles II came to the throne he gave his old tutor a pension and helped protect him against a parliamentary bill put together by enemies who claimed that the Great Fire of London and the Plague of 1665-6 were both a result of God's wrath against England for harbouring such a terrible man – an atheist. The bill was passed by the Commons but did not become law. However, Hobbes was banned from publishing any future books in England, and for the rest of his life most of his books were published in Holland. Hobbes was, indeed, so alarmed at the ban that some of his books dealing with controversial topics were not published until after his death. Hobbes wrote well into his 80's and published *Behemoth: a history of the causes of the Civil Wars of England*, translations of the *Iliad* and *Odyssey* and an autobiography in Latin verse. He also wrote a good deal of poetry.

Although Hobbes was an absolutist, who believed that unlimited centralised authority should be vested in a monarch, his work also contained many of the principles of developing liberalism.

Throughout his life Hobbes was looked after by the Cavendish family. He died at Hardwick Hall.

William Hogarth (1697-1764)

Every artist and designer in the world owes a huge debt of gratitude to William Hogarth. So, too, does every comic strip artist.

Hogarth was born in London. His father was a textbook author and school teacher who, when Hogarth was a boy, opened a coffee house, went bust and ended up in the Fleet Prison for five years as a debtor.

After an apprenticeship with an engraver, Hogarth set up in business designing coats of arms, letter headings and plates for booksellers. He spent his free time wandering around London sketching what he saw.

The first works he sold were satirical drawings. For example, in 1721 he produced a savagely satirical drawing called *Emblematical Print on the South Sea Scheme* which satirised the South Sea Bubble. During the next few years he produced an extraordinary mixture of engravings. Some were book illustrations, others were satirical sketches.

By the 1730's, he was producing oil paintings of actors, politicians and families – probably because these were more easily saleable. But he continued with his commentaries on social and political life. In 1731, he produced a series of paintings with a powerful moral message, entitled *A Harlot's Progress*. The originals are now lost but the paintings survive as a series of six engravings. The series tells of a country girl who arrives in town, becomes a prostitute and dies of venereal disease. Despite its melancholic tone the series was a huge success and Hogarth quickly followed it with a sequel entitled *A Rake's Progress*, a series of eight pictures which show the reckless life of the son of a rich merchant who wastes his father's money on gambling, whoring and luxurious living and ends his life in Bedlam, the lunatic asylum.

These paintings, which showed a sequence of events, were the forerunners of the strip cartoon.

Starting in 1743, Hogarth painted the six pictures in his Marriage-a-la-mode series. These paintings show how a marriage for money (something common in upper-class 18th century society) can be a complete tragedy. Hogarth's satire became hugely successful. The paintings were engraved, and they sold enormously well as prints.

In 1747, Hogarth produced twelve engravings and prints with the title *Industry and Idleness*. These showed the lives of two apprentices; one who is hard working and the other who is lazy. The series showed how the individual who works will be rewarded while the layabout will come to no good. In Hogarth's series, the idle apprentice ends up becoming a highwayman and living with a harlot. In the final frame of the series the industrious apprentice, now rich, successful and a respectable magistrate, sends the idle apprentice to the gallows.

In the early 1750's, Hogarth, who was still politically motivated (one of his paintings showed the French as cringing, emaciated and superstitious people), produced his famous *Beer Street and Gin Lane* series, which shows the dangers of alcoholism. The series was published in support of the Gin Act and may well have been produced by Hogarth in response to a request from his friend the magistrate Henry Fielding (who was continuing the new business of writing realistic novels, invented by Daniel Defoe, and who would later produce the book *Tom Jones*). In the same year, Hogarth, who loved animals and hated to see them being abused, also produced a series in which he showed a criminal starting off by torturing and ill-treating animals and ending up murdering a woman. In the final picture in the series, the murderer is dissected by doctors after his execution. (Hogarth was apparently aware of the now proven connection between cruelty to animals and cruelty to people. It is now accepted that mass murderers often start their evil by torturing cats and dogs.)

Amazingly, Hogarth also became a popular portrait painter. In 1746, he painted the actor David Garrick, playing Richard III. For this one painting he received £200. It was more than any English artist had ever received for a portrait.

Hogarth was a prolific artist and he lived at a time when artists were beginning to earn a living by selling their work not solely to rich patrons but also to shop and tavern owners. Engravings of popular paintings sold well in printshops and successful artists could earn good money from their work. Hogarth introduced moral tales and humour into his drawings and these went down extremely well in 18th century England. It was Hogarth who had the original idea of painting and engraving modern moral subjects and creating stories as a mixture of writer and playwright. It was Hogarth who invented the whole concept of the strip cartoon.

In 1729, Hogarth married Jane Thornhill, herself the daughter of a successful artist. He died in London in 1764. His friend, the legendary actor David Garrick composed the following inscription for Hogarth's tombstone:

Farewell great Painter of Mankind
Who reach'd the noblest point of Art
Whose pictur'd Morals charm the Mind
And through the Eye correct the Art

If Genius fire thee, Reader, stay,
If Nature touch thee, drop a Tear;
If neither move thee, turn away,
For Hogarth's honour'd dust lies here.

There is one more reason for Hogarth to deserve his place in my 100.

Hogarth had never been a man to allow anyone to take advantage of him professionally. For example, when he wasn't paid for a design he made in 1727, when he was still at the beginning of his career, he sued the man who had commissioned the work and won.

In 1734, Hogarth, together with other 'artists and designers of paintings, drawings, and engravers of original prints' petitioned the House of Commons for copyright protection for their work.

The House of Commons reported that Hogarth and his friends claimed that they had 'with great industry and expense, severally invented designed or engraved divers sets of new pictures and prints, in hopes to have reaped the benefits of such their own labours, and the credit thereof, but that divers printsellers, printers, and other persons, both here and abroad, have, of late, too frequently taken the liberty of copying, printing, publishing, great quantities of base, imperfect and mean copies and imitations thereof, to the great detriment of the petitioners and such other artists, and to the discouragement of Arts and Sciences in this Kingdom.'

Hogarth put politics into art and invented the cartoon strip. He also helped give artists, writers, designers and others copyright protection for their work. The fight for copyright protection, which Hogarth began in the House of Commons in England, eventually spread to other countries around the world. Writers and artists today could do with Hogarth to protect their interests.

Robert Hooke (1653-1703)

Robert Hooke didn't have a good start to life. Born on the Isle of Wight, he grew up with a pronounced curvature of the spine, he had smallpox when he was a boy (which left him badly scarred) and, when he was just 13 years old, his father, a clergyman, hanged himself. When he decided to train as a painter he found that he was allergic to paint fumes. And then he fell in love with a girl called Grace Hooke who, unfortunately, happened to be his niece.

But, after that unpromising beginning, Hooke's life became a massive success. He learned to play the organ, secured a place as a chorister at Oxford and became an assistant to Dr Thomas Willis.

He met Robert Boyle and discovered a passion for science and mathematics.

A complete list of his discoveries and inventions would fill a book. He invented the marine barometer and was one of the first men to build and use a reflecting telescope. He invented sash windows, the circular flywheel (used in clocks), the anchor escapement (used in clocks), the hygrometer (used to measure humidity), the anemometer (used to measure wind), the helioscope (used for studying the sun), the refractometer (used to measure the refractive index of liquids), the marine chronometer (decades before the one John Harrison invented in 1761), the wheel barometer, the altimeter (used for measuring height), and the equatorial quadrant (used to aid astronomical observations). He invented synthetic fibres, microdots, mercury amalgam (later used as a filling material by dentists) and the hypodermic needle (after studying bee stings under a microscope). He discovered the principles of respiration (working with Robert Boyle, whose work on gases is remembered by the laws which bear his name, Hooke expanded the significance of Harvey's work on the circulation of the blood with a complementary piece of research which showed that the movement of the lungs draws air into the body), developed the hypothesis that the earth's magnetic poles are not fixed and was the first man to study fossils. He was the first man to discover sun spots and the fact that the earth and the moon follow an elliptical orbit around the sun. He discovered the planet Neptune. He discovered the relationship of vibrations to musical notes (eighty years before the formal discovery of the wave nature of sound), the principles of light refraction (he proposed the wave theory of light to explain diffraction – which he also discovered), the existence of binary star systems and the nature of combustion. In 1667, he announced in his *Micrographia* that he had 'by the help of a distended wire, propagated the sound to a very considerable distance in an instant, or with as seemingly quick a motion as that of light.' He also pointed out that sound could be transmitted through a wire even if the wire was bent. He found out how to measure gravity by using a pendulum and demonstrated the law describing planetary motions. He suggested that Jupiter rotates on its axis, and his detailed sketches of Mars were used to determine its rate of rotation. He found that matter expands when it is heated and he developed the kinetic theory of gases. It was Hooke who coined the word 'cell' to refer to the basic unit of life (after examining a piece of cork under a microscope he decided that the smallest parts of the material reminded him of monastic cells) and, as an architect, he helped rebuild London after the Great Fire. He was responsible for designing the Bedlam mental asylum, the London College of Physicians and the London Monument to the Great Fire. His law of elasticity, a crucial discovery, states that the deformation of a material is linearly proportional to the force applied to it. He was one of the first proponents of the theory of evolution (years before Darwin wrote about it). He was the first to state that air is made up of particles separated from each other by relatively large distances.

Oh, and he invented the universal joint, without which a vast number of other inventions would never have been possible. And he invented the steam engine but, not surprisingly, never actually got round to building one.

It is difficult to believe that anyone has ever done more for mankind than Robert Hooke, or that the world has ever known a more terrifyingly brilliant and wide-ranging genius.

In 1696, he began to write his autobiography. Not surprisingly, he never managed to find the time to finish it. Pity. He knew Isaac Newton and Christopher Wren well and had a lasting friendship with John Aubrey. He was Curator of Experiments for the Royal Society for 40 years. He was in many ways an unusual, as well as a great, man. When he died in London he had amassed a considerable sum of money. The cash was found in his room.

Edward Jenner (1749-1823)

Throughout the 18th century, smallpox was one of the most dangerous and feared diseases. It killed hundreds of thousands.

Many attempts had been made to control the disease.

In China and India, twenty-five centuries before, it had been discovered that putting material from smallpox scabs or pustules into the nose or skin of a healthy individual would protect that individual to the extent that if they contracted smallpox they would suffer a less serious attack – and probably not die.

It was not, however, until the beginning of the 18th century that this method of preventive medicine, an early form of inoculation, was introduced into Europe from Turkey. Material from a smallpox pustule was rubbed into a scratch made with a clean needle on the arm of the person to be inoculated. Prior to that time, the only way to minimise the deadly effect of the disease had been for healthy individuals to mix with people who had a mild version of smallpox. Aware of this, local 'wise women' in Europe (a cross between early midwives, district nurses and GPs) had encouraged mothers to allow their children to play with other local children who had a mild case of smallpox.

After Lady Mary Montagu, the wife of the British Ambassador to Turkey, had her daughter publicly inoculated against smallpox with a needle, the method became fashionable. Experiments performed on prisoners from Newgate Prison in London seemed at first to show that the technique was relatively safe and effective.

Thomas Dimsdale, an English practitioner in the town of Hertford, was invited to Russia to inoculate the family of Catherine II. His fee for this was to receive £10,000, an annuity of £500 and his expenses. He was also made a baron, a councillor of state and a major general.

However, it quickly became clear that this crude form of inoculation was rather dangerous.

When a Society for the Inoculation of the Poor was founded in London, Dimsdale objected on the grounds that in the overcrowded conditions in which the poor of London lived, inoculation would simply spread smallpox and produce an epidemic of the disease. He was right. One doctor reported that a single inoculated child had infected a total of 17 people, eight of whom had subsequently died. Inoculation worked for the rich but not for the poor, who lived in close contact with one another and who could not all be inoculated at the same time, the method was simply too dangerous.

Throughout the 18th century, smallpox continued to kill hundreds of thousands. One of the greatest epidemics to affect London occurred in 1772. In 1774, the disease claimed the life of King Louis XV of France.

In 1774, however, there was a breakthrough in the fight against smallpox. Frightened by the news of a local outbreak of smallpox, a Dorset farmer called Benjamin Jesty vaccinated his wife and two sons with cowpox (a similar but mild disease contracted by cows) in the hope that this might protect them against smallpox. Jesty had noticed that the girls working on his farm who had contracted cowpox did not develop smallpox. Although Jesty's experiment was ignored by the medical profession, the Dorset farmer had discovered vaccination – a very different form of protection to inoculation.

Inoculation requires the person to be protected to be given the infection against which they are seeking protection in the hope that they will merely suffer a mild case of the disease. It is an obviously dangerous business. Vaccination, however, involves giving the patient a harmless disease, or a mild and harmless version of a disease, in the hope that by being forced to prepare its defenses the body will acquire a defence against the similar but potentially lethal disorder. The hazards with vaccination are considerable but not as immediately obvious.

Jesty's idea was eventually revised by a general practitioner called Dr Edward Jenner.

Jenner was born, worked and died in Berkeley, Gloucestershire, where his father was the vicar. He was a keen naturalist and an intelligent and thoughtful man. 'The deviation of man from the state in which he was originally placed by nature,' he once wrote, 'seems to have proved to him a prolific source of diseases.'

In the area of Gloucestershire where Jenner worked it was well known that dairymaids who developed cowpox did not develop smallpox and Jenner slowly collected evidence for this phenomenon until, in 1796, he was certain enough of the theory to repeat the experiment which had been first tried by Jesty in 1774.

With great professional courage Jenner put material from a cowpox pustule on the hand of a dairymaid called Sarah Nelmes into a scratch he made on the arm of an eight-year-old boy, James Phipps.

Then, seven weeks later, to test whether young Master Phipps really was protected, Jenner injected him with material from a genuine smallpox pustule.

To Jenner's undoubted relief the boy remained healthy.

With the remarkable pig-headedness that has characterised the scientific and medical establishment through the ages, the Royal Society, did not think Jenner's account of his daring experiment worthy of publishing (though they had happily published one of his earlier papers describing the natural history of the cuckoo).

Undeterred by the lack of interest shown by the profession, Jenner continued with his experiments and within two years had performed 22 similar vaccinations, many performed in an arbour in his garden. He described his work in a booklet which he published himself in 1798.

This small self-published publication resulted in the results of his work spreading around the world. People everywhere wanted to be vaccinated with the Jenner method. In some areas, an infected cow would be led from door to door so that material could be scraped off and used to vaccinate the waiting citizens. In 1805, the Emperor Napoleon, ruled that all his troops who had not had smallpox should be vaccinated at once. The technique became popular in North, Central and South America, throughout Europe, in Russia and eventually in China, where the original form of inoculation had been first used so many centuries earlier. (The French often claim that Pasteur invented vaccination. In fact, Pasteur's first vaccine, against rabies, was not tested until 1885.)

Jenner did not prove as popular or as influential in his own country, of course. The theory of vaccination met with considerable opposition from jealous members of the medical profession. Some argued that there was a risk of transmitting syphilis. Others argued that preventing smallpox was interfering with the will of God. A few claimed that by limiting deaths from smallpox, vaccinators would put an intolerable burden on family men who might otherwise expect their liabilities (and the size of their families) to be limited.

Jenner was never critical of the establishment and remained graceful, despite the criticism. 'The scepticism that appeared, even among the most enlightened of medical men when my sentiments on the important subject of the cowpox were first promulgated was highly laudable. To have admitted the truth of a doctrine at once so novel and so unlike any thing that ever had appeared in the annals of medicine without the test of the most rigid scrutiny, would have bordered upon temerity.'

Parliament eventually gave Jenner a grant to continue his experiments, though by that time his technique had been accepted in most parts of the world.

Jenner's work may have helped end smallpox's reign of terror (though better living conditions also played a large part) and in the 19th and early 20th century vaccination proved effective in controlling other dangerous, potentially fatal, infectious diseases. Sadly, vaccination has been subsequently wildly over-promoted and over-used to protect against far less threatening disorders. The profession which had rejected Jenner's discovery as too dangerous, embraced it with diminishing reservations and unbridled enthusiasms, ignoring the risks and side effects as the profits to be made (both by the manufacturing industry and the medical profession) grew and grew; the glimpse of unending profits encouraging the development of too many vaccines which were neither effective nor safe.

Those whose enthusiasm for vaccination remains undimmed should perhaps be aware that Jenner himself had his own reservations. He tried out the first smallpox vaccination on his own 10-month-old son. Tragically, his son remained mentally retarded until his death at the age of 21. Jenner refused to have his second child vaccinated.

Samuel Johnson 1709-1784

Dr Samuel Johnson was a poet, translator, literary critic and author. But it is as the compiler of the most famous dictionary in the world that he is best remembered.

Johnson was born in Lichfield, in the English Midlands, where his father ran a bookshop (though not terribly successfully). Possibly because he was surrounded by books as a child (and spent much of his time reading his father's stock) he did well at school and at Oxford University. But because his father was poor he did not finish his degree course.

Johnson's hearing and his sight had both been damaged by childhood illnesses and although famous for his pugnacious conversational skills, his seemingly inexhaustible capacity for friendship, his endless curiosity, his wonderful sense of humour and his extraordinary wisdom, he was nevertheless a nervous, often depressed, individual; he constantly feared death and worried about going insane. After leaving Oxford without a degree he had difficulty finding work. His lack of qualifications, his involuntary tics and his physical infirmities all made life a constant torment.

At the age of 28 Johnson moved to London, and for twenty years he worked as a freelance journalist, writing essays, articles and biographies. He wrote just about anything that would bring in money. He was often poor and on one occasion he was sent to prison for debt. It was, without doubt, those years of poverty that forged his everlasting concern for the poor, the mentally ill, the underprivileged and those other outcasts living on the edge of society.

Samuel Johnson's *Dictionary of the English Language*, the book that became a classic and gave him immortality, was published in 1755. The dictionary, which consisted of two volumes, weighed an impressive 20 lbs and cost £4 10 shillings (over £500 in modern money). It contained 42,773 entries and had taken Dr Johnson eight years to compile. It was, to say the least, an impressive achievement. In France, 40 scholars took 40 years to produce the French equivalent. 'Forty times forty is sixteen hundred... so is the proportion of an Englishman to a Frenchman,' said the wise doctor.

Johnson refused to include French words such as 'blonde' and 'champagne' in his dictionary and there were no words beginning with X, though this was possibly because neither X-rays nor the xylophone had then been invented.

Robert Cawdrey was the first person to create an English dictionary (his book *A Table Alpheticall* had been published in 1604) but Johnson's was the first to include clear definitions and common usages and to show how writers used words. Johnson included over 100,000 quotations in his dictionary, and his definitions were often spiced with humour and prejudice. For example, he defined 'oats' as 'a grain which in England is generally given to horses, but in Scotland supports the people' and a stockjobber as 'a low wretch who gets money by buying and selling shares'.

Johnson continued to write in old age and was more comfortable in his later years after he was awarded a pension for services to literature. His final major work *Lives of the English Poets* was published just a few years before his death.

John Keats (1795-1821)

Born in London, the son of a livery-stable owner who kept horses for hire, John Keats was the eldest of five children. His father died when he was only eight and Keats grew up with his grandmother in Edmonton. He was apprenticed to a surgeon in Edmonton at the age of 16 and studied medicine at Guys Hospital in London from 1815 to 1816.

But his love was poetry. Leigh Hunt, his neighbour in Hampstead, introduced him to Percy Bysshe Shelley, and Keats published his first sonnets in a magazine called *The Examiner* in 1816 when he was 21 years old. He gave up medicine to concentrate on poetry, living on a small legacy from his grandmother. The following year his first book of poems was published and in 1818 he published a long mythological poem entitled *Endymion* which, in 4,000 lines, told of the love of the moon goddess Cynthia for the young shepherd Endymion. The opening line is: 'A thing of beauty is a joy for ever.'

Sadly, his work was not well received.

He returned from a long and exhausting walking tour of Scotland to find that *Endymion* had been savaged by all the critics. They hated it. Even worse was the news that his younger brother Tom was dying of consumption (tuberculosis), the disease which had already killed much of his family.

Despite all this he found the strength to keep writing and in 1820 published a volume of poetry entitled *Lamia and Other Poems*. This book included a series of well-known odes including: *On a Grecian Urn*, *On Melancholy* and *To a Nightingale*. It also included *To Autumn* and just about all his other best poems. Keats, at the age of 25, had suddenly become one of the greatest poets of the age. Most of his great poetry had been written within a single twelve month period. His work astounded the critics who were enormously impressed by the way he created vivid word pictures to praise beautiful things. Keats believed that the purpose of poetry should simply be to glorify beauty and not as a vehicle for philosophy or religion. He wrote that the poet's true function is to be simply an artist, and not a teacher or a prophet. The two words that perhaps best sum up his style are 'tender melancholy'.

That same year Keats himself became seriously ill with consumption. He travelled to Rome to find some sunshine and escape England's cold winter, and died there in a house at the foot of the Spanish steps; a house which became a target for literary pilgrims from all around the world.

Although his life was short and intensely tragic, Keats is also remembered for his letters which throw a great deal of light both on his development as a poet and also on his often sad love affair with Fanny Brawne – the girl he had met in 1818 and whom he loved but was too poor to marry. It was a love affair which seemed to cause him as much pain as pleasure.

Keats greatly influenced many writers who followed, including Tennyson, Swinburne, Rossetti and Morris. Robert Bridges, the famous English poet and critic wrote: 'If one English poet might be recalled today from the dead to continue the work which he left unfinished on earth, it is probable that the crown of his country's desire would be set on the head of John Keats.'

Stephen Langton (1150-1228)

The Magna Carta is the document which guaranteed political liberty and basic human rights for all Englishmen. It was signed at Runnymede, in a meadow by the River Thames, by King John on 15 June 1215 under pressure from a group of rebellious barons who were angry at the high taxes the King had introduced. If one man can be credited with *The Magna Carta*, it is Stephen Langton, who was Archbishop of Canterbury at the time, and the driving force behind the document.

The Magna Carta included clauses reforming law and justice, providing for a free church and controlling the behaviour of royal officials. *The Magna Carta* may have been superseded and rendered impotent by a sequence of treaties signed with the European Union but it is still traditionally regarded as the only written basis of an English constitution.

The Magna Carta set the tone for constitutions and declarations around the world and was the first example of citizens demanding, and obtaining, a formal charter of their basic rights. It has been, for the best part of a thousand years, the blueprint for just about every democratic constitution ever written.

Stephen Langton was born in Surrey and educated at the University of Paris, where he lectured on theology until 1206. While in Paris he met the future Pope Innocent III who subsequently called him to Rome and made him cardinal-priest of San Crisogono. He had then become the most eminent English churchman and in

1207, against the wishes of King John, he was made Archbishop of Canterbury.

King John, who could pick a quarrel with his own reflection, immediately announced that anyone who recognised Stephen Langton as Archbishop would be proclaimed a public enemy. The new Archbishop duly left the country and moved to France. The Pope excommunicated the King and the King confiscated the property of the clergy. The Pope then issued a bull deposing King John and instructing Philip II of France to replace him. Things had now got very silly and in 1213 King John, who was extremely unpopular at home, realised that he was out of his depth. The hapless King gave in and did some royal grovelling. Stephen Langton led churchmen and barons in demanding that King John renew the charter of Henry I which had guaranteed basic rights to the English people. Barons, clergy and ordinary people were united in demanding that King John should keep his oath and restore the laws of Henry I which he had brushed aside. No one liked King John who was cruel, badly behaved and very full of his own self-importance. He was a despot whose corrupt administration and crushing taxes alienated all groups of citizens. (In a fit of pique he once tried to convert England to Islam.)

The energetic Archbishop of Canterbury kept up the pressure but after King John had made peace with the Pope he managed to get the Pope on his side and the Pope excommunicated the Barons. When Stephen Langton refused to publish the excommunication he was suspended from his post by the Pope. Things which had become complicated had now become even more complicated. But Langton stood firm and still demanded that the King sign a document promising to give the people the laws and the protection they wanted.

An English army, led spiritually by the Archbishop and given military strength by the barons, met the King at Runnymede where the King capitulated and signed *The Magna Carta*.

Naturally, once the barons and the army had disbanded and gone home, King John broke his word and reneged on everything he had signed. The barons called over the French dauphin (the future Louis VIII) to be their leader. As a result, King John was now in even bigger trouble. He got out of it by dying in October 1216. It was his only way out of the mess he had got himself into through dishonesty and arrogance. Helpfully, Pope Innocent III also died.

Everyone in England now rallied to support the new King, Henry III. Stephen Langton, still the Archbishop of Canterbury, worked for the political independence of England. In 1223, he acted as leader and spokesmen for the barons and demanded that King Henry III confirm the contents of *The Magna Carta*. This the King did. Langton then won concessions from the new Pope that were favourable to the English church and opened a council which produced decrees (known as the *Constitutions of Stephen Langton*) which are still regarded as binding canons in the English church.

Stephen Langton died in Sussex in 1228 and was buried in open ground next to Canterbury Cathedral. A chapel was later built over his grave. He remains England's most important churchman. He can be truly said to have had the courage of his convictions.

John Lilburne (1614-1657)

Oliver Cromwell and the Puritans (also known as Levellers) wanted England to have a properly accountable Parliament, responsible to the people and representing the people's wishes. They wanted to get rid of a monarch who believed that it was his God-given right to rule the country, and to do what he wanted regardless of the people's wishes.

Cromwell was tough, single-minded and determined. But alongside John Lilburne he sometimes looks slightly mealy-mouthed and uncertain.

Lilburne, known as Freeborn John, was a pamphleteer and campaigner who fought with his life, and apparently without fear, for the rights of the ordinary Englishman. Between 1638 and 1640 he was whipped and imprisoned by the country's Star Chamber for importing Puritan literature. He then rose to the rank of lieutenant-colonel in the Parliamentary army during the English civil war but resigned in 1645 because he disapproved of the Solemn League and Covenant, an agreement between the English and the Scots in which the Scots agreed to support the English Parliamentarians in their dispute with the King, and to work for a civil and religious union of England, Scotland and Ireland.

Lilburne also believed (and said loudly) that Cromwell's republic was too aristocratic.

He agitated consistently and noisily on behalf of the Levellers (who believed that sovereignty should rest solely with the House of Commons) and with enormous courage he indefatigably demanded greater liberty of conscience and more and more reforms. He was repeatedly put in prison for writing and publishing pamphlets which were regarded as treasonable. But nothing would stop him telling what he believed to be the truth and fighting for a cause which he believed, with all his heart, to be important. On both the occasions when he was tried for treason he was acquitted.

John Lilburne was just 42 years old when he died of a fever. He had given most of his life fighting for freedom and true democracy.

Joseph Lister (1827-1912)

In the middle of the 19th century surgeons still operated without giving any thought to the dangers of infection. They knew that infection killed many of their patients. But they regarded the hazard as unavoidable. Surgeons wiped their instruments on their blood and pus-stained coat tails, while their assistants carried needles in their coat lapels ready-threaded with silk for sutures. One eminent New York surgeon is said to have whetted his scalpel on the sole of his shoe. Surgeons used dirty old rags to clean out wounds and to stop bleeding. The introduction of anaesthesia had made life considerably less painful for the patient. But mortality rates were still horrendous. In Paris a mortality rate of 63 per cent was recorded. In Edinburgh, a mortality rate of 43 per cent was considered acceptable. It was no exaggeration to say that in the 19th century it was more dangerous to be in a hospital ward than it had been to be on the battlefield at Waterloo.

All that changed as the result of the work of an English doctor called Joseph Lister (later Lord Lister). Joseph Lister was born in Essex. His father was a scientist. The young Lister graduated from London University with an arts degree and a medical degree.

While working as Regius Professor of Surgery at the University of Glasgow in 1860, Joseph Lister learned about the work of Louis

Pasteur, the French chemist who had discovered the principles of fermentation – and how small, unseen organisms could multiply and affect the environment around them.

Worried by the fearful mortality rate among surgical patients, Lister had been studying the problem of infection for some time and accepted the idea, then prevalent among surgeons, that the majority of deaths were caused by some poison in the hospital atmosphere. Lister did all he could to try to prevent infection in his operating theatre. He removed his frock coat before operating. He used fresh towels in such abundance that the hospital managers complained. And he washed his hands before operating.

It was through discussing the problem with the Professor of Chemistry at the University that Lister heard about Pasteur's work. From the papers he studied, Lister came to the conclusion that it was not the air that was the problem as much as the small organisms in the air. The solution, he decided, would be to find some way to keep the hospital atmosphere free of these small, invisible organisms.

Pasteur had suggested that the organisms which cause fermentation, putrefaction and decay could be controlled by using heat or antiseptics. Lister decided that the same sort of approach might work for the organisms which cause infection and since it was clearly not practical to keep surgical patients at a high enough temperature to kill the unseen bugs he started experimenting with other ways to prevent the development of infection. He decided that bacteria on surgical instruments, on the surgeon's hands, and in the air itself, might start an infection in an exposed wound and then cause the patient's death. He concluded that the answer was to make hospitals as clean as possible and to make sure that operating theatres were kept especially clean. After unsuccessfully trying out various chemicals he hit upon a substance called German creosote, a substance which had already been used to clean up a sewage plant in Carlisle. He obtained a specimen of the dark brown, harsh-smelling creosote and found it easy to dissolve in water. It was not difficult to apply to dressings. Lister's method was to use a piece of lint impregnated with creosote to make an artificial scab over a surgical wound. The first patient, who had suffered a compound fracture, did well. In 1865, a chemical firm in Manchester began to produce a purified form of creosote. They called their product carbolic acid and Lister changed from creosote to this new product. He would clean the wound with a piece of cotton material soaked in carbolic acid and held in a pair of clean forceps. He would then put a piece of lint, again soaked in carbolic acid, directly over the wound, overlapping by half an inch in all directions. He would place a thin sheet of flexible metal on top of the lint to prevent evaporation of fluid from the cloth. The metal sheet would be lifted regularly and fresh carbolic acid painted on the outside of the lint. When he found that the carbolic acid dissolved better in oil than in water he switched to oily dressings. He found that the oil acted as a reservoir, keeping the wound soaked with antiseptic for longer periods. He used a soft putty made of common whitening and linseed oil, impregnated with carbolic acid, because this could be spread thickly over the wound itself. An additional advantage was that the putty didn't irritate as much as the more watery solution. He was delighted to see that the wounds healed completely and without infection.

In 1867, after some research and some more experiments, Lister published in the *Lancet* a paper entitled *On the Antiseptic Principle in the Practice of Surgery*. He subsequently wrote to his father and said: 'I now perform an operation for the removal of a tumour etc., with a totally different feeling from what I used to have: in fact surgery is becoming a different thing altogether.'

The paper Lister published in the *Lancet* was, without a doubt, one of the most important scientific papers ever published. It revolutionised surgery and saved countless lives. Lister's paper provided the answer to the problem that had for centuries faced all surgeons.

Naturally, the medical establishment did not accept Lister's work without a struggle. His critics ignored the evidence and attacked his recommendations with the tragic result that it was several decades before all surgeons accepted, and began to practice, the sort of technique the English doctor had advocated.

Convinced that he had found the solution to the age-old problem of post-operative infection, Lister ignored the criticism and continued to experiment. He next developed a steam-powered carbolic spray which would enable him to fill the operating theatre with a fine mist of carbolic acid. Since he operated in the middle of this mist, and since the carbolic acid inevitably covered his hands, his instruments and the patient, Lister's new invention proved extremely successful, and the number of patients dying in his operating theatre was immediately reduced yet again. Lister was even able to open up joints and operate on them without fear of infection.

In the years which followed Lister's early experiments, other investigators showed that it was not necessary to smother the patient or the surgeon with antiseptics, but that an equally good result could be obtained by thoroughly cleaning all instruments and by dressing surgeons and their assistants in clean gowns, caps and gloves.

But it was Lister's imagination and courage which first led to the conquering of this major problem. And it was Lister's pioneering work which enabled surgeons around the world to begin performing operations never before dreamt possible. Within Lister's lifetime, surgeons were operating within the human chest and skull without fear of failure because of infection.

It is difficult to think of any doctor who contributed more to medicine than Lord Joseph Lister. Lister also made important observations about inflammation and the coagulation of blood but it was his introduction of an antiseptic approach to surgery that earned him immortality. It is extraordinary to realise that when he discovered the principle of using an antiseptic to prevent disease, Lister had never even seen the microbes which can cause infection. He believed that they were there and he had the imagination and the genius to understand the problem and to see the solution.

John Locke 1632-1704

Born in Wrington in Somerset and educated at Oxford University, where he studied medicine and science, John Locke was elected to the Royal Society at the age of 36. He was friends with many important scientists of his age, including Isaac Newton and Robert Boyle.

Although Locke had qualified in medicine, he practised only occasionally but was family physician and adviser to the future 3rd Earl of Shaftesbury. When Shaftesbury was imprisoned by King Charles II because of his political activities both he and Locke moved to the Netherlands. Locke remained there until King James II had been removed by the revolution of 1688. He returned to England shortly afterwards and became commissioner of appeals, a post he held until his death.

John Locke is remembered as a philosopher; the first writer to put together the basic ideas of a constitutional democracy. If Oliver Cromwell was the practical man behind the birth of English democracy then John Locke was the brains behind its development.

Locke is, perhaps, most famous for a classic philosophical book entitled *An Essay Concerning Human Understanding* which he published in 1690 and in which he discussed the origin, nature and limits of human knowledge. He was hugely influenced by two other Englishmen, Francis Bacon and Thomas Hobbes, but his work, in turn, influenced many subsequent philosophers. Locke argued that knowledge begins in sensation or introspection and that it is through reflection that the mind receives ideas, which are themselves the building blocks of knowledge.

It was, however, Locke's books on politics which had most impact.

In 1689 (writing at first anonymously) Locke published *A Letter Concerning Toleration* in which he argued that the State should not interfere with man's freedom to choose and practise his own religion. He argued that we should all be tolerant of our neighbours – whether they be Christian, Pagan, Mahometan or Jew. (He did, however, draw the line at accepting Catholics whom he said owed their allegiance to a foreign potentate and could not, therefore, be given the same level of freedom by the State.) His strong and well-based arguments were a big factor in the growth of public support for this point of view and although elements of his book may now seem strangely intolerant he was, for his time, extremely tolerant and broad-minded.

In the same year, Locke published *Two Treatises of Government* in which he described his basic ideas for a liberal, constitutional democracy. He argued that every citizen has natural rights, including personal liberty and the right to hold property of his own.

He pointed out that the main purpose of government is to protect the lives and property of the citizens. Locke rejected the notion of the divine right of kings and claimed that governments have authority only through the consent of the people. He argued that when governments attempt to take away the rights of the people, or to reduce them to slavery under arbitrary power and the use of force, they lose the right to govern and the people no longer have the responsibility to be obedient.

He pointed out that the people always have a right to remove the government and that if normal processes do not work then the people have the right to take back their authority by revolution.

Locke believed in the principle of majority rule but also repeatedly argued that governments, once elected, do not have unlimited rights and must not violate the natural rights of men. He claimed that the legislature should be superior to the executive and, since he considered the judiciary to be part of the executive, superior to the judiciary too. He believed that the legislature, elected by the people, should have all the power. It is hard indeed to see Locke accepting the sort of executive control favoured by the European Union.

Locke firmly believed that individual citizens have basic, natural rights and that governments, and those who work for them, have limited authority and must always serve the public good. His work influenced both the French and the American revolutionaries. It was Locke's defence of the right of revolution that influenced Thomas Jefferson and other American revolutionaries, and the constitution of the USA was written with reference to Locke's work. Indeed, Locke had described all the major ideas of the American Revolution a century before the American Revolution took place. Locke's views and soundly argued beliefs preceded and strongly influenced such men as Voltaire as well as Jefferson.

Thomas Malthus (1766-1834)

Malthus was born near Dorking, in Surrey and went to Cambridge University where he graduated in 1788. He was ordained an Anglican clergyman in the same year.

Thomas Robert Malthus was a little known English parson, just 32 years old, when he published a book called *An Essay on the Principle of Population as It Affects the Future Improvement of Society*. To begin with, the book was published anonymously. But, later as the book gained fame, so Malthus's name was associated with it and he was named as the author. He repeatedly revised and expanded the book as the years went by and new editions grew steadily longer.

The basic thesis of Malthus's book was that the growth of the population tends to be faster than the growth of the available food supply. In the first edition of his book he claimed that the population tends to increase in a geometric fashion, doubling at regular intervals (as with the numbers 1,2,4,8,16 and so on) while the food supply increases only arithmetically (as with the numbers 1,2,3,4,5 and so on).

In later editions, Malthus abandoned this specificity and stated merely that the size of the population tends to increase until it reaches the limit of the food supply.

But the conclusion he drew remained the same: that most men, women and children are doomed to live in poverty, constantly bordering on the edge of starvation. He concluded that in the long run no advances in technology would change this basic premise because 'the power of population is indefinitely greater than the power of the earth to produce subsistence for man'.

He pointed out that the usual, traditional forms of population growth restraint (war, pestilence and famine) are obviously pretty nasty and provide only temporary relief. Once the war, pestilence or famine is over the population starts to grow again.

His theoretical answer was to suggest that people should remain chaste before they married, should marry late and should restrain their sexual impulses. In practice, however, he realised that most people would not follow this suggestion. And he concluded that mankind inevitably faced a future of poverty and hunger.

Malthus never suggested that men and women used contraceptive devices to keep down the population growth (such things were pretty primitive in those days and he disapproved of them on moral grounds). Today, however, advocates of the use of control of population through the use of contraceptives usually refer to themselves as neo-Malthusians.

Another Englishman, Francis Place, had read Malthus's book and in 1822 he wrote a book advocating contraception. He also disseminated birth control information among poorer people. He was, without a doubt, the true father of contraception.

Malthus's book had a dramatic effect on economists. Those who had read his book concluded that overpopulation would prevent wages from rising much above the subsistence level. An English economist, David Ricardo, stated that: 'The natural price of labour is that price which is necessary to enable the labourers, one with another, to subsist and to perpetuate the race, without either increase or diminution.' This theory became known as the 'iron law of wages' and became a critical element in the theory of surplus value and the development of communism.

Malthus also influenced another Englishman, Charles Darwin, who admitted that Malthus's book gave him an important link for his theory of evolution by natural selection.

In 1804, Malthus, who was then 38, married, and the following year he was made professor of history and political economy at the East India Company's College at Haileybury. He stayed there for the rest of his life and wrote several other books on economics. One of them, *Principles of Political Economy*, influenced many important economists (including John Maynard Keynes).

Malthus died near Bath at the age of 68.

Few men have had such a dramatic effect on the world as Thomas Malthus. He strongly influenced Charles Darwin and most major economists. His theory influenced Karl Marx. And although he personally did not advocate contraceptives, his book undoubtedly triggered the idea of using them. Malthus was the first person to draw attention to the significance of over-population.

And now his work is about to become even more pertinent.

The use of oil-based fertilisers, and the use of machinery running on oil, changed the rules for a while – for those fortunate enough to live in countries rich enough or powerful enough to obtain the oil – but now that the oil is running out it seems that Malthus's basic premise is, once again, about to be proven entirely accurate.

Henry Maudslay (1771-1831)

The Industrial Revolution started in England and so it is hardly surprising that most of the men who led the revolution were English. Henry Maudslay was one of the leaders.

Born the fifth child of a storekeeper at the Royal Arsenal, Woolwich, London, Henry Maudslay was one of the most significant inventors of the era. At the age of 12 the young Maudslay got a job at the Arsenal, filling cartridges. He then transferred to the blacksmith's shop to learn the trade of blacksmith. By the time he was 18 years old he had such a reputation that Joseph Bramah heard of him and hired him for his workshop in Denmark Street, London. Maudslay made a significant contribution to the development of Bramah's hydraulic press.

Maudslay's first invention of his own was a much-improved version of the lathe. Up until that time lathes were worked by a treadle, and the workman had to hold his tool against whatever he was working on. Maudslay's improved lathe enabled workmen to produce components which were all precision made – rather than subject to the vagaries of the workman's hand. It is no exaggeration to say that Maudslay's lathe revolutionised the production of machine components.

Having been made manager of Bramah's workshop, Maudslay married Braham's housemaid in 1791. He was now just 20 years old.

In 1797, having had a request for a modest pay rise turned down, Maudslay set up his own engineering business just off Oxford Street. He was 26 years old and clearly ambitious.

His first major job was to manufacture 42 machines to make rigging blocks for the Royal Navy. Each machine had to be capable of making 130,000 ships' blocks a year. Some of the machines are still in existence and functioning. Thanks to Maudslay, specialised machinery was now being used in an assembly line.

In 1800, Maudslay developed the first practical screw-cutting lathe, making it possible to turn out thousands of identical and standardised screws for the first time. Before this invention bits and pieces of machinery had not been interchangeable. Nuts and bolts, for example, had to be used together because they could not be swapped around.

Over the years that followed, Maudslay invented a number of pieces of machinery which were crucial to the development of the Industrial Revolution. His astonishing variety of inventions also include a method for printing calico cloth, the slide rule and a method of de-salinating salt water. He also invented the micrometer, a measuring machine that was accurate to 0.0001 inches. He called his micrometer the 'Lord Chancellor' as it was used to settle any questions about the accuracy of workmanship. He also designed and built many stationary and marine engines. And his company built the tunnelling equipment used by the Brunels to build the Thames tunnel.

A number of outstanding English engineers and inventors, including James Nasmyth, Joshua Field and Sir Joseph Whitworth, learned their trade in Maudslay's company.

In 1831, Maudslay caught a chill while crossing the English Channel and died four weeks later.

John Stuart Mill (1806-1873)

John Stuart Mill was born in London and taught at home by his historian father. He was taught Greek at the age of three, Latin and arithmetic at eight, logic at 12 and political economy at 13. His only recreation was a daily walk with his father. During those walks his father conducted oral examinations. No toys, no games. Life can't have been much fun.

After visiting France at the age of 14 the young but well-educated Mill studied law, history and philosophy, and at the age of 17 began a career under his father at the India Office. He remained there until the dissolution of the East India Company in 1858, when he retired at the age of 52. It was, it seems, an undemanding job which allowed him plenty of time to write.

Mill never seemed to resent his lost childhood. On the contrary he claimed that his forced education gave him an advantage of a quarter of a century over his contemporaries.

In 1822, he began publishing articles in the newspaper *The Traveller* and he helped form the Utilitarian Society which met for readings and discussions in the home of Jeremy Bentham. In 1824, he was arrested for distributing birth control literature to the poor in London.

In 1826, at the age of 20, Mill had a nervous breakdown, probably a result of the fact that in his 20 years he hadn't been allowed a moment in which to relax or have any fun. The breakdown was followed by a depression. Afterwards Mill mellowed a little and humanised utilitarianism by recognising that there are differences in the quality as well as the quantity of pleasures. (Bentham, the prime advocate of utilitarianism was, perhaps, rather too keen on measuring joys and delights quantitatively rather than qualitatively and so, to the traditional utilitarian, five minutes spent walking, reading the paper, looking at an amazing sunset, eating, enjoying the sunshine or making love were all interchangeable.)

In 1830, Mill met Harriet Taylor, the wife of a wealthy London merchant and although she remained faithful to her husband, she and Mill had a long and intense romance. They married in 1851, two years after the death of the almost but not quite cuckolded Mr Taylor. She died in 1858 but helped and encouraged Mill in his writing.

During his late thirties, Mill owned and virtually edited the *London Review*, which was later incorporated with the *Westminster Review*. As a result of these periodicals he became the prophet of the philosophical radicals.

His first major work, *A System of Logic*, was published in 1842. His next significant book *The Principles of Political Economy* appeared in 1847 and his most brilliant and popular book *On Liberty*, in which he defines and defends the freedoms of the individual against social and political control, was published in 1859.

In 1863, Mill published *Utilitarianism* and in 1869 he wrote *The Subjection of Women*; an analysis of the status of women, which caused a great deal of controversy and attracted much antagonism.

He published many other books but his autobiography, published in 1873 is one of his most revealing and important books. It is a simple, honest and sincere book and in it he describes the mental crisis he suffered in 1826.

John Stuart Mill was elected to Parliament in 1865, at the age of 59, and campaigned for women's suffrage. In 1872 he became godfather to Bertrand Russell, who would later himself become a noted philosopher. Mill spent his final years in France, and died in Avignon.

There is no doubt that Mill was driven by a genuine desire to do work for the public good, nor that much of his life was devoted to social service and political reform. Like his chum Jeremy Bentham, he probably wasn't the sort of person you'd want by your side on a dull Sunday afternoon, but he wrote about serious topics with great freshness and sensitivity and he greatly influenced the development of society in England and the rest of the world.

John Milton (1608-1674)

Born in London and educated at Cambridge University, John Milton was one of the world's greatest and most celebrated poets and essayists. As a poet he is recognised as having had a sensitive feeling for the rhythm and flow of words. As a result his poetry is both majestic and, at times, ethereal.

Milton's father was a rich lawyer and composer who had a house in the country as well as a London home and after leaving Cambridge John Milton spent the next six years of life studying privately at his family's country home. He had begun writing poetry at 16 and he gradually became a serious scholar of Greek, Latin and Hebrew. He had originally intended to become a priest but decided instead to devote his life to God through his poetry.

His poem *Lycidas* was completed when he was 29 but his promising career was interrupted by the English Civil War. In 1642, Milton temporarily abandoned his poetry and started writing political essays supporting Oliver Cromwell. In 1649, he became Secretary for the Foreign Tongues for Cromwell. He was the official spokesman for the revolution and also wrote pamphlets criticising censorship. At about that time he became aware that he was slowly losing his sight.

In 1659, Cromwell's new Commonwealth collapsed and the English monarchy was temporarily restored. Not surprisingly, Milton found himself in disgrace. But with enormous bravery he continued to publish pamphlets supporting the principles and practice of republicanism even as the restoration was taking place. Almost inevitably he had to go into hiding. His books were burned by the hangman in London and he was imprisoned for about two months. By then, however, he was famous as an essayist and poet. Indeed, he was regarded as Europe's leading scholar and poet. Although he had defended the idea of regicide in print, Charles II and his advisers didn't fancy the idea of executing a famous, blind poet. And so they let him go. Milton retired from public life and from writing political essays and went back to poetry. He desperately wanted to write an epic poem that would rival those of the ancient 'greats' such as Virgil and Homer.

By now completely blind (he was blind for the last twenty years of his life) he dictated *Paradise Lost*. His life was in ruins. His son had died, his daughters were estranged, two marriages had ended, he was in disgrace, his friends had been hanged or had flown abroad. *Paradise Lost*, which was published when Milton was 55, tells the story of how Satan was ejected from Heaven and came to earth to corrupt Adam and Eve. Milton's experience of England's civil war is reflected in the themes of war and conflict which appear in the poem; a magnificent and definitive exploration of evil.

Four years later Milton wrote and published *Paradise Regained*.

Thomas More (1478-1535)

Thomas More was an enlightened champion of the freedom of the mind and of religious toleration. He gave his life as a martyr and is the only saint on my list.

Born in London, the son of a judge, More qualified as a lawyer but then, as soon as he had finished his training, spent four years in devotion and prayer. In 1504, towards the end of Henry VII's reign, he became a member of parliament and under-sheriff of London.

More married twice and the manner of his marrying tells us much about the man. His first marriage took place in 1505 when More met an Essex gentleman called Colte who had three daughters. More rather fancied the second daughter ('the fairest and best favoured') but 'considered that it would be both great grief and some shame also to the eldest to see her younger sister preferred before her in marriage'. And so 'of a certain pity' he 'framed his fancy' towards the eldest daughter, Jane and duly married her.

Jane was very young and quite uneducated but More shaped her character and taught her about books and music. She had four children but, tragically, died in 1511. More almost immediately married again, choosing this time a widow whom he described as neither beautiful or well-educated. More reported that she had no sense of humour either (not, at least, as far as More's jokes were concerned) but, perhaps as punishment for this, he made her learn the guitar, flute, cithern and harp and made her practise every day. She was, by all accounts, a good housekeeper rather than a passionate wife. An anecdote, reported in Arthur Cayley's book *Memoirs of Sir Thomas More* (published 1808) defines the relationship between More and his wife (and well illustrates More's impartiality and innate sense of justice). More was sitting in his hall one day when a female beggar came in to complain that Lady More had a small dog which belonged to her. More sent for his wife, asking her to bring the dog with her. He then took the dog and sent his wife to one end of the hall and the beggar to the other. Having done this he told the two of them to call the dog. Without hesitation the dog ran to the beggar. More then told his wife that if she wanted the dog she had to purchase the animal from the beggar.

During his first marriage More had lived in the City of London. For his second marriage he moved to the peaceful, riverside hamlet of Chelsea where he lived in quiet comfort, surrounded by his children, his pictures and his books.

When Henry VIII came to the throne More quickly became a favourite and rose to be, in order, Master of Requests, Treasurer of the Exchequer and Chancellor of the Duchy of Lancaster. He was also speaker to the House of Commons and acted as the King's personal ambassador on missions to France. It was during a spell when he was envoy to Flanders that More wrote the first draft of his description of an imaginary island of Utopia. The book was finished in 1516 and describes More's search for the best possible form of government. In the text, More meets a traveller called Raphael Hythloday who has discovered a country called Utopia or Nowhere land where everyone (male or female) is entitled to a free education and where there is complete tolerance of religious views. Every man has to work at a craft and spend some time each day on husbandry. The hours of manual labour are strictly limited to six a day. The principle of government More describes is, in essence, communism. The people who live in Utopia have contempt for gold and silver and precious stones. Diamonds and pearls are treated as children's toys. Those who break the law are chained (with solid gold fetters) but allowed to go free when they promise to mend their ways and to use their liberty wisely. The book was quickly translated into

French, German, Italian and Spanish. It was not, however, translated into English until 1551. (It was written in Latin.)

Unusually for such a religious man, More was something of a wag. He was for ever cracking jokes. He was enormously fond of animals, tame or wild, and although he had a large household he lived, for the time, a life relatively free of luxury. His friends included many artists (the German artist Holbein stayed with More and his family and painted portraits of them) and he was a great collector of furniture and plate, as well as books and paintings.

In 1529, when Wolsey fell out of favour, partly as a result of his evasiveness over the question of Henry's divorce from Catherine of Aragon and partly as a result of his unnatural greed and arrogance, More was appointed Lord Chancellor, even though he really didn't want the job. More could, no doubt, see what was coming and obviously regarded the post as a poisoned chalice. But the King was insistent and More had little choice.

It was an uncomfortable couple of years and in 1532 More finally managed to resign. This meant a serious reduction in his income and meant that he, and his family, had to become accustomed to living simply. (Although he had to dismiss many of his servants he did his best to find them all situations with bishops and noblemen of his acquaintance.)

But that was just the beginning of More's problems. In 1534, Henry VIII declared himself to be head of the English Church. More refused to accept the King's position, insisting that the Pope was the only head of the church. More was willing to swear fidelity to the new Act of Succession but he refused to take an oath that would impugn the Pope's authority and he refused to accept the King's divorce from Catherine of Aragon. The King had More imprisoned and sentenced for high treason. There is no little irony in the fact that More's sentence was widely considered to be harsh, for More himself was, despite his legendary reputation as a kindly man, a tough disciplinarian who, when he had the power could be as ruthless as any judge. He had an old-fashioned belief in the value of corporal punishment. One of his own servants was whipped for 'talking lightly of sacred things' and a madman who had been arrested for brawling in churches was sentenced by him to be beaten. More was a religious zealot who genuinely believed that physical torture, and even burning at the stake, were sometimes essential. And we must not forget that More spent many years working with, and at the top of, a Government which was run on principles which he had condemned in his book *Utopia*. The Government he helped lead made no effort to get rid of poverty but, rather, maintained, protected and perpetuated the existing inequalities.

The King desperately wanted More to recant. But More, torn between his loyalty to his King and his loyalty to the Pope, refused to do so. In prison he wrote letters and tracts and made jokes. When his wife begged him to ask the King for pardon he replied that he had no intention of leaving his cell and that prison was as near to heaven as was his own house. His family, by now struggling with poverty, had to pay for his food and lodging in prison. His letters were regarded as conspiratorial and he was deprived of pens or paper. He continued to write on scraps of paper, using pieces of coal as writing implements.

The King's one final favour to his once loyal friend was to commute the sentence of hanging to that of beheading.

And Thomas More was duly beheaded in 1535.

'I pray thee, see me safely up,' he said to the warder who was leading him up the steps of the wobbly scaffold. 'As for my coming down, I can shift for myself.' He then added, 'Pluck up thy spirits, man; be not afraid to do thine office; my neck is very short.' He then moved his beard from the block, saying that it had never been found guilty of treason, and prayed God to send the King good counsel. His head was exhibited on a pole on London Bridge and his body was buried in St Peter's in the Tower of London. His favourite daughter, Margaret Roper, found the money to purchase his head a month later, and kept it preserved in spices until her own death, nine years afterwards. The head then passed down the family and is now believed to be in the vault belonging to the Roper family in a church in Canterbury.

More's martyrdom startled the world and greatly damaged the reputation of Henry VIII. Writers throughout Europe likened him to the great heroes, Seneca, Socrates, Cato and Aristides.

But it isn't primarily for this monumental spat (and his undoubted courage and determination to die a martyr) that More is remembered here. We remember him as an author; notably for *Utopia* (1516) and his *History of King Richard III.* He was a prolific author (writing in both Latin and English) and his work influenced many in the 16th century (including, most notably, Desiderius Erasmus, the Dutch priest and humanist who was considered to be one of the great scholars of the century). More wrote many polemical tracts and treatises but also wrote poetry. Whatever he wrote, he wrote with passion and humour. In the 17th century, most European critics regarded Shakespeare and Bacon as his inferiors.

In a way, it is strange that More is best remembered for *Utopia* for it is a book which contrasts vividly with his other work. There is a paradox in the fact that a man who represented a corrupt and dying system, and who was a man of fixed and stern religious views, should also be the author of such a hopeful and imaginative book.

Saint Thomas More was, undeniably, a true Renaissance man and yet he was one huge contradiction. He created a new and revolutionary ideal and yet died a martyr to ancient and restrictive beliefs.

William Morris (1834-1896)

William Morris mastered many skills. He was a novelist, essayist, poet, architect, lecturer, printer, bookbinder, militant socialist, weaver, typesetter, calligrapher, furniture designer and builder, politician, textile designer and decorator and an artist in oils, stained glass and ceramic tiles. He didn't just dabble in these things: he mastered them. He was one of the very first conservationists in the world and the founder of the Society for the Protection of Ancient Buildings. He was the first man to argue that 'small is beautiful' and firmly believed that men would be happier if they had few wants and few belongings and spent their free time doing things they enjoyed. It was Morris who wrote that people should have nothing in their homes that was not beautiful or useful (or, preferably, both).

He wrote: '...suppose people lived in little communities among gardens and green fields, so that you could be in the country in five minutes walk, and had few wants; almost no furniture for instance, and no servants, and studied (the difficult) arts of enjoying life, and finding out what they really wanted: then I think one might hope civilisation had begun.'

He worked towards unifying life, art, beauty and progress and believed that society had to change if men and women were going to enjoy the real beauty of life. He considered many aspects of Victorian England ugly and therefore hateful. This led him, inexorably, to an interest in politics and his interest and involvement in politics led him to found the Socialist League, a forerunner of the modern Labour Party.

Born the son of a rich businessman, in a village on the edge of Epping Forest, in 1834, Morris went to Oxford in 1853. He didn't like it but met there two men who were to become life-long friends: Edward Burne-Jones and Dante Gabriel Rossetti.

In 1856, he trained as an architect and in 1857 he met Jane Burden whom he married two years later. (Sadly, Mrs Morris later admitted that she had never loved her husband. She spent a lot of time with Rossetti who was undoubtedly her lover. He was overwhelmed by Jane Morris's beauty and he painted her countless times.)

The years that followed were a blur of artistic activity. Together with Rossetti, Burne-Jones and others, including Philip Webb and Ford Madox Brown, Morris founded The Firm, a Decorative Arts business which, over the ensuing decades produced an enormous amount of furniture, stained glass, tiles and other furnishings. But, despite these huge responsibilities, he never stopped writing. He wrote poems, translated the *Aeneid*, the *Odyssey* and *Beowulf* and wrote hugely influential and popular books of fiction and non-fiction.

Between 1865 and 1870, Morris published a long narrative poem called *The Earthly Paradise*. Like Chaucer's *The Canterbury Tales*, Morris's long poem has a prologue and 24 stories told by different narrators. The poem earned Morris great popularity and a chance to become Poet Laureate (he turned it down).

In other work he predicted that art would perish and that man would, in the generations to come, become hopeless, lifeless and without desire. 'A progress which puts art to one side,' he wrote, 'will tend towards the intellectual death of the human race.'

In 1872, Morris was one of the first designers when the Royal School of Needlework was founded. He developed a passion for colour and dyeing materials, he became interested in tapestry production and in 1877 he started silk weaving.

Morris, who believed that craftsmanship and design were an essential part of human fulfilment and self-expression, and that a decent, whole society should reflect this, gave us the Arts and Crafts Movement. He believed that art, design and literature have a common creative base: nature. Together with Rossetti he was one of the inspirations behind the Pre-Raphaelite movement.

William Morris was a real Renaissance Man. His influence on the arts, and the world in which we live, was enormous. He undoubtedly dominated those around him, but he was, according to those who knew him, also enormously loveable and kind.

Eadweard Muybridge (1830-1904)

Born Edward James Muggeridge in Kingston on Thames, the man who became Muybridge was the world's first cinematographer. It was Muybridge, an Englishman, who is the true father of the modern cinema.

Muybridge emigrated to California in 1852, to make his fortune, and became a professional photographer in 1866 – eventually becoming chief photographer to the American Government. His photographs of San Francisco and Yosemite showed the grandeur of the West, and Muybridge initially became famous for his landscape photography.

In 1872, he was commissioned by a former Governor of California, Leland Stanford, to take a series of action photographs of moving horses in order to settle an argument about the way horses move. Stanford was a racehorse owner and businessman who believed that all four of a horse's hooves left the ground when it was galloping. The debate may well have been accompanied by a substantial wager. However, it wasn't until 1877, when faster photographic plates became available, that Muybridge was able to take the famous photographs that show that a horse which is trotting has all its feet off the ground at the same time.

Muybridge pioneered the use of multiple cameras to capture motion. To take the photographs of the horse he used 12 stereoscopic cameras, 21 inches apart, to cover the 20 feet taken by one horse stride. He took pictures at one thousandth of a second. Trip wires attached to the camera shutters were triggered by the horse's hooves.

In 1880, Muybridge invented something he called the zoopraxiscope (a name which was never going to catch on) to show the picture sequences he had obtained. This was the first cinematography. In 1893, he built his Zoopraxographical Hall in Chicago and showed his pictures to the paying public. His Zoopraxographical Hall was, therefore, the world's first motion picture theatre.

In 1883 and 1885, working for the University of Pennsylvania, he carried out an extensive survey of the movement of humans and animals. He took around 100,000 images and his photographs included people walking down stairs, boxing and carrying buckets of water. Most of the models were naked, or wearing very little clothing, and this didn't go down too well with some people. (It was alleged that some of the models who had taken off their clothes were prostitutes and this went down even less well.) The results of his survey were published in his extraordinary book entitled *Animal Locomotion*, in 1887. Muybridge's work helped in the foundation of the study of biomechanics.

Muybridge does not appear in many history books, and is not widely credited as the inventor of the cinema because he was considered to be a rather unsavoury character. This is unfair and unreasonable.

Muybridge's problems arose in 1874 when he was living in San Francisco. When he discovered that his wife had a lover, a Major Harry Larkyns, Muybridge met the major and greeted him with the words: 'Good evening, Major, my name is Muybridge and here is the answer to the letter you sent my wife.' He then shot the Major and killed him.

Muybridge was tried for murder but he was acquitted on the grounds of 'justifiable homicide'. Stanford paid for his defence. Muybridge's subsequent reputation was not helped by the fact that during the trial part of his defence was a plea of insanity. The jury did not accept this part of his defence, preferring to concentrate on the fact that the killing was a 'crime passionelle'.

Critics inevitably described Muybridge as a madman and a murderer who took photographs of naked prostitutes.

In 1894 Muybridge returned to England, published two additional books based on his work and died in 1904 in Kingston on Thames – where he had been born. He died at the home of his cousin.

Horatio Nelson (1758-1805)

Born in Burnham Thorpe in Norfolk, Nelson entered the navy at the age of 12 and served in the West Indies from 1777 to 1783. Nelson is remembered as the most successful fighting seaman of all time; the most skilled and audacious admiral in naval history.

Before Nelson's knockout victory at Trafalgar, English and French fleets had been clashing for 50 years. Nelson achieved a decisive victory, despite facing a larger Franco–Spanish force, through devising a dramatically new strategy. The usual form of naval attack during the late 18th and early 19th centuries had always been to place the 'ships of the line' parallel to those of the enemy in what was known as 'line ahead'. Both sides would then fire broadsides at one another. Speed of firing and accuracy would eventually result in a sort of victory for one side. But relatively few ships were sunk by this method of fighting and the side which was losing could usually still sail away.

Nelson's tactical genius was first apparent in 1797 at the battle of St Vincent where he disobeyed orders (risking a court martial) and sailed out of line in order to intercept French vessels. His tactic was successful and instead of being court martialled he was knighted and promoted to Rear Admiral. (The idea of attacking the enemy at right angles first appeared in print in a book called *Naval Tactics*, written by James Clerk. But it was Nelson who put the idea into practice.)

In 1798, at the Battle of the Nile, Nelson attacked from both sides, cut through the line of enemy ships and, in a pincer movement, captured 11 out of the enemy's 13 ships. It was a stunning victory. In 1801, at Copenhagen, Nelson famously put his telescope to his weak eye and, ignoring a hesitant commanding officer, took a naval advantage from a prospective defeat. (It is a myth that Nelson was blind in one eye and another myth that he wore an eye patch. His eye looked 'normal' and worked reasonably well, though it had been damaged during fighting in Corsica in 1794.)

At Trafalgar, on 21 October 1805, Nelson used his knowledge and experience to create a meticulously designed battleplan. He told his captains to attack in two columns, at right angles to the Franco-Spanish enemy line. He foresaw that when he cut through the enemy lines his ships would be able to deliver devastating broadsides up and down a defenceless enemy line that was unable to return fire. The plan required great courage as well as vision. During their approach the English ships were on the receiving end of continuous enemy broadsides from a much larger fleet. They could not return fire because they were sailing towards the enemy. Nelson's ships approached the enemy under full sail in order to minimise the time they would be under fire without being able to retaliate. The wind was lighter than expected and it took 20 minutes for the English fleet to reach the enemy. Nelson's own ship, Victory, was severely damaged. But as the British ships cut through the Franco-Spanish lines they discharged double-loaded broadsides at the enemy. Heavy cannon fire, delivered at very short range, demolished the enemy ships and killed many of their crews. No English ships were lost but 18 ships from the French and Spanish fleets were captured. As an inspiration to his men Nelson walked around on his deck wearing all his medals. He was an obvious target for sharp-shooters (snipers) in the rigging of the enemy ships. Shortly after the English ships had broken through the enemy line, and turned the battle in England's favour, a musket bullet from a sniper in the rigging of the French ship Redoutable hit Nelson and killed him. His body was taken back to England, preserved in a cask of brandy and under armed guard. Following a state funeral he was interred in the crypt of St Paul's Cathedral, buried in a coffin made with planks taken from the French ship L'Orient, which had been destroyed at the Battle of the Nile in 1798.

Thomas Newcomen (1663-1729)

Enthusiastic Scots sometimes claim that James Watt invented the steam engine. He didn't. Watt wasn't born until 1736 and Newcomen, the real inventor of the steam engine, had already been dead for seven years by then. Thomas Newcomen's design for a steam engine was dated 1712.

Born in Dartmouth, Devon, Thomas Newcomen was an ironmonger by trade and many of his biggest customers were the owners of Cornish tin mines. They had one huge problem: as their mines went deeper and deeper so they tended to fill with water. The old-fashioned way of removing the water was to pump it out manually or use teams of horses to haul out buckets with a rope.

In 1698, a man called Thomas Savery had designed a pump which used a vacuum to draw up water. His small steam engines were designed to pump water out of flooded mines. But they weren't terribly effective. Newcomen was 35 years old when he became a partner of Thomas Savery.

Newcomen designed the first really powerful steam engine. He created an engine in which steam raised a piston within a cylinder. The steam then condensed, creating a vacuum. And the vacuum drew the piston back down again. Newcomen was the first man to design a practical engine using a piston within a cylinder.

Because it was difficult to cast cylinders and pistons which fitted tightly together, Newcomen deliberately made the pistons smaller than the cylinders and then sealed the gap with a ring of wet leather.

Newcomen's engine was large and rather cumbersome but it worked – and worked well. Despite his local connections, his first working engine was installed at a coalmine in Dudley Castle in Staffordshire in 1712. The engine had a cylinder 21 inches in diameter and nearly eight feet long and it could raise ten gallons of water from a depth of 156 feet – giving it approximately five and a half horsepower.

A number of Newcomen engines were made and continued to work for a hundred years or more. Newcomen engines were strong and reliable. By the time he died there were over a hundred of them in England and the rest of Europe.

The Scottish born James Watt didn't work on steam engines for another fifty years.

Isaac Newton (1642-1727)

Mathematician, physicist and, without a doubt, the greatest scientist who ever lived, Newton was born prematurely (so prematurely in fact, that he wasn't expected to live) at Woolsthorpe Manor-house, Lincolnshire on Christmas Day in 1642 to Hannah Newton. Sadly, the baby's father, whom Isaac was named after, never got to see his son. The uneducated, prosperous farmer had died three months before his child was born.

Very shortly after Isaac Newton's third birthday, his mother re-married and moved a mile and a half away from Woolsthorpe to be with her new husband (a wealthy rector called Barnabas Smith). She left her son behind in the care of his grandparents.

Unsurprisingly, having been left with his grandparents later caused Isaac much anger, bitterness and, probably, lasting emotional damage. His anger was so great that he once threatened to burn his parents' house down with them in it.

Newton's stepfather, the Rev. Barnabas Smith, died in 1653. Newton's mother – now a wealthy woman – left the rectory at North Witham and moved back to Woolsthorpe with her son and two daughters from her second marriage.

When Isaac was 12 years old, he attended King Edward VI Grammar School in Grantham which was around 7 miles away from Woolsthorpe. While at school there, Isaac stayed with William Clark, an apothecary in the town, who was a friend of the Newtons. Whilst lodging there, Newton became very good at identifying different medicinal herbs and was soon allowed to mix herbal medicines.

Although very clever with his hands (having constructed windmills, sundials, water clocks and other mechanical pieces as a boy), Isaac was said to have been inattentive at school and didn't show much promise. However, all that was soon to change when, one day, Arthur Storer, (William Clark's stepson) attacked Isaac while they were both on their way to school. Isaac – a rather serious and quiet boy – wasn't one to be bullied. After school, he challenged his antagonist and defeated him in a brutal fight. Once he had beaten him he rubbed his attacker's nose against a wall. That incident changed him. Isaac then made it his mission to study hard so that he could be intellectually superior to his bully, and not just physically superior. Through much hard work, Newton rose from next to the bottom of the class to the highest place in the school – his mission more than accomplished.

During Newton's years at Grantham, he had a romantic

entanglement with William Clark's stepdaughter, Miss Storer, who was a few years younger than him. Being amazingly gifted with his hands, Isaac used to make dolls' furniture for Miss Storer and for her friends.

In 1659, Isaac's mother decided to take her eldest son out of school so that he could manage the farm. Isaac proved utterly useless at this because the work didn't interest him. Instead of working on the farm, he was often found with his head stuck in a book. He could be absent minded, in that way academics are often said to be. One day he was in such deep thought whilst coming home from town that he didn't realise his horse had slipped out of its bridle. He walked all the way home totally oblivious to the fact that he was holding an empty bridle. Later in life, when working, he would often forget to eat. Thankfully, with the help of the school principal, Mr Stokes, and Isaac's uncle, the Reverend William Ayscough, Isaac was sent back to Grantham school to continue his studies.

In 1661, (older than most of his fellow students because of his interrupted education), Isaac attended Trinity College Cambridge as a subsizar (carrying out menial tasks for wealthy students in order to earn his keep). Isaac largely ignored the official university syllabus and pursued his own studies. He immersed himself in the learning of René Descartes' geometry (which inspired his love of the subject), and in the works of Aristotle, Thomas Hobbes, Franciscus van Schooten, John Wallis, Henry More, Robert Boyle and many other great intellects. Newton could absorb literature like a sponge and possessed amazing powers of concentration.

Newton worked hard at university, often staying up all night to study. In 1664, he was elected to one of the 44 scholarship vacancies that were available and his days of carrying out menial tasks for the other students were over. A year later Isaac received his Bachelor of Arts degree.

In 1665, a plague epidemic forced the university to close and Newton returned to Woolsthorpe. The 16 months away from university proved to be a very productive time for Newton. He discovered that white light is, in fact, composed of many colours, he laid the foundations of calculus, and started work on the laws of universal gravity. Legend has it that it was seeing an apple fall (the story of the apple falling on his head is almost certainly a myth) in the orchard that triggered Newton into studying gravity. Whatever the truth is about the original idea, the theory of gravity took nearly 20 years of study to develop. Newton collated his ideas about gravity two decades later in *Philosophiae Naturalis Principia Mathematica* (commonly known as *Principia*) – now regarded as the greatest book in the history of science.

Isaac Newton put himself forward as a candidate for a fellowship when the university reopened in 1667. He was elected a Minor Fellow of Trinity and was elected a Major Fellow after being awarded his Master's Degree in 1668. He concentrated most of his mental energy on optics. And in 1668, he constructed (with his own hands) the first functioning reflecting telescope, which later gave him great recognition in the scientific community. Newton found the mechanics of vision and the nature of light fascinating. So great was his fascination that in order to investigate his theory of colours, he once carried out a hazardous experiment on himself where he inserted a bodkin into his eye. Through a series of experiments using glass prisms and a ray of sunlight, he proved that white light was made up of the colours of the rainbow and was not pure – a theory which people had believed for centuries.

In 1669, Newton was elected Lucasian Professor of Mathematics at Cambridge. He remained at the university, lecturing in most years, until 1696.

It was Newton's friend Edmond Halley who encouraged Newton to publish the book on gravity; he even financed its publication. As well as containing his ideas on gravity, *Principia* (published in 1687) contained Newton's three laws of motion and many other very important ideas. It was this book that made Newton famous throughout Europe.

Newton's formula of calculus, devised during his productive 16 months away from university, was undoubtedly the single most important contribution to mathematics and one of the major scientific breakthroughs. Calculus made possible most of the subsequent progress in modern science and is used in everything from construction to electrical engineering. Through its two primary tools, the integral and the derivative, calculus allows scientists to calculate precisely rates of change and amounts of change in a system. Despite its importance, Newton's work on calculus went unpublished for over 30 years. Newton was often reluctant to have his work published for fear of criticism; which meant that a lot of his theories weren't made public until many years after he'd first thought of them.

During the last 25 years of his life, Newton became embroiled in battles with a number of colleagues. He got into a nasty debate with Robert Hooke over the authorship of some of the theories of gravitation. Hooke also accused him of stealing some of his optical results. Fearing further criticism, Newton withheld publication on one of his major works *Opticks* until after Robert Hooke's death in 1703. Newton was renowned for being a difficult man. He was neurotic; he had a temper; he harboured resentments; he suffered from bouts of melancholy; and he could be vindictive. He also despised being contradicted or criticised. However, Isaac Newton was extremely hard working (working right up until his death), sensitive and very generous to his family and friends.

Having been a firm opponent of King James II's demand that Sidney Sussex College award an MA to a Benedictine monk who hadn't taken the statutory oath of allegiance to the Church of England, Newton – who was a Protestant – was elected member of parliament for the University of Cambridge in 1689. Isaac Newton's involvement with the Cambridge rebels put him at serious risk of being hung, for early on in King James II's reign, 300 rebels were sent to the gallows.

During his Parliamentary career, Isaac Newton made just one speech. He said: 'There's a bit of a draught. Can you close that window?' Not exactly Churchillian, perhaps, but then Churchill didn't discover gravity.

In 1696, Newton was appointed Warden of the Mint, and in 1699 he was made Master of the Mint – an office he retained right up until his death. During his time at the Mint – a job which he put his heart and soul into – he did much to improve the organisation's efficiency and he went to great lengths to combat forgery (sending quite a number of counterfeiters to the gallows). Newton also supervised recoinage. Isaac Newton moved to Jermyn Street in London when he worked for the Mint. In London, he invited his niece, Catherine Barton to run his household. Catherine Barton was charming, intelligent, beautiful and a brilliant conversationalist.

Newton was very fond of her, and she caused quite a stir amongst London society.

In 1703, Newton was elected President of the Royal Society of London and was re-elected annually for the rest of his life. In 1705, Isaac Newton was knighted by Queen Anne. He was the first scientist ever to be knighted.

Isaac Newton was an extraordinary man. He suffered two nervous breakdowns, was a keen student of alchemy (something he kept secret) and spent 25 years searching for the Philosopher's Stone. He studied Christianity extensively – he possessed 30 bibles in many languages – almost blinded himself by staring at the sun for hours during one of his experiments (for several days afterwards he had to stay in a darkened room until his eyesight returned to normal) and designed Queen Anne's Coronation Medal.

In 1662, he underwent a religious crisis and wrote a list of all his sins, one of which included squirting water on a Sunday. As this suggests, he was something of a practical joker. When he was at school he used to tie lit lanterns onto the tails of kites and fly them at night knowing that this strange sight used to frighten the people living in the neighbourhood.

On 20 March 1727 Isaac Newton died at Kensington at the age of 84. It wasn't a bad age considering that he wasn't expected to survive past the first day of his life. Newton died a wealthy man and was one of the most famous men in England. His discoveries helped change the world.

Isaac Newton, who had once said: 'If I have seen further, it is by standing on the shoulders of giants', was buried in Westminster Abbey and was the first scientist to be buried there.

Thomas Paine (1737-1809)

Thomas Paine, the writer, revolutionary, politician and political commentator, was born in Thetford, in Norfolkshire, to a very religious Quaker family. His father was a smallholder and corset maker.

Paine's early thinking had been influenced by the work of the philosopher John Locke and the scientist Isaac Newton. Sadly, Paine's early years were less than successful. At the age of 13 he became a corset-maker. He then became a sailor and a schoolmaster. In 1771 he became an exciseman (customs officer). By the age of 36 he had married twice and had been fired from his job as a customs officer for publishing a demand for higher wages. He was regarded as an agitator.

Having travelled to London, Paine met the American Benjamin Franklin who, in 1774 found him a job helping to edit the *Pennsylvania Magazine* in Philadelphia. Once in America, Paine quickly established a reputation as a fearless and controversial writer. He wrote articles demanding rights for women and freedom for slaves, and acquired a reputation as a radical journalist.

And then, in 1775, the American Revolution (aka the United States War of Independence) started. Paine left the magazine and joined George Washington's army. In 1776, he wrote a 50-page pamphlet called *Common Sense* in which he outlined the history of the events that had annoyed the colonists, and advocated American independence. The pamphlet quickly sold more than half a million copies and had a massive effect on the determination of the American colonists to break away from England. He also wrote a series of 16 separate papers with the heading *American Crisis*. Each was signed *Common Sense* to link them to the best-seller. These were all stirring, patriotic works and, although an Englishman, Paine became a leading spokesmen for the independence cause. The first of the 16 pamphlets began with the words 'These are the times that try men's souls' and was, upon the order of George Washington, read to the American troops at Valley Forge. Paine fought with the American rebels during the war, and after it ended he became secretary to the congress committee on foreign affairs. In this role he went on a mission to France in 1781 and published *Dissertations on Government* in 1786.

In 1787, Paine travelled to England and became involved in debates about the French Revolution. His book *The Rights of Man* (which he wrote in 1791-2) endorsed republicanism, advocated the abolition of the British Monarchy and supported the French Revolution (and, indeed, the spirit of revolution itself). He also proposed that Britain become a republic. *The Rights of Man* was written as a reply to Edmund Burke's *Reflections on the Revolution in France*.

Since his book was regarded as a dangerous threat to the English monarchy it was banned and Paine was indicted for treason and declared an outlaw in his home country. He escaped from England and went to Paris where he was made a citizen of France. He fought for the Revolution. Then, instead of writing about politics he became a politician; being elected to the National Convention as deputy for Pas-de-Calais and helping to draft the constitution for the new French republic.

Paine was not, however, a man who sat easily within the establishment. He criticised the Reign of Terror and in particular the execution of the French King and naturally this didn't go down too well. Robespierre had Paine's French citizenship rescinded and then had him arrested and imprisoned as an enemy Englishman.

Just before being imprisoned Paine had written *The Age of Reason Part I*, a powerful attack on accepted religion. While in prison Paine wrote *The Age of Reason Part II*. The books, an analysis of The Bible, were mistakenly assumed to be a denial of the existence of God. Naturally, this annoyed the church and ended with Paine being wrongly branded an atheist. His former friends, including George Washington, were angry with him and were alienated. Paine had now annoyed the English, the French, the Americans and, presumably, God.

When the reign of terror was over, Paine managed to get out of prison in France by arguing that he was an American citizen, not an English one. He stayed in Paris for a while, writing and studying and then in 1802 returned to the USA. Sadly, when he got there, in poor health, he found that he was being widely criticised for his misunderstood attacks on the church. He was ostracised as an atheist and a 'free thinker'. His influential support for the American Revolution had been forgotten.

Paine died in America in poverty a few years later, quite alone and shunned by those who had once revered him. He died on a farm at New Rochelle that had been given to him many years earlier by the once grateful state of New York.

Today Paine is remembered by some as a hero and by others as a traitor. It is uncomfortable for many to remember that an Englishman helped inspire the American Revolution and helped found the French Republic. He was, without a doubt, the most influential and controversial individual in both America and Europe during the two bloodiest and most famous revolutions the world has seen. He was the only man to play a major part in both revolutions and the only man to have been a senior politician in both countries at their most important times.

Robert Peel (1788-1850)

There are a number of reasons why Sir Robert Peel should be remembered, and on this list. He was a member of parliament from the age of 21, Under Secretary for the Colonies in 1811 and Chief Secretary for Ireland from 1812 until 1818. He was Prime Minister from 1834 until 1835 and again from 1841 until 1846. In addition he was a principal founder of the Conservative Party. In 1842 he imposed income tax to try to restore the nation's finances after the expensive war against Napoleon. (The initial rate was 7d in the pound, to be levied for three years. Peel softened this new burden by abolishing or lowering the duties on a number of important items.) He reorganised the Bank of England and initiated important reforms in Ireland. (He was so fiercely attacked by Daniel O'Connell that he challenged him to a duel.)

Peel was a member of the land-owning, aristocratic Tory party and might have been expected to support the Corn Laws, which protected farmers from foreign competition and kept the price of corn high. But when he was Prime Minister, Peel regarded the Corn Laws as unfair to huge numbers of people, particularly the poor, and so in 1846, after the potato rot in Ireland was followed by a terrible famine, he repealed the Laws, splitting his own party and forcing him to resign.

Peel's courageous decision changed the nature of the Tory party and helped create a more moderate and progressive Conservative Party. After his resignation, Peel continued to support free-trade principles and he is now regarded as the chief architect of the Victorian age of prosperity and stability. A successor, Benjamin Disraeli built on Peel's foundation.

But it is not for any of this that Robert Peel is best remembered.

Before he became Prime Minister, Peel was home secretary (from 1822 to 1827 and from 1828 to 1830) and during his tenure he reorganised England's criminal code. He reduced the number of offences carrying the death penalty from 200 to 12 and, most important of all, he established the world's first proper police force (initially in London). The members of the force were widely known as 'Bobbies' or 'Peelers', in reference to their founder. Even today, policemen in England (and elsewhere) are often known as 'Bobbies'.

Robert Peel was born near Bury, in Lancashire. His father was a wealthy cotton manufacturer and calico printer who was created a baronet in 1800. Robert Peel inherited a fortune from his father and took a great interest in literature and the arts. He was a keen sportsman and died after being thrown from his horse in 1850. He was 62 years old.

Peel was one of the most thoughtful and gentlemanly of England's Prime Ministers. But it is his creation of the world's first police force for which he is, quite rightly, best remembered.

Samuel Pepys (1633-1703)

Pepys was a naval administrator, but whatever he did in that role is long forgotten and would certainly have not earned him a place in this or any other book of great English heroes and heroines. Pepys, who was born in London and died in London, is remembered and honoured for his diary, sometimes saucy and always full of gossip, which provides an extraordinary insight into his own weaknesses, and domestic arrangements (he had a most particular view of the responsibilities of female domestic servants). His diary provided an excellent picture of 17th century England in general and of London society in particular. It was, perhaps, the first and most influential social history ever written.

Pepys started the great English tradition of diarists and inspired a thousand imitators (some good, some bad and some so dull and self-serving, and so written for effect rather than content, that they were a waste of good paper and ink) but few people have ever managed to keep such a complete and well-honed account of their lives, or such a valid social documentary of their times. When reporting that a surgeon called Richard Lower had put lamb's blood into an unfortunate patient Pepys noted that the transfusion had aroused much interest, including the comment that 'it might be entertaining to let the blood of a Quaker into an archbishop'.

Pepys never intended his diary to be read by other people (diarists didn't in those days) and he wrote it in a private, multilingual shorthand to protect his privacy. He was a meticulous and clever observer and he wrote about the people he knew, the people he saw and the people close to him. Most important of all he wrote about himself without restraint and without fear. There is no self-aggrandisement and no attempt to create or protect an image. He is honest about his failings and shortcomings and details his life without censorship. He mixes domestic and national issues, anecdotes and sermons and his honesty about personal issues encourages the reader to have faith in his accuracy on other matters. He never revised or edited what he wrote (where he forgot a name the blank remained) and as a key civil servant he revealed how public employees and members of parliament were as corrupt then as they are today. He even showed how parliamentary estimates were doctored back in the 17th century and he details his own personal accounts. He wrote about the Plague of 1665 and the Great Fire of London in 1666.

He started his diary at the age of 27 and abandoned it at the age of 36, only when he thought he was losing his eyesight and stopped writing it. Why did he keep it? Who knows. But he was an obsessive, meticulous man and it seems most likely that he really did write it simply as his own personal record.

What a pity it is that he didn't continue with it. Pepys lived another 34 years after ending his diary. He became Secretary to the Admiralty and a member of parliament and enjoyed friendships with eminent contemporaries such as Wren and Newton. It was an extraordinary life for a man who started from humble beginnings and whose first job was as a clerk in the office of the Exchequer.

In 1679, he got into terrible trouble as a result of an association with the Duke of York, and in the panic and confusion over the Popish Plot he was sent to the Tower of London for six weeks, suspected of, but not charged with, treason. But he bounced back and in 1684 he became the King's Secretary of Admiralty Affairs (a post invented for him).

When he retired he spent his final years finishing his library. He collected 3,000 books and his library, intact and unaltered, and still in the original bookcases he had specially made, survives together with the six, leather-bound volumes of his diary, at Magdalene College, Cambridge.

William Petty (1623-1687)

Born in Romsey, Hampshire, William Petty was a man of many great skills and huge achievements. He was a doctor, scientist and philosopher, an entrepreneur and a politician. Most of all he was also the first great political economist. His theories on trade and taxes were, many decades later, repeated to great acclaim by the Scotsman Adam Smith.

Born the son of a clothier, the young William Petty first went to sea as a cabin boy when he was 14 years old. After breaking his leg on board he was set ashore in France. Alone and in a foreign country he applied, in Latin, to study with the Jesuits in Caen. He supported himself by teaching English. After a year he returned to England with a good knowledge of French, Greek, mathematics and astronomy. He then joined the Navy before leaving to continue his studies in Holland where he discovered an interest in anatomy, which he subsequently studied in Utrecht, Amsterdam, Leiden, Paris and Oxford. A genuine polymath he became Professor of anatomy at Oxford and Professor of Music at Gresham College in London. When Petty was just 29, Oliver Cromwell appointed him physician to the army in Ireland.

While in Ireland he won the contract to begin a survey of the Irish land which had been forfeited in 1641 and which was being used to repay those who had lent money to Cromwell's army. Petty completed this in 1656. His reward was an estate of 30,000 acres in the southwest of the country and a fee of £9,000. He started lead-mines, ironworks, sea fisheries and other industries on his new estate. By the time he was 35 Petty was a rich man and a leading member of English society. Charles II was so impressed by Petty's brilliance and hard work that he made him surveyor-general of Ireland. Petty then spent much of his life proposing remedies for Ireland's poor state and poverty.

In addition to his extraordinary activities in Ireland, Petty was also an inventor. In 1647 he invented the first copying machine and in 1663 he invented a double-keeled sea boat (the first catamaran). He was a founder member of the Royal Society.

But it is not his work as an inventor, a doctor, a surveyor or a businessman which earns him a place in this book. Petty, who somehow managed to find time to work as personal secretary to Thomas Hobbes for a while, was also a statistician and economist and the originator of something he called 'political arithmetic' – which he defined as 'the art of reasoning by figures upon things relating to government'. (Petty himself was for a while a member of parliament.) He based his new economic theory on the work of Francis Bacon, who had argued that all rational sciences should be based on mathematics and the senses. Petty announced that his work would use only measurable phenomena and would rely on quantitative precision. His work on 'political arithmetic' was the foundation for modern census techniques.

In 1662, the year after he was knighted, he wrote *Treatise of Taxes and Contributions* in which he explained why he believed it was important to give free rein to 'the forces of individual self-interest'. However, he also declared that it was a duty of the State to maintain a high level of employment, and argued that a strong labour force makes a strong nation and a strong currency. He coined the term 'full employment'. This, and other subsequent books, was the foundation of economics.

Petty recommended that taxes should just be high enough to pay for providing support for the elderly, the sick and for orphans and that government expenditure in other areas should be kept to a minimum. He recommended that imports should be taxed, but only to put them on a par with domestic produce. He favoured taxes on consumption rather than income and recommended collecting statistical information in order to find ways to raise taxes more fairly.

Petty introduced precision into national accounting. He worked out that the average income in England at the time was £6 13 shillings and 6 pence per annum and that, with a population of six million, that meant a national income of £40 million.

Petty warned that governments should not over-interfere in the economy. He introduced the concept of 'laissez-faire' government and pointed out that it was as dangerous for a government to over-interfere with the economy as it would be for a physician to over-treat a patient. His *Essays in Political Arithmetick* and *Political Survey of Anatomy of Ireland* included calculated estimates of population and social income. His ideas of monetary theory and policy were developed in *Verbum Sapienti* and *Quantulumcunque Concerning Money*. It was Petty who first stated that the price of land equals the discounted present value of expected future rent on the land.

Perhaps the greatest contribution Petty made was to base his theories on data and statistics rather than on anecdotal evidence and prejudice. He was a prolific author on economics but wrote precisely and with humour. His work greatly influenced every writer on economics who followed him – particularly, for example, Adam Smith and Karl Marx. Adam Smith knew of Petty's work but does not credit him as the originator of his own ideas on the economy. Smith's derivative book *Inquiry into the Nature and Causes of the Wealth of Nations*, was not published until 1776, over a century after Petty had written his masterpiece *Treatise on Taxes and Contributions*. It was Englishman William Petty, not the Scot, Adam Smith, who invented many of the concepts that are still used in economics today.

Petty married Baroness Shelburne. He died at the age of 64. His great grandson was the government minister William Petty Fitzmaurice, 2nd Earl of Shelburne and 1st Marquess of Landsdowne.

Francis Place (1771-1854)

Born in a debtor's prison in Drury Lane, where his father worked as an overseer, Francis Place first aroused attention when he was identified as one of the leaders of a strike in 1793. He afterwards found it impossible to work as a maker of trousers (the trade he had taught himself).

Having decided that working men needed the vote he joined a group called the London Corresponding Society, whose leaders were all in prison. He was soon offered, and accepted, the post of chairman. He held this position until 1797 when he resigned in protest at the violent tactics used by some members of the group.

In 1799, unable to get employment because of his record as a militant, Place opened his own shop in Charing Cross Road. Part of the premises he ran as a tailor's shop but the other part was a lending library of radical books. Not surprisingly, the shop soon ended up as a meeting place for reformers.

In the early 19th century the people of England wanted freedom and parliamentary reform. But leading politicians refused to budge. In 1830, on the opening day of Parliament, the Prime Minister, the Duke of Wellington, sniffily stated that he was not prepared to introduce any reforms, despite the many demands which had been made for constitutional change.

It was a mistake by Wellington.

Just thirteen days after that Wellington's Government was defeated and the Iron Duke resigned. He had defeated Napoleon but a London born tailor called Francis Place, together with the English reformists, had proved too much for him.

The new Prime Minister was Earl Grey, a member of 'The Friends of the People', a society which wanted reform of parliamentary representation. Meetings had been held all over the country and many messages of support and encouragement had been sent to Lord Grey.

Despite his victory in the polls, Grey didn't find the battle for reform an easy one. Eventually, however, he managed to obtain enough support, and the Reform Bill was introduced into the House of Commons in March 1831 and finally passed in June 1832.

Sadly, although this bill enfranchised the well-to-do commercial classes, the lower middle class and working class wage earners still had no vote. In that respect the bill turned out to be a disappointment. Social conditions were subsequently allowed to deteriorate so much that the workhouses and debtors' prisons immortalised by Charles Dickens became a part of English society. Not surprisingly, the lower middle classes felt disappointed and let down.

In 1836 Francis Place, John Cleave and William Lovett founded a new society called the London Working Men's Association. The society, aimed at artisans who had been ignored in the Reform Bill, drew up the People's Charter. The author of the Charter was Francis Place, who was one of the most effective, persistent and influential English reformers.

Followers of Place's ideas were known as Chartists and their campaigning eventually gave them the parliamentary representation they wanted. They were told by Place, and William Lovett, a cabinet maker and revolutionary colleague, that 'true liberty cannot be conferred by Acts of Parliament or decrees of princes, but must spring up from the knowledge, morality and public virtue of our population.'

Place and his followers argued that England's social and political structure had to be based upon the intelligence and morality of the people if they were to avoid exchanging one despot for another and one set of oppressors for another set. No one in modern political history did more to extend the freedom of English men and women than Francis Place. He was an untiring and determined campaigner for reform.

In addition to his political battles, Place was also the first person to campaign in favour of contraception. In 1822 he wrote *The Principle of Population*, a book which caused a considerable storm. Ironically, although Place advocated the use of contraception, he himself fathered fifteen children.

Walter Ralegh (1552-1618) (aka Raleigh)

Walter Ralegh was a sailor, adventurer, pirate, poet, soldier, courtier, explorer and entrepreneur. He was one of England's great 16th century heroes and we should remember him for much more than laying down his cloak so that Queen Elizabeth I didn't have to step in a puddle.

Colonial expansion may sometimes begin because a nation's leaders want more land, more wealth or more power. Occasionally, a nation may launch expeditionary forces to pre-empt attacks on its shores or on existing colonies. But, very often, colonial expansion begins, builds and is sustained through the ambition of individuals who want to venture beyond the normal horizon in search of adventure, knowledge or wealth. Sometimes, adventurers set out because they are bored or because they are inspired by something as simple as curiosity. And often explorers, adventurers and emigrants leave in search of greater freedom and independence. The Greeks and the Romans were enthusiastic colonisers. And, throughout history, the Spanish, the French, the Italian and the English have all been keen colonisers too.

By the second half of the 16th century it was clear that the English had fallen behind in their western adventures. Columbus and Cabot (an Italian who sailed from Bristol) had discovered America and the West Indies but English explorers had been rather caught napping.

Things changed in Elizabethan England. Encouraged by their Queen, men acquired new ambitions and were encouraged to see them through. Sir Philip Sidney, a cultured Englishman, who was a poet, diplomat and politician, was one of the first of a new breed of men eager to engage in colonial exploration. But Sidney died young and it was Walter Ralegh who epitomised the English approach to exploration and adventure in the 16th century.

Ralegh was a man of action but he also had a passion for books. He was born in Devon, near to the peaceful seaside village of Budleigh Salterton, and after spending a little time in Oxford and then studying law in London, he joined the army and went to war. He fought with the Huguenots in France against the French Government (which was determined to destroy the Protestant movement the Huguenots had organised) and then crossed to the Netherlands to join the Dutch Protestants who were fighting the Spanish.

It was there that he learned to loathe the Spanish. Filled with contempt for their religious doctrine and stirred by curiosity he decided to sail to the New World where the Spanish had established more than a foot-hold. At the age of 26, by now a seasoned warrior, he joined his half-brother, Sir Humphrey Gilbert on a rather unproductive voyage to the West Indies.

Having returned to England he then enlisted in the Irish wars. It was there that he first acquired personal wealth. He was given 40,000 acres of confiscated land in what is now Waterford and Cork. Ralegh was also given a famous house called Myrtle Grove and the land upon which he later built a larger mansion. He didn't much like the Irish (who he was quite happy to kill as and when required) but liked the Irish countryside. For a while, he stayed on his newly acquired lands, gardening and writing poetry.

But when, in 1583, his half-brother took possession of Newfoundland in the name of Queen Elizabeth, Ralegh was inspired to travel again. His half-brother had been granted permission to take personal possession of an almost infinite area of land on the North American continent but tragically Gilbert died when his ship was wrecked on his return and the Queen transferred to Ralegh most of the privileges she had previously given his half-brother.

The story that Ralegh first won the Queen's affection by laying down his cloak for her first appeared in a book called *Worthies* written in 1662 by Fuller. 'Captain Raleigh coming out of Ireland to the English court in good habit found the queen walking, till meeting with a plashy place, she seemed to scruple going thereon. Presently Raleigh cast and spread his new plush cloak on the ground; whereon the queen trod gently, rewarding him afterwards with many suits, for his so free and seasonable tender of so fair a foot cloth.' Thus Ralegh became a favourite of the Queen and a puddle became a legend.

Ralegh behaved like a lover and the Queen lapped up his flirtatious attention. He promised everlasting love. She took him at his word and refused to let him leave her side. The expedition he had organised to take advantage of his new lands in America had to leave without him.

When word came back that the expedition had gone well Ralegh, desperate to join in the foreign fun, had a brain wave. He asked the Queen for permission to call the new territory Virginia (as a tribute to his virgin Queen). He wanted to make a new England out of Virginia. It would, he told her, be a permanent memorial to her greatness. The Queen happily accepted the suggestion.

He sent out colonists, many of whom simply disappeared. In 1587, for example he sent out a band of emigrants, including 89 men, 17 women and two children. They were left there while their leaders came home for supplies. When the leaders and the supplies went back the settlers had all disappeared.

Ralegh never got to Virginia himself, though he spent around £40,000 of his own money in his efforts to colonise the area. He was the first English colonialist. His sailors brought back two products, the potato and tobacco, which were to play a large part in England's future prosperity (though not its health). Tobacco smoking quickly became an almost universal habit. (There have been attempts to suggest that Ralegh was not responsible for bringing either of these substances to England. It is always difficult to be sure about what happened 400 years ago but having studied the evidence I am not convinced by the doubters. Ralegh may not have clambered ashore clutching bundles of tobacco leaves or a bag of potatoes but whether it was him or his agents who were responsible is largely irrelevant. It was Ralegh who brought potatoes and tobacco to Europe.)

The rivalry between England and Spain reached a zenith in 1588 when Spain tried to conquer England itself by sending a Spanish armada into the channel. The Spaniards were repulsed by a fleet led by Sir Francis Drake. Ralegh played his part in that victory. A little later an expedition under his control captured a Spanish vessel homebound from the West Indies with a cargo estimated then to be worth at least half a million pounds. Ralegh, who had funded the capture, was awarded a share of the plunder and realised that here lay an excellent way to become extremely rich (instead of merely very rich).

It is important to understand too that Ralegh had a cultured side. He wrote poetry and was great friends with Edmund Spenser (author of the *Fairie Queene*) and Christopher Marlowe (the dramatist, founder of English tragedy and tutor of Shakespeare). He also met and talked often with Ben Jonson and William Shakespeare himself.

When he heard reports of a city in South America known as El Dorado, Ralegh was fired by ambition. The word was that the city contained fabulous wealth. Ralegh sent out agents, but they came back with no useful information, and so in 1595 he went himself. He obtained a commission from the Queen allowing him to wage war on the Spanish and upon the South Americans if they got in his way and impeded his chances of acquiring treasure. This was, of course, just another example of the legalised and officially sponsored piracy which was prevalent in the 16th century.

Ralegh reached Trinidad and took the Spanish governor prisoner. The Governor told Ralegh of limitless gold to be found on the banks of the river Orinoco. So, naturally Ralegh set off with a hundred men on a voyage up the river. In 'unsavoury and loathsome' conditions they rowed up the river and lived off the land.

The expedition was a failure. Ralegh brought home tons of something which he thought was gold but which allegedly turned out to be nothing more than iron pyrites or fool's gold. (Ironically, many years later it turned out that there was a gold source very close to where Ralegh had prospected.)

Ralegh's book about the expedition, *The Discovery of Guiana*, is one of the most vivid and exhilarating travel books ever written.

When he returned to England, Ralegh immediately took part in the English fleet which attacked Cadiz in 1596, and in 1597 he attempted to intercept Spanish treasure ships off the Azores. In 1600 he became governor of Jersey and did much to improve the economy of the island.

Sadly, Ralegh's final years were disastrous.

He had lost the Queen's patronage when he had married Bessie Throckmorton in 1592 (Bessie had been one of the Queen's maids of honour and Ralegh had conducted a secret affair with her for some years) and although he regained some of the Queen's affection, his temper and inability to take orders meant that he made many enemies at court. These included the powerful Earl of Essex, Lord Howard of Effingham and Sir Robert Cecil.

When Elizabeth died, Ralegh knew little of the new monarch, King James I. Ralegh had failed to pledge himself to support the new King and this did not go down well with the suspicious Scot. Ralegh's position at court quickly became insecure. He was falsely accused of trying to assassinate the King and of trying to put Arabella Stuart, the King's relative, on the throne. Desperate and alone he tried to commit suicide. This was regarded as a sign of guilt. He was tried in Winchester and condemned to a traitor's death. His estates were forfeited. He waited in prison for three weeks and then James decided not to sign the death warrant. Ralegh was kept a prisoner in the Tower of London but told he was not to be executed. His wife and sons were allowed to stay with him and he was allowed to move around within the Tower. He built a laboratory where he carried out a series of chemical experiments. He managed to obtain fresh water from salt water. He created several new drugs. And he began to write an ambitious *History of the World*, using his library of six or seven hundred volumes for source material.

But he still wanted to have one more adventure. He wanted to return to South America. He petitioned the King and the Privy Council. And, after five years of petitioning, Ralegh was released from prison. He had been in the Tower for 13 years.

English enthusiasm for exploration had been fired by a popular play called *Eastward Ho!*, written by George Chapman, Ben Jonson and John Marston and published in 1605. The play encouraged those who saw it to believe that the New World was awash with gold and replete with honest men. It was, said the playwright, a nation where no public office could be procured except through merit. It was, the trio said, a nation where corruption in high places was unknown. Ah, the wisdom of ignorance.

Ralegh was now 65 years old and in poor health. He had little money and no friends. He had been released from prison on condition that he return to Guiana and secure the gold mines. But for a long while it seemed that he had little realistic hope of making the journey. The Spanish Ambassador in London protested that Guiana belonged to Spain and Ralegh's many enemies did everything they could to make things impossible for him.

But Ralegh persisted and eventually he managed to find a ship and to put together a crew of drunkards and crooks. And he reached South America. But the journey was a disaster. His elder son, Walter, died and the new Spanish settlers prevented him travelling up the Orinoco. And, contrary to the promises he had made in London, he molested a Spanish settlement.

He arrived back in Plymouth a failure and in despair. He was taken to court and the Spanish minister in London ensured that the old offence was revived. Ralegh was sentenced to death again. He smoked a pipe and was taken to a scaffold erected outside the Houses of Parliament. He read a short statement he had written, in which he thanked God for allowing him to die in the light and commented that 'I have a long journey to take and must bid the company farewell'. He felt the edge of the axe, smiled at the sheriffs and said: 'This is a sharp medicine, but it is a sure cure for all diseases.' And then, with two blows, the executioner severed his head from his body. His widow, Elizabeth, had his head embalmed. She kept it in a red leather bag by her side for the rest of her life.

The night before he went to the scaffold Ralegh wrote these words:

'Even such is time, that takes in trust
Our youth, our joys, our all we have,
And pays us but with earth and dust;

Who, in the dark and silent grave

When we have wandered all our ways,
Shuts up the story of our days.
But from this earth, this grave, this dust,
My God shall raise me up I trust.'

Walter Ralegh was a courageous, resourceful and versatile Englishman. He was a soldier, sailor, author, poet, traveller and coloniser. He was a philosopher, a politician and a historian. He had boundless energy and imagination. He acquired a fortune but was not afraid to use it when he needed it. His *History of the World* was highly regarded. Oliver Cromwell told his son to read it. 'It's a body of history,' he said, 'and will add much more to your understanding than fragments of story.'

It was thanks to Ralegh that the great English settlements of Virginia and New England came into being. Walter Ralegh was a man of his time; a great romantic, a great hero and a great Englishman.

Note: The spelling 'Raleigh' is commonly used today but I've spelt Ralegh's name the way he chose to spell it.

Cecil Rhodes (1853-1902)

He wasn't fifty when he died but Cecil Rhodes, the Colossus of Africa, had achieved more by then than most men would hope to achieve in a hundred lifetimes. Today, he is regarded with a mixture of disdain and contempt by the narrow-minded, the bigoted and the politically correct, but Rhodes was a man of great vision, enormous ambition and huge amounts of compassion for his fellow men. He was a statesman, businessman, financier and empire builder. He was enormously controversial in his lifetime and today his life reads like something out of a boy's adventure magazine but it is impossible to exaggerate the importance of his role in the development of Africa, the Empire and, of course, the mining industry.

He was born in Bishops Stortford, in Hertfordshire, the son of the local vicar; a clergyman whose boast was that he had never preached a sermon that lasted longer than ten minutes. As a boy, Rhodes grew up in the English countryside. No one loved his country more. 'Remember that you are an Englishman, and consequently won first prize in the lottery of life,' he once said. He believed that England was the greatest country in the world.

Cecil was a sickly child who suffered from asthma and heart problems and when he was a teenager he was sent by his parents to Natal, South Africa to help Herbert, his older brother, who operated a cotton farm.

In 1871, after just a few years farming, Rhodes obtained finance from Rothschild and Sons and headed to the diamond fields of Kimberley where he proceeded to buy up all the small diamond mines in the area. At about this time a doctor gave him just six months to live.

As his holdings grew, so Rhodes became increasingly interested in South African politics. In 1884, he became a member of the Cape House of Assembly and quickly took office in the ministry. He was asked by General Gordon to go with him to Khartoum as secretary but declined because of his new political responsibilities in the Cape. Still only in his thirties, but aware that his poor health meant that his life expectation was short, Rhodes had become a major force in Africa. His ardent enthusiasm for his home country meant that he succeeded in extending British territory. In 1884, wanting to expand to the north and to build a railway connecting Cairo and the Cape, he secured Bechuanaland as a British protectorate and in 1889 he took over the territory which was later to become Rhodesia. The British Government chartered the British South Africa Company and put Rhodes in charge. He then extended control to two northern provinces which were eventually named after him as Southern Rhodesia (now Zimbabwe) and Northern Rhodesia (now Zambia). His aim was to establish a federal South African dominion under the British flag.

Meanwhile, as his political power grew, Rhodes was becoming richer and richer. By 1888, Rhodes had virtually obtained a monopoly of the world's diamond supply and had formed the De Beers Consolidated Mines Company. His own company was mining over 90% of the world's diamonds. He turned his position of control into a complete monopoly in 1888 by arranging a partnership with the Diamond Syndicate in London. Rhodes agreed to control the supply of diamonds in order to keep prices high.

In 1890, Rhodes became Prime Minister of Cape Colony but he resigned this six years later after complications arose as a result of an unofficial raid into the Transvaal which was condemned by the South African Commission and the British Government. However, in the same year, 1896, he succeeded in quelling the Matabele rebellion by personally negotiating with the local chiefs. Although he is today often attacked for his alleged imperialist views, Rhodes advocated more self-government for the Cape Colony and wanted the empire to be controlled by local settlers and local politicians and not by the Government in London. In reality, Rhodes was directly opposed to imperialism in which colonies are controlled from a distant city.

Rhodes was also responsible for founding the modern Cape fruit industry of South Africa. In 1898, he financed a fruit export business on a farm in the Cape area of the country. This grew into the Rhodes Fruit Farms.

In 1899, during the Boer War, he played a major part in defending Kimberley during the siege. He and his company manufactured an armoured train and a super-gun (called 'Long Cecil'), constructed fortifications and provided water and refrigeration facilities for the defence of the town.

Rhodes's final years were badly affected when he was stalked by a Polish princess called Catherine Radziwill. The princess asked Rhodes to marry her and then, despite his refusal, falsely claimed that she was engaged to him. She obtained her revenge by falsely accusing him of loan fraud. He was found innocent after a trial but the stress proved too much for him and he died shortly afterwards.

When Rhodes died in 1902 he was one of the richest men in the world. He left a will which gave huge amounts of money to Cape Colony. He left a large area of land on the slopes of Table Mountain to South Africa. He also founded the Rhodes Scholarships at Oxford University for Americans, Germans and colonials. Amazingly, during his short and astonishing career he had somehow managed to enter Oriel College, Oxford and take a degree. He started his degree in 1873 but ill health meant he had go back to South Africa. He returned for his second term in 1876 and completed his degree. As a student at Oxford he was influenced by a lecture given by the ubiquitous John Ruskin. In 1899, Rhodes was made a doctor of civil law by Oxford University.

Peter Mark Roget (1779-1869)

Few men's names are better known than Roget's. And yet surprisingly little is written about this extraordinary English doctor.

Born in London, the son of a minister, Roget had an unhappy childhood. His father died young and his favourite uncle committed suicide in his presence. His wife died young. It is perhaps not surprising that he struggled with depression throughout his life.

Peter Roget qualified and worked as a physician. His first job was as physician to the Manchester Infirmary when he was 25 years old. Four years later he was appointed physician to the Northern Dispensary in London.

But he was far, far more than a physician. In 1814, he invented a slide rule for calculating the roots and powers of numbers and in 1828 he helped found both the Royal Society of Medicine and the University of London. He was Fullerian professor of physiology at the Royal Institution from 1833 to 1836 and secretary of the Royal Society from 1827 to 1849. In 1834, he wrote *Animal and Vegetable Physiology*. He even designed an inexpensive pocket chessboard and, as a hobby, created chess problems.

However, those are still not the achievements for which he is best remembered. In 1840, he retired from medical work to work on the most notable work of his life. This was, of course, his *Thesaurus of English Words and Phrases*, a most comprehensive and classified collection of synonyms which enables writers to find an alternative word when they are creating a letter, an article or a book and do not wish to keep repeating themselves. Roget was the first person to create a thesaurus. He had always loved lists and had something of an obsession for list making when he was eight years old.

He started work on the thesaurus in 1805 and it was, for him, a way of escaping from his depression. The book was first published in 1852 when it was given the snappy title: *Thesaurus of English Words and Phrases Classified and Arranged so as to Facilitate the Expression of Ideas and Assist in Literary Composition*. The book was reprinted 28 times during Roget's life. After he died at 90, while on holiday in Malvern, his son, John Lewis Roget took over the job of keeping the book up-to-date. And when he, in turn, died, his son Samuel Romilly Roget carried on the family tradition.

John Ruskin (1819-1900)

The men and women in this book have been selected for their influence on England in particular and on the world at large. When a man discovers gravity or electricity or invents the railway train it isn't difficult to conclude that his life must have had a profound impact on the world around him – and, indeed, on future generations.

But sometimes the influence a man or woman has on his and future generations isn't quite so immediately obvious. John Ruskin is one of those and I spent a good deal of time wondering whether or not to include him in this book.

Although John Ruskin was a writer and a critic, few of his books survive and apart from knowing that he wrote a series of books called *Modern Painters* I could not have named any of his other books before I started to research his life.

But Ruskin is in my 100 because of the influence he had on 19th century England and because of the way his life influenced others who helped shape the future. He had a profound and lasting influence that has slowly spread throughout the world.

Born in London, the only child of wealthy parents (his father was a wine merchant) he was taught at home by a private tutor and then at Oxford University. At home, as a boy, he was protected from the world and was undoubtedly a rather spoilt child. He wasn't allowed to mix with other boys of his own age. His parents worked hard to stimulate and guide his taste by taking him around England and the European Continent. He was only 24 when he wrote the first of his five volumes called *Modern Painters*. These were very subjective books in which Ruskin wrote solely about the painters he admired. He was a great fan of J. M. W. Turner, whom he met, and Ruskin championed his work with an enthusiasm that Turner found almost embarrassing.

Ruskin married Euphemia Chalmers Gray in 1848 but the marriage was legally annulled fairly quickly (she then married the painter John Everett Millais) and Ruskin, who still often travelled around Europe with his parents, began a crusade on behalf of another group of painters whom he felt had been ignored – the pre-Raphaelite brotherhood. This group was led by Dante Gabriel Rossetti and Millais and favoured a faux-mediaeval style which honoured the simple way that nature was depicted in Italian art before Raphael. William Morris later became a member of the Brotherhood.

While writing the later volumes of *Modern Painters*, Ruskin also extended his writing to cover architecture. In his books *The Seven Lamps of Architecture* (1849) and *The Stones of Venice* (1851-3) he wrote praising mediaeval architecture. He believed that architects and craftsmen who were inspired by their religious beliefs when building cathedrals had created great art. He loved gothic architecture.

Ruskin's writings about the Pre-Raphaelites made him the art critic of the day. But his work, which also contained moral and social criticism, made him into a sort of 19ᵗʰ century guru. When he had finished his five part series of books on painters in 1860, he took an increasingly active interest in important social questions of the day. He felt resentment about the social injustice and the squalor which had resulted from the unbridled capitalism created by the Industrial Revolution. He was horrified by the knowledge that children and adults worked in appalling conditions, lived in appalling conditions and were paid a pittance. They worked long hours and their work was often dangerous. Towns and cities were grey, smoky, dangerous places. Ruskin argued that the quality of life which a man leads is the only really important criterion and that money-grabbing is an anathema to civic and social welfare. He argued that things which cannot be bought and sold (such as love, friendship and truth) do and must have a real influence on supply and demand. He said that to treat a worker as a machine (and, therefore, as something less than a man) is to lower the economic value of his work. He pointed out that in the long run it is more profitable to pay a higher wage to an efficient workman who enjoys his job, and takes pride in his work, than a lower wage to an inefficient workman who hates his job.

Ruskin developed a philosophy which was has been described as a 'sort of Christian communism' and, naturally, this didn't go down terribly well with the establishment which was largely run by fat, wealthy men who had made their fortunes out of the factories which were springing up all over the country. He blamed the ugly cities which were developing throughout England on the enthusiasm for mass production and blamed bad working and living conditions on the industrial age. This may seem obvious now but at the time it was revolutionary, and considered heretical. He wrote urging that working and living conditions should be improved for factory workers and his books and articles on the need for social reform changed the way people thought, first in England and then elsewhere. Ruskin did everything he could to reach out to people who were privileged to try to make them aware of society's new problems. He was attacked, of course, and his suggestions and advice were often treated with contempt.

However, not everyone ignored him. After all he was still a noted art critic and quite wealthy too. And he knew lots of influential people. (He was a brilliant networker.) The Industrial Revolution had started in England and now the reaction to it, the feeling that the workers had been forgotten, started too.

In 1689, at the age of 50, Ruskin was made the first Slade professor of fine art at Oxford University. Instead of living in Oxford he settled at Coniston, in the Lake District, where he continued to battle for better conditions for working men; always writing vividly and with great colour. His early art criticism had often been extremely wordy – one sentence in Modern Painters contains more than six hundred words and eighty commas – but when writing about social conditions he did so far more crisply and intensely.

Between 1871 and 1884, Ruskin wrote a series of papers addressed *To the Workmen and Labourers of Great Britain* in which he explained in detail his social philosophy. His writing was always powerful and passionate. He argued that life cannot be compartmentalised; that, in art, in thought, in morals and in the workplace, 'nothing can be beautiful which is not true'. He believed that industrial prosperity should go hand in hand with social prosperity. He constantly tried to awaken the spiritual in the material.

Ruskin tried to make a difference by example too. He founded the John Ruskin school in Camberwell and the Whitelands College in Chelsea. He opened a non-profit making shop in Paddington Street.

Ruskin's name comes up time and time again when influential figures of the 19ᵗʰ century are investigated. So, for example, consider Octavia Hill, the daughter of a corn merchant and banker who was born in Wisbech Cambridgeshire in 1838. Hill was a social reformer and humanitarian whose campaigning for the availability and preservation of open spaces for public use led to the establishment of the National Trust – she wanted to bring beauty and tranquillity into the lives of ordinary people. More importantly, being well aware that there was a real need for better housing for the poor she also played a great role in helping the development of social housing, including council housing. But it is doubtful whether she would have got anywhere without Ruskin, for it was John Ruskin who funded Octavia Hill's first ventures in housing reform by financing the lease of several slum properties in London.

In 1879, Ruskin, weak, ill and depressed and exhausted after losing a libel suit brought against him by James McNeill Whistler, resigned his Slade professorship. But even in his final years he still found enough strength to attack the railways which were, he believed, disturbing rural beauty. He died at Coniston, looked after by his cousin and her family.

Ruskin's last regret was reported to have been that he had failed to get rid of all his money before he died.

Ruskin is worthy of respect and remembrance for his original ideas and for the passion and power with which he expressed them. A. C. Benson wrote that what Ruskin did was 'to break utterly to pieces the old leisurely feeling about art as a pleasant and dignified adjunct to life. He taught men and women to look close, to compare, to discriminate, to wonder, and above all to care for art as the passionate expression of one of the deepest and strongest of human qualities, the love and worship of beauty.'

Ruskin was a man who always meant what he said. He made people think and his influence is lasting.

William Shakespeare (1564-1616)

William Shakespeare, poet and playwright, universally acknowledged as the greatest writer the world has ever seen, contributed more than any other individual to the English language. If it were not for Shakespeare, many phrases in our English language today would simply not exist. His entire work contains between 25,000-30,000 different words (far, far more words than most writers use); some of these words were invented by Shakespeare, many were given new meanings by him.

Shakespeare was born in a house on Henley Street, Stratford-on-Avon in 1564. He was one of seven children. Very little is known about his life but his parents were John Shakespeare and Mary Arden. Shakespeare's father was quite a big wheel in the small town; he owned a profitable glove-making business and by 1568, John Shakespeare had risen to the position of high bailiff, after joining the town council in 1557.

In the 1570's, touring actors would frequently stop off at Stratford-on-Avon where they would perform plays. These plays no doubt made a strong impression on the growing Shakespeare, and probably sowed the seeds for his future career in acting and writing.

By the time he left school, William Shakespeare's father had fallen into debt and William himself was not well off. Nevertheless, in 1582, at the age of 18, he married Anne Hathaway who was eight years his senior. The couple had two daughters and a son: Susanna (who was the eldest) and twins, Judith and Hamnet. Sadly, Hamnet died in childhood.

Little is known about what Shakespeare did for a living at this time but in the late 1580's he seems to have left his family and headed for London to seek his fortune. There is no documentary evidence of what happened to him and these are often referred to as 'the lost years'. Little is known about his life because Shakespeare was a poor man with no contacts at court and no status.

In 1594, after having spent some years being involved in the theatre in London, Shakespeare became a member – and a shareholder – of a newly founded theatre company called 'The Lord Chamberlain's Men' (later named the King's Men after King James I succeeded the throne).

As well as being a shareholder, William Shakespeare acted in the company and wrote plays for them to perform. Indeed, documents suggest that Shakespeare acted throughout his professional life.

Before he joined the Lord Chamberlain's Men, Shakespeare was already making a name for himself as a playwright; the first reference to him in this capacity was in 1592 and by 1596, Shakespeare had made enough money to buy a house called 'New Place' in Stratford-on-Avon for himself and his wife and children.

From 1599, Shakespeare's company of players performed at the Globe Theatre in London. Nearly all of Shakespeare's new plays were presented at the Globe, and he soon earned a reputation as one of England's greatest playwrights. His comedies include *Love's Labour's Lost, The Taming of the Shrew, A Midsummer Night's Dream* and *The Comedy of Errors*. The history plays include *Henry VI (Part I, II and III), Richard III* and *Richard II*. His tragedies include *Romeo and Juliet, Hamlet, Othello, Julius Ceasar* and *Macbeth*. Nobody is really certain in what order many of his plays were written and first performed.

The day before the second Earl of Essex led a rebellion against Queen Elizabeth I, the supporters of Essex arranged with the Lord Chamberlain's Men to put on a performance of Shakespeare's tragedy *Richard II,* which involved a monarch being overthrown. As a celebration of the pre-planned rebellion, the Earl of Essex encouraged his supporters to watch the play which was held at the Globe. When Queen Elizabeth found out about it, she suspected Shakespeare's company of being involved in the rebellion. An investigation followed but luckily Shakespeare and the rest of the players were found not guilty of any crime.

On the 29 June 1613, the Globe's thatched roof caught fire when a cannon was fired during the performance of the play *Henry VIII* (which Shakespeare had written with the new chief playwright of the King's Men, John Fletcher). The Globe theatre was destroyed in less than two hours, but was soon rebuilt. The fire at the Globe prompted Shakespeare to break away from the King's Men and to sell his shares in the company.

William Shakespeare wrote 37 plays and 154 sonnets. It is widely believed that Shakespeare's sonnets were printed without his consent, and one theory is that someone who knew Shakespeare betrayed him by handing his sonnets to a publisher.

William Shakespeare, the writer whose plays are still performed more often than those of any other playwright, died on 23 April 1616. He was just 52 years old. Nobody really knows for certain what caused his death, though since he is believed to have had some sort of fever he presumably died of an infection.

Before he died, Shakespeare wrote his own epitaph of which the last line reads: 'And curst be he that moves my bones'. In his will, Shakespeare left his wife Anne his second-best bed. However, this was not as bad as it seems, as the best bed around that period was usually reserved for guests, and the second bed was often the marital bed. Anne died seven years after her husband's death.

It wasn't until 1623 that the first collected edition of his plays was published. There is evidence to suggest that Shakespeare wrote another play called *Cardenio* but, sadly, this has never been found.

There has, over the years, been a considerable amount of discussion about whether or not William Shakespeare really was the author of the Shakespearean plays. Many academics have written books proposing alternative authors and suggesting that the name 'William Shakespeare' was used as a convenient pseudonym.

Does it really matter?

Whoever wrote the plays was happy to use the name 'William Shakespeare' during his lifetime. Maybe we should respect that wish and simply be happy to remember William Shakespeare as the greatest playwright who ever lived.

John Snow (1813-1858)

Most of the people in this book were quite elderly when they died (many were well past their biblical allowance of three score years and ten and a good number were elderly even by modern, 21st century standards). John Snow, however, was in his mid forties when he died. Nevertheless, he made his mark. Two marks to be exact. First, he was the one of the very first anaesthetists, and arguably the one who made anaesthesia acceptable. Second, he proved the relationship between cholera and contaminated water supplies.

The first effective and safe anaesthetic was nitrous oxide. It was first used in 1799 by the English inventor Sir Humphry Davy. He was in pain and used the gas to obtain relief from an erupting wisdom tooth. Michael Faraday, another English inventor, described the anaesthetic qualities of ether a little later. Americans, who always like to claim to have invented everything, credit a dentist called Morton with 'inventing anaesthesia' but in truth Morton was nearly half a century behind Davy and Faraday.

And it was Snow who made anaesthesia fashionable and acceptable. It was in 1853 that Snow administered chloroform to Queen Victoria when she was giving birth to Prince Leopold.

For years a huge battle raged between those who believed in anaesthesia and those who claimed it was unnatural. Doctors argued that anaesthesia made surgery and childbirth easier for surgeons and more comfortable for patients. Male church leaders were horrified. They argued that it was unnatural for a woman to suffer no pain while giving birth.

Heaven knows how long the argument would have raged if Dr John Snow hadn't played a trump card in 1853 by anaesthetising Queen Victoria. Once the royal approval had been given the opposition melted away.

By then, however, Snow had already earned his own place in history.

During the 1848-9 cholera outbreak in London, thousands of people died. The main problem was that no one knew how the disease was being spread. Because of this it was, inevitably, impossible to stop it spreading.

And then Dr John Snow decided that the only explanation for the way the disease was spreading was that it was carried in the water supplies. He argued that the solution was to keep sewage away from drinking water. He considered that since the two commonest symptoms, vomiting and diarrhoea, involved the alimentary tract, the disease must be transmitted by something ingested rather than breathed in.

Snow, a physician, general practitioner and (at the time, budding) anaesthetist, spent much of his own time investigating his theory. His first conclusive proof came from a survey of the district around Golden Square in the centre of London. At that time piped water was not supplied to all the houses in the area and many people took their water from pumps and wells. A pump in Broad Street supplied the majority of local inhabitants and Snow's enquiries showed that a cholera epidemic in the area was linked directly to the use of the Broad Street pump. His investigations then showed that the brick lining of a cesspool about three feet away from the well had decayed and cracked. This, Snow decided, was responsible for contaminating the previously drinkable water obtained from the Broad Street pump. To stop the spread of the disease Snow recommended that the handle be removed from the pump so that water could no longer be drawn from that source.

Snow continued his investigations and eventually managed to show a consistent relationship between the incidence of cholera and the supplies of water in different areas of London. He showed that customers whose water came from a polluted or contaminated source were more likely to develop cholera than customers whose water came from a pure source.

It was the work of Dr Snow and Edwin Chadwick (who is also in this book) which helped tame the three major killers of the 19th century: smallpox, cholera and tuberculosis.

Dr Snow is now largely forgotten (although there is a public house in his name in Soho in central London) but although he was not an officially trained or employed public health official his work helped protect millions throughout the world. He can rightly be called the father of epidemiology.

Edmund Spenser (1552-1599)

Born in London, where his father was a cloth-maker, and educated at Cambridge University, Edmund Spenser was one of the world's greatest poets. His first important publication, *The Shepheardes Calender*, published in 1579, is known as the first work of the English literary Renaissance. In it Spenser writes about a maiden he met on a visit to Lancashire. He disguises her under the anagram of Rosalinde. He fell in love with her but she gave her heart to a rival.

By the time he was in his late twenties, Spenser was part of a literary circle led by Sir Philip Sidney (to whom *The Shepheardes Calender* was dedicated) and was working for the Earl of Leicester. He rather hoped for a nice post at court but he blotted his copybook (something he wrote offended the powerful but rather touchy minister, Lord Burghley, the former William Cecil, who was principal adviser to Elizabeth I) and instead he was appointed secretary to the lord deputy of Ireland, where he spent much of the rest of his life.

In the late 1580's, Spenser was appointed clerk of the council of Munster and took over Kilcolman Castle, a large property near Cork which came with around 3,000 acres. The castle was given to him by Queen Elizabeth. Spenser was now further away from London than ever and wasn't even able to mix with Dublin society.

In 1590, with encouragement from Sir Walter Ralegh, who had also ended up in the wilds of the Irish countryside, Spenser published the first three books of *The Fairie Queene*, a long allegorical poem, a glorification of England and Elizabeth I and a poetic vindication of Puritanism and Protestantism. The Fairie Queene of the poem is Elizabeth. Her kingdom is England.

Spenser dedicated the book to the Queen, in the hope that she would invite him to return to the court in London. But the invitation never came and Spenser had to be content with a pension of fifty pounds a year as a reward.

Returning to his castle, Spenser met a local woman, Elizabeth Boyle whom he married in 1594. He then resigned his job as clerk to Munster and, although he did visit London again, spent much of his time working on the later volumes of *The Fairie Queene*.

In another attempt to get back into favour at court he wrote a poem glorifying the Earl of Essex but when this didn't work he realised that his future lay at his comfortable castle in Kilcolman.

Spenser intended that *The Fairie Queene* would consist of no less than twelve separate books but he completed only half of the planned work. It is, nevertheless, regarded as one of the greatest poems ever written. Spenser used a revolutionary nine-line stansaic pattern which has often been used by other poets.

Spenser's other work include a satire on court life called *Colin Clouts Come Home Againe*, which he wrote when Queen Elizabeth did not invite him to return home from Ireland.

Much of his other work has disappeared, presumably lost for ever. One of the problems he had was that although he was writing in Ireland he was publishing in London. Moving manuscripts between the two places was a time consuming and risky business.

Spenser has one other important claim to fame: he was one of the first major writers to write in his own language. By choosing to write in English, rather than Latin (he used the standard English of the period, together with words and dialect borrowed from around the country, together with neologisms of his own invention) he helped encourage others throughout Europe to abandon Latin in favour of their own national language.

In 1598, Spenser was recommended for the post of Sheriff of Cork and he was rather looking forward to this when his home was burned down in the Munster rebellion of that year. Spenser escaped and returned to London with his family. He was however, depressed and despairing at the loss of a home he had grown to love and he died shortly afterwards. As some recognition of his talent, skills and achievements he was buried near the poet Chaucer in Westminster Abbey.

George Stephenson 1781-1848

George and Robert Stephenson, father and son, did more than anyone to 'create' railways. I have chosen to include George (the father) in this list solely because although Robert Stephenson (1803–1859) made an enormous contribution to the development of the train he was continuing his father's work rather than branching out on his own.

George's family were almost all employed in the local coal mines. His father worked as a coal-mine mechanic and George himself started his working life in a colliery near Newcastle as his father's assistant. He proved so good at his job that he became chief mechanic – and his dad's boss – at the age of 17. It was at that colliery that George Stephenson learnt how to operate the steam engine which was used to pump water out of the coal mines so that the miners could work underground and dig out the coal.

It wasn't long before the young Stephenson had the idea of using the pumping engine to drive some sort of vehicle. And so he invented the 'travelling engine' or 'steam locomotive'; originally designed not to pull coaches carrying passengers but to pull wagons full of coal out of the pits. In 1815, he developed a powerful system called 'steam blast' which made the whole idea practical. He obtained financial backing (often the most difficult part of any entrepreneurial activity) and built his first locomotive which he called the Blucher, after the Prussian general who fought alongside the Duke of Wellington at the Battle of Waterloo.

Strictly speaking Stephenson's locomotive wasn't the first to be designed. Another Englishman, Richard Trevethick, had built a steam car some years earlier and in 1808 had built a locomotive that could travel at five miles an hour. The problem was that Trevethick's engines were impractical. They were unreliable, they were so heavy that they broke the rails, they were so slow that people could walk alongside them and they tended to explode rather more than was thought entirely acceptable.

George Stephenson's train, on the other hand, was practical, quick and efficient. George even invented special cast-iron rails and an improved system to enable the wheels to run on the rails more smoothly and more safely. George Stephenson was, without a doubt, the world's first and greatest railway engineer.

Stephenson's locomotive was a success and he was quickly invited to build two locomotives for the Stockton and Darlington railway – the world's first commercial railway. These new engines were capable of pulling passenger coaches carrying 450 people at a speed of 15 miles per hour. In 1829, George Stephenson built his best locomotive which he called the Rocket. His son Robert helped him with the work (and became an important and significant railway engineer in his own right).

The new locomotive was capable of travelling at 36 miles an hour and when a competition called the Rainhill Trials was held to help celebrate the building of the Liverpool and Manchester Railway, the Rocket was the winner. The Rocket was the model for subsequent locomotives. George Stephenson's company built all eight locomotives for the Liverpool and Manchester Railway.

George Stephenson is remembered for a number of other inventions too. He designed a safety lamp for miners (at the same time as Sir Humphry Davy invented one) and, rather bizarrely but ingeniously, he invented a baby's cradle that could be automatically rocked by smoke from a chimney stack.

When George Stephenson retired, in 1838, he was a rich man. He lived in a huge mansion and continued to invent and study.

He had a habit of taking blood from his guests and examining it under a microscope, and he worked out a way of growing straight cucumbers.

The Stephensons have much in common with that other famous family, the Brunels. And like the younger Brunel, Isambard Kingdom Brunel, the younger Stephenson also built some famous bridges. Robert Stephenson was, for example, the creator of the Britannia bridge over the Menai Straits and of a six arch iron bridge which spanned the River Tyne. The Britannia bridge was built with a unique tubular system which was subsequently widely used in England and elsewhere.

Joseph Swan (1828-1914)

Sir Joseph Swan was an English chemist and physicist (he was born in Sunderland) who should be much better known than he is.

In 1860, twenty years before Thomas Edison, who is usually, but wrongly, credited with inventing electric light, Swan produced, and patented, the first electric lightbulb. He had begun working on his lightbulb in 1850, using carbonised paper filaments in a glass bulb. Swan's house was the first in the world to be lit by an incandescent electric light bulb. When Swan visited the Paris Exhibition in 1881, the whole city was lit with electric light, thanks to his invention and there were exhibits of his inventions. (Thomas Edison, in America, was just getting round to developing his first light bulb at this time.)

Swan received the Legion d'honneur from the French for inventing the electric light bulb though, naturally, he had to wait until 1904 to be recognised with a knighthood in his own country.

In 1878, Swan received another patent for a much improved electric light bulb which had a better vacuum and a carbonised thread as a filament. (This was similar to the bulb which Edison eventually produced. Edison obtained patents in America for a copy of the Swan lightbulb and dishonestly ran an advertising campaign claiming that the invention was his own.)

In 1871, Swan invented the dry photographic plate, an invention which revolutionised photography and made it convenient and popular. In 1879, he invented bromide paper for photographic printing. Similar paper is still used for black and white photographic prints. While searching for a way to make a better filament for his light bulbs he also patented a process for manufacturing nitrocellulose fibres (by squeezing the nitrocellulose through small holes). This latter invention revolutionised the textile industry by making it possible to manufacture artificial silk.

Many reference books and encyclopaedias describe the American Thomas Edison as the inventor of the electric light bulb. It is understandable, perhaps, that Americans should seek to perpetuate this myth. It is, however, sad that even some English publications should give credit to the American rather than to the Englishman who was the real inventor of electric light.

William Henry Fox Talbot (1800-1877)

Talbot was born at Lacock Abbey near Chippenham, in Wiltshire and he was trained as a chemist though his interests were wide ranging. He was an amateur polymath and published numerous articles on mathematics, physics and astronomy.

Ignore whatever else you may have heard: William Henry Fox Talbot, the squire of Lacock, invented photography.

Talbot's father was a Dragoon Guards officer with a spending problem. When he died, leaving Lacock Abbey to his son, he also left huge debts. The only way the young Talbot could pay off these debts was by letting out the Abbey and living with friends of his well-connected mother and by studying at Cambridge University. (His mother, Lady Elisabeth, was the daughter of the 2nd Earl of Ilchester.)

By the time he left Cambridge (having mastered Greek and Hebrew, and studied Astronomy, Archaeology, Chemistry and Physics) the debts had been paid off and he was able to reclaim possession of the Abbey and move back in as resident squire of the village.

Unlike his father, who was a bit of a wastrel, young Talbot was a hard worker. He served as MP for Chippenham in the first

Reformed Parliament, published important papers on mathematics, deciphered inscriptions on archaeological finds at Nineveh and developed a new method of estimating the distance of some fixed stars. And he invented an extraordinary internal combustion engine which was sparked by a belt containing small pieces of gun cotton. He continued writing scientific papers, especially on mathematical subjects, all his life.

He began the researches which would lead to the invention of photography quite early on, contributing relevant papers to scientific journals in 1826 and 1827, but it was his hobby of drawing which in the end led to the invention of photography. In 1833, while on his honeymoon near to Lake Como, he was tracing over the images produced through a 'camera obscura' when he decided he wanted to find a way to make such images permanent. Two years later, in 1835, he invented the paper negative and in 1840 he invented the calotype, or talbotype, an early photographic process which involved the use of a photographic negative from which multiple prints could be made. He started taking photographs in that year and the oldest photographic negative in existence in the world is an image of a latticed window in Lacock Abbey which was taken in 1835 by Talbot. In 1844, he published *The Pencil of Nature*, the first book in the world to be illustrated with photographs. He described his discoveries in that book.

Having spent many thousands of pounds developing his photographic process, Talbot took out a patent for his calotype in 1841. He charged professional photographers up to £300 a year to use his process, though amateurs could use it for free. The idea of scientists taking out patents to protect their inventions was fairly new and Talbot was widely criticised for this.

Four years after Talbot first started taking photographs, a Frenchman, Louis Daguerre, exhibited pictures he had taken using a different method which he called the 'daguerrotype process'. (The Frenchman made a good deal of the claim that he was offering his patent free to the world but in fact he too took out a patent in England.) The daguerrotype process was rarely used and was abandoned by 1865. The main problem with it was that copies could not be made.

In the years which followed, photography became increasingly popular. Journalists sent photographs back from the Crimean War. Visiting cards started to include photographs and numerous eminent people (including Queen Victoria and Lewis Carroll) started taking and collecting their own photographs. In 1899, the final year of the century in which Talbot invented photography, more than 100,000 box Brownie cameras were sold in England.

Richard Trevethick (1771-1833)

Born in Cornwall, and poorly educated, Richard Trevethick was just 19 years old when he became an engineer working for several mines in his home county. At the time huge, low-pressure engines were used for hauling ore out of the mines and Trevethick thought these were inefficient and clumsy. In 1797, after conducting experiments with high-pressure steam, he invented a small light engine as a replacement.

The success of this invention led him, four years later, to build the world's first car – a steam carriage – which he subsequently drove in London. Trevethick's creation puts him nearly a century ahead of the engineers who are usually credited with inventing the car. His problem was that no roads had been built and the tracks and bridle paths that existed were entirely unsuitable for transport that, unlike a horse, couldn't pick its way between the ruts and through the mud.

In 1803, after another two years work, Trevethick built the world's first steam railway locomotive. He built a small circular track in London, near the site of the mainline Euston station, to show off a locomotive which he called Catch-Me-Who-Can. Sadly, it wasn't a success. The locomotive was extremely slow and unfortunately, despite much work, the designs had to be abandoned. The main problem was that the iron rails available at the time were too fragile to carry the weight of the engine. It would be another Englishman, George Stephenson who would solve the problems and create the world's first operating steam locomotive.

But Trevethick didn't abandon his engine and he adapted it to create the world's first steam dredger. Sadly, even this didn't prove to be commercially successful and in 1816 the frustrated Trevethick sailed to South America to deliver engines to Peruvian silver mines hoping to make himself rich there. However, the expedition was not a success and Trevethick, a great inventor but a poor businessman, returned to England penniless in 1827. When he died a few years later he was still a poor man.

Jethro Tull (1674-1741)

Jethro Tull, an English inventor and the world's first scientific agronomist, was born in Berkshire, the same county where he died 67 years later. He was educated at Oxford.

Tull took the Industrial Revolution into farming and designed machinery that enabled farmers to work far more efficiently and productively.

After leaving Oxford, Tull became ill with a respiratory problem and travelled throughout Europe searching for a cure. When he returned home he married a girl from Warwickshire, with whom he had three children.

In 1701, Tull perfected a horse-drawn seed drill that sowed seeds in neat rows. His drill enabled farmers to sow their seeds without waste. He then invented a horse-drawn hoe for clearing weeds and improved the design of the plough. It was Tull who first stressed the importance of breaking up the soil to release the nutrients before planting seeds (a simple development that would revolutionise farming and crop production).

Tull's inventions and innovative farming methods were, at first, widely attacked. Farm labourers worried that their jobs would disappear if farmers started using mechanical aids. But within a relatively short period large landowners throughout England, and then the rest of Europe, recognised the importance of Tull's recommendations, and modern agriculture was born.

Few people in history have made a bigger or more important contribution to human life than Jethro Tull. He transformed agricultural practices, both by improving farming methods and by inventing practical implements designed to make farm work more efficient. Modern versions of his inventions still look remarkably like the ones he designed.

It is no exaggeration to say that Jethro Tull is the father of modern agriculture.

Joseph Mallord William Turner (1775-1851)

Commonly known as 'the painter of light', Turner was one of England's greatest painters. His early work was concerned with accurate depictions of the places he painted but later on, he became much more interested in the dramatic effects of light and colour and his experiments made his style of painting unique, something which provoked much venom from his critics. But Turner, who could have easily conformed in order to please his critics, had enough self-belief to continue experimenting in his highly innovative style, which is probably why he is regarded as the most important painter of his time.

The son of a barber and wig maker, J.M.W. Turner, was born in 1775 in Maiden Lane, London to William and Mary Turner. The month and day Turner was born remains something of an enigma because no recorded birth document has ever survived. However, Turner later claimed that he was born on 23 April – St George's Day and the traditional birth date of William Shakespeare.

Sadly, Turner's childhood was blighted by much tragedy: his younger sister died just before her fifth birthday and his mother, Mary, suffered from mental illness. In 1800, she was confined to a mental asylum. Her mental illness made her prone to violent fits of temper, which must have been fairly traumatic for her son to witness. Turner spent some of his childhood with relatives in Brentford and later on in Margate. At Brentford, he attended the Brentford Free School in the High Street. On his way to school, he used to amuse himself by drawing figures on the walls with chalk. Turner showed artistic talent from an early age, and his father used to display his sketches for sale on the walls inside his barber's shop in Maiden Lane.

Turner's artistic talent led him to work in the drawing office of the architect, Thomas Hardwick, where he sketched and painted. Around the same time, Turner also studied in the studio of architectural draughtsman, Thomas Malton. There, Turner learned perspective, a skill that was necessary for architectural drawing.

In 1789, at only 14 years of age, Turner, who spoke with a Cockney accent and who was described as having a 'vulgarity of pronunciation' by *New Monthly Magazine* in 1816, entered the Royal

Academy as a Probationer where he learnt much from the Academy's President, Sir Joshua Reynolds. (Turner was elected an Associate of the Royal Academy in 1799 and became a full Academician in 1802. He was also elected Professor of Perspective in 1807, but for some unknown reason, perhaps nervousness, did not start giving lectures on the subject until four years later.)

After a short period of study at the Royal Academy, the gifted Turner who was still only 14, exhibited a watercolour for the first time. Turner exhibited his work at the Royal Academy right up until the year before he died.

As his studying progressed, Turner's growing talent and artistic skill gained attention from others and in 1793, he was awarded – the first and last prize he ever received – the Greater Silver Pallet by the Society of Arts. The favourable press Turner received for his work contributed to him becoming one of the leading artists of his day – though he was not yet 23.

In 1791, in search of new material, Turner travelled to the West Country on a sketching tour paid for by the Royal Academy. Throughout his life, he toured extensively throughout Britain and Europe. Turner loved Venice and was fascinated and entranced by the light of the city. Five years later Turner exhibited his first oil-painting, Fishermen at Sea at the Royal Academy. This painting which sold for ten pounds was inspired by his visit to the Isle of Wight during one of his sketching tours.

In 1799, the same year Turner was elected an Associate of the Royal Academy, he moved to Harley Street in Marylebone after having made enough money from his art to buy himself a smart home. At his residence in Harley Street, he built his own gallery (he built another gallery at his later London address in Queen Street West) so that he could exhibit his work. It is said that Turner hated selling his favourite paintings, sometimes refusing to sell them at all.

Some of Turner's works include: The Shipwreck (1805), Sun Rising through Vapour (1807), The Battle of Trafalgar, as Seen from the Mizen Starboard Shrouds of the Victory (1806), Ulysses deriding Polyphemus (1829), Burning of the Houses of Lords and Commons (1835) (which he produced after witnessing the fire), The Fighting Téméraire Tugged to her Last Berth to be Broken up (1839), Fishing

Boats with Hucksters Bargaining for Fish (1842) and Rain, Steam and Speed – The Great Western Railway (1844).

Turner's reputation was badly damaged by the critics during the 1830's and onwards but his career was revived by the writer and art critic John Ruskin who was a huge supporter of the painter's work and who often defended him against some of his fierce critics.

After the death of his mother in Bethlehem Hospital (Bedlam) for the insane in 1804, Turner invited his father to live with him. The two men were very close, so close in fact that after his father's death in 1829, friends reported that Turner was never the same man. His father's death had a profound effect on him. As well as being a friend and confidant, William Turner happily became his son's studio assistant and housekeeper. William Turner was proud of his son and one of his greatest admirers.

Turner was said to have been short and stout; extremely private; often eccentric; absent-minded; and prone to parsimony. It was said that he kept Manx cats rather than cats with tails because he had heard that they helped keep the heat in rooms because they were able to enter and exit much more quickly, thus saving money.

Turner never married, but he did have a relationship with a widow, Sarah Danby, by whom he had two illegitimate daughters. And later, he had a close relationship with another widow, Sophia Caroline Booth, who was the landlady of the boarding-house he often stayed at in the seaside town of Margate – a town where he lived for a short period as a child.

Around 1846, Turner left his gallery and residence in Queen Anne Street West and moved to a small house in Chelsea, which he shared with Mrs Booth.

At his Chelsea residence, he lived under the assumed name of Admiral Booth. It was here that he died on 19 December 1851. The painter of light's last words were reputed to be: 'the sun is God'.

Turner was buried in St Paul's Cathedral (next to Sir Joshua Reynolds as he requested) and he bequeathed most of his work to the nation. The prolific artist produced around 300 paintings, and over 20,000 drawings and watercolour sketches.

Wat Tyler (1350-1381)

Wat Tyler was one of the most charismatic leaders of the peasants' revolt and the dramatic march on London which took place in the 14th century. Tyler (almost certainly so named because he was a tiler) came from Essex and was accompanied by his side-kick Jack Straw. Tyler, who was elected to be the mob's spokesman after they had successfully taken Rochester Castle, was, like those who accompanied him, angry at attempts at forced labour which had been introduced after the Black Death a few years earlier. Peasants weren't allowed to sell their labour freely but were treated more like slaves.

The demonstration led by Tyler started in Essex and then moved on to Canterbury, Blackheath and finally London. The demonstration they organised in London was intended to be peaceful, and essentially it was, though there was a little looting, burning and killing when a few wilder elements attacked rich men's homes. Some lawyers and government employees were murdered. No one, not even King Richard II, much minded about the lawyers or the government employees and the demonstrators even got away with destroying the palace of John of Gaunt, the hated uncle of the King and a principal minister.

The young King then decided it would be a good idea to meet the protestors before things really got out of hand. He came to meet them at Smithfield, offering to agree to their demands for freedom and promising to seal documents confirming this. But Wat Tyler ended up quarrelling with some of the King's attendants, and the then Lord Mayor of London, William Walworth, stabbed Tyler and badly wounded him. When he found out that Tyler had been taken to St Bartholomew's Hospital, the Mayor had the rebel leader dragged out of the hospital and beheaded. Tyler was falsely said to have attacked the King. This was early 'perception management' (now known as 'spin').

Naturally, the mob got angry. There was much fighting. Jack Straw, John Bull and a number of other revolting peasants were caught and executed. In all, over 1,500 rebels were hung or beheaded.

In order to try to quieten things down, and to persuade the

troublesome peasants to go back home, King Richard offered all sorts of reforms. Indeed, he promised to do everything the peasants had requested, and signed all the relevant documents. Satisfied, the peasants eventually dispersed.

But as soon as the rioters had gone, King Richard behaved like a politician and went back on his word.

Technically the Peasants' Revolt was a failure and for a while it must have seemed as though Wat Tyler's death was pointless.

But within the next few decades everything the peasants had demanded was given to them. The feudal system ended and peasants were no longer tied to individual landowners or treated like slaves.

William Tyndale (1494-1536) (aka Tindale and Huchins)

William Tyndale, who was probably born in Slymbridge, Gloucestershire and certainly educated at Oxford University, was the man who first published an edition of The Bible in the English language. To do so he had to risk his life. And in the end he died for his work.

After spending time at Cambridge, Tyndale became chaplain and tutor to a household in Little Sodbury but his sympathy with the new ways of thinking (and his enthusiasm for using English rather than Latin) aroused suspicion. Probably wisely, Tyndale left his post and went to London where he tried to persuade Bishop Tunstall to support his plan to translate The Bible into English. His pleas were refused and in 1524 Tyndale went to Hamburg where he visited Luther. His plan was to print an English version of The Bible and to smuggle copies into England. In 1525 he travelled to Cologne where he began printing his own English translation of the *New Testament*.

Unfortunately, Tyndale hadn't got beyond the gospels of Matthew and Mark when problems caused by the intrigues of a German theologian called Johann Cochlaeus meant that he was forced to flee to Worms, carrying with him the parts of The Bible that had already been printed. It was there that the first 3,000 copies of his *New Testaments* were finally printed by Peter Schoeffer.

Bishop Tunstall and others denounced the book and hundreds of copies were burned but Tyndale's bible began to circulate and it was clear that there was a need for it. Nevertheless, Tyndale's life was in danger and he had to flee from Cardinal Wolsey's men who were after him. Sir Thomas More had also become an enemy.

In 1527, Tyndale moved to Marburg, under the protection of Philip the Magnanimous. Two years later he was shipwrecked on the way to Hamburg. In 1531, he went to Antwerp and published an attack on the Pope and the bishops. He temporarily won some approval from Henry VIII because his outspoken views on the church seemed to coincide with the King's interests.

In 1534, Tyndale published a revised version of his *New Testament* and printed a special copy of his new version on vellum for presentation to Anne Boleyn. Tyndale then got into trouble again for denouncing the King's divorce proceedings.

In the same year emissaries of King Henry VIII, who had been chasing him for some time, managed to arrest Tyndale in Antwerp, because of the treachery of a man called Henry Philips. Tyndale was imprisoned, tried for heresy and then strangled and burned.

During his short life Tyndale wrote and published a number of other books including *The Parable of a Wicked Mammon* (1528), *The Obedience of a Christian Man* (1528) and *Practyse of Prelates* (1530).

Victoria (1819-1901)

Queen Victoria – Queen of Great Britain and Ireland, and later, with the help of Tory Minister, Benjamin Disraeli, Empress of India – was born on 24 May 1819 at Kensington Palace.

Queen Victoria's father was Edward Augustus, Duke of Kent (King George III's son). Her mother was the widowed Princess Victoria of Saxe-Coburg-Saalfeld. Queen Victoria was Christened Alexandrina Victoria (nicknamed Drina throughout her childhood) and was her father's only legitimate child. Queen Victoria's mother already had children from her previous marriage with the Prince of Leiningen.

Queen Victoria's father died suddenly on 23 January 1820 when the young princess was less than a year old, leaving her mother, the

Duchess of Kent, a widow for the second time. Just under a week later, Queen Victoria's grandfather, King George III, died, making his granddaughter's chances of becoming Queen much more likely. When learning at the age of about 11 that she was closer to the throne than she thought, Queen Victoria was reported to have famously said: 'I will be good'. Although she was thoroughly spoilt, the young Victoria had a lonely childhood without many children of her own age to play with; her half siblings were quite a lot older than her. Instead, the young princess had a vast collection of dolls (just over 130) for company.

Brought up well aware of her importance from a very early age, the young princess was overheard one day telling a young visitor who was about to touch her toys: 'You must not touch those, they are mine; and I may call you Jane, but you must not call me Victoria'.

Right up until her succession to the throne, Queen Victoria slept every night in the same room as her mother. She was not allowed to walk downstairs or upstairs without somebody holding her hand. Her mother wanted to protect her daughter from any physical harm from her 'wicked uncles' (who she thought would try to murder the Princess) as she, along with Victoria's late father, had a firm belief in their daughter's future destiny as Queen.

The tiny (she was just 4ft 11in tall) Princess acceded to the throne in 1837 after her uncle, King William IV died. Victoria received the news that she was Queen at six in the morning while she was still in her dressing gown. Queen Victoria wrote about the news of her accession in her journal (which she religiously wrote in throughout her life on the instruction of her childhood tutor, advisor and much cherished friend, Fraulein Lehzen): 'Since it has pleased providence to place me in this station, I shall do my utmost to fulfil my duty towards my country; I am very young and perhaps in many, though not all things, inexperienced, but I am sure that very few have more real good will and more real desire to do what is fit and right than I have.'

Tragically, after Queen Victoria passed away her daughter, Beatrice, rewrote and censored her mother's diaries and destroyed the originals.

When Princess Victoria became Queen, she was barred from the throne of Hanover because she was female. This meant that the

120-year-old constitutional link with the German kingdom had now come to an end.

Early on in her reign, the young Queen began to depend on the Prime Minister, Lord Melbourne, for political guidance and advice, and she socialised with him regularly. There were even rumours that there was something more to their friendship, especially as Lord Melbourne was single after divorcing his wife many years earlier for her infidelities (including an affair with the very busy Lord Byron).

Queen Victoria made the mistake of allowing herself to be surrounded by Whigs and was even nicknamed 'Queen of the Whigs' by the Tories, whom she quickly grew to despise. When Whig leader Lord Melbourne resigned after his party's majority was reduced in the General Election, Queen Victoria was bereft at losing her friend and advisor. Her loss was heightened by the fact that she disliked the new Tory Prime Minister, Robert Peel immensely.

The new Prime Minister was disliked even more after he had a discussion with the Queen about her Household. Peel felt that Queen Victoria couldn't possibly give her full support to the Tories if her Household contained wives of opposition MPs. This predicament was famously known as the 'Bedchamber Crisis'. Much to Queen Victoria's delight, Lord Melbourne returned as Prime Minister when Robert Peel was defeated after Melbourne gave a speech to Parliament explaining the Queen's predicament over the 'Bedchamber Crisis'.

After a second election victory in 1841, Robert Peel returned as Prime Minister and Queen Victoria eventually grew to like and respect him.

It was Queen Victoria who proposed to her first cousin Prince Albert of Saxe-Coburg and Gotha. She had to do this because royal etiquette would not allow the Prince to propose to the Queen. On seeing Prince Albert during his visit on 10 October 1839, she later wrote in her journal: 'It was with some emotion that I beheld Albert – who is beautiful'. Queen Victoria and Prince Albert were married on 10 February 1840 in the Chapel Royal at St James's Palace. Queen Victoria's dependence on Lord Melbourne for political guidance and advice was now transferred to her beloved husband, Prince Albert. Royal policy was his policy.

Queen Victoria and Prince Albert went on to have nine children: five girls and four boys. Queen Victoria used chloroform when giving birth to her eighth child, Prince Leopold in 1853. The chloroform was administered by English physician Dr John Snow. Despite public outcry from religious moralists who believed that women should endure pain when giving birth Victoria used chloroform again when giving birth to her ninth and final child.

Amazingly, Queen Victoria survived seven assassination attempts. The first assassination attempt was by 18-year-old Edward Oxford. He fired a shot at Queen Victoria and Prince Albert from one of the two pistols he was carrying. He was sentenced to 27 years in a mental asylum for his crime.

Sadly, Prince Albert (who had become the Prince Consort when Victoria became Queen) died from typhoid fever on 14 December 1861 at the age of 42. Queen Victoria did not attend her husband's funeral because it was established protocol for women not to attend funerals in the 19th century. In mourning for her beloved husband, Queen Victoria withdrew from the political and social scene for quite some time, and wore black for the remaining 40 years of her life (even wearing black to her children's weddings). Her lengthy mourning earned her the nickname the 'Widow of Windsor', and made her very unpopular for a long time with the public.

Queen Victoria remains the longest reigning British monarch (63 years). She was 81 when she died from a stroke on January 22nd 1901 at Osborne House in the Isle of Wight. The Queen was buried with an alabaster of Prince Albert's hand that was placed into her own hand and with some personal mementoes, which she had requested be buried with her. One of the mementoes was a photograph of her Highland servant, John Brown, plus a lock of his hair.

Queen Victoria and Prince Albert first met John Brown when they were developing their estate at Balmoral. Prince Albert had even made him his personal gillie. Much to the horror of those around her, the rather rough Highlander used to address Queen Victoria as 'Wumman!' Queen Victoria enjoyed his straight talking, no-nonsense attitude, and formed a very close friendship with Mr Brown who was allowed more freedom than anyone, even senior courtiers and close relatives. There have even been rumours that Queen Victoria secretly married her servant.

Queen Victoria's reign saw the birth of the modern world. She grew up to reign over the largest empire in the history of the world. She wanted England to be dominant and she believed it was the nation's destiny to rule as much of the world as possible. Victoria's empire was an empire based on trade; the English had acquired naval bases, colonies and coaling stations around the globe.

The Queen's ambitions for England were realised. Well before her death, the English had become the richest and most powerful people in the world.

Robert Walpole (1676-1745)

England's first Hanoverian king, George I (1660-1627), never learned to speak English and naturally this rather hindered any attempts he made to run the country. He became King of England in 1714 but from 1721 onwards he left the nation's affairs to his chief minister Robert Walpole who became, effectively, the nation's first Prime Minister.

Born in Houghton in Norfolk, and educated at Eton and Cambridge, Walpole, a younger son of a wealthy family, was originally destined for a career in the church. However, his two older brothers died before they had chance to have sons of their own, and Robert was left the family estate. Naturally, this changed things and a career in the church was no longer necessary or appropriate. Instead, the young Walpole used his unexpected wealth to enable him to follow a career in politics.

He entered the House of Commons in 1701 as the Whig member for Castle Rising in Norfolk, and in 1702 as the member for King's Lynn. He was a powerful, formidable speaker and he found himself rising fast within the party. He was secretary at war from 1708 to 1710 and treasurer of the navy from 1710 to 1711. In 1712, the Tory Government, worried by his growing power and influence, impeached him for corruption and had him expelled from the House of Commons. But he was back in 1714 and by 1715 he was first Lord of the Treasury and Chancellor of the Exchequer.

The new King, George I, could not speak any English and quickly found himself bored by the proceedings of the House of Commons.

He simply stopped attending, and left the elected politicians of the House of Commons in charge of the country. This gave Walpole a considerable amount of freedom and discretion. Gradually, Walpole established his position and began to chair a small group of ministers who held regular meetings to discuss the nation's affairs. These were the first cabinet meetings. In 1732 MPs, recognising Walpole's status, began to call him the 'Prime Minister', though the title was not officially recognised until 1905. Walpole is still the longest serving Prime Minister – having effectively held the office from 1721 until 1742.

Walpole wanted peace and industrial prosperity for England and he skilfully managed the House of Commons. He set up the first 'sinking fund', abolished export duties, lowered or abolished import duties on essential raw materials and made it illegal to export materials (such as wool) which were used by English manufacturers. He also clamped down on smuggling and forbade Ireland and America to produce goods or raw materials that would compete with English ones. Well aware that wars are costly, disruptive and bad for a nation's economic health, Walpole avoided all foreign entanglements as much as he possibly could. He kept England neutral until 1739 but then found himself forced into the War of Jenkins' Ear in 1739. (This was a war between England and Spain that began in 1739. A Captain Jenkins had appeared before a House of Commons committee and had produced his own amputated ear, which he claimed had been cut off by Spanish coast guards who had boarded his ship in 1731 when he was in the West Indies. MPs used the incident to stir up public outrage and to force Walpole into a war he didn't really want.)

When George II became King in 1727, Walpole cultivated his support and cleverly used royal patronage for political ends.

Walpole survived a number of scandals (including the South Sea Bubble) and as a reward for his years of service Walpole was given No 10 Downing Street (which was to become the permanent London home of all future Prime Ministers) and was made the Earl of Oxford. His famous art collection, which was sold to Russia in 1779, became part of the Hermitage Museum collection.

Robert Walpole, the first Earl of Oxford, died in 1745.

Charles Wheatstone (1802-1875)

The electric telegraph was invented not, as is usually claimed, by an American, Samuel Morse, but by an Englishman – Sir Charles Wheatstone, working with Sir William Cooke. Of the two men, Wheatstone is the most significant.

Charles Wheatstone was born in Gloucester, where his father was a music seller, who later moved to London and became a flute teacher. As a result, Wheatstone was educated first at a village school and then at private establishments in London.

Apprenticed at the age of 14 to his uncle, who made and sold musical instruments, Wheatstone showed little interest in either manufacturing or selling though he did write two songs which his uncle published (though not knowing they had been written by his nephew). The young Wheatstone had one vice: books. Most of his money was spent buying books. One of his earliest purchases was an account of Volta's work on electricity. Since the book was written in French his next purchase was a French dictionary. Once he'd succeeded in translating the book for himself he tried out the experiments described within it. At one point he ran out of money to buy copper and so used the copper coins which were all he had left. The boy was clearly determined, hard working and brilliant.

Wheatstone duly became a physicist. His first experiments were into sound. He invented the concertina in 1829 and became professor of experimental philosophy at King's College, London at the age of 32. Also in 1829, expanding on work done by Robert Hooke in 1667, he estimated that sound would travel at a speed of 200 miles a second through solid rods and suggested building a telegraph between London and Edinburgh to enable people in the south of England to talk to people in Scotland. He called the arrangement a 'telephone'. (Alexander Graham Bell is officially regarded as having invented the telephone in 1876 but it was Wheatstone who had the idea for it and thought up the name.)

In 1838, Wheatstone was the first to explain the principle of the stereoscope. He later invented a sound magnifier (for which he introduced the term 'microphone'), an instrument which doctors could use when listening to patients' chests (the modern stethoscope) and gave his name to Wheatstone's Bridge, a device which is used for the comparison of electrical resistances. He invented the portable harmonium and in 1840 devised a chronoscope, an instrument for measuring minute intervals of time, which was so accurate that it could be used to determine the speed of a bullet.

But it was in the 1830's that Wheatstone took out the first patent for an electric telegraph.

He began his experiments in 1835, suggesting that an electric telegraph would be extremely useful for transmitting information around the world. He proposed laying a line across the river Thames but before he could do any more with the idea he began a collaboration with William Cooke, an army officer who was home on leave studying medicine.

Cooke had built a telegraph of his own and had exhibited it in 1837. He showed it to Dr Roget (the man who created the thesaurus, who was also a physician) who suggested that he visit Wheatstone.

The two men eventually agreed to work together, with Wheatstone contributing the scientific part of the partnership and Cooke providing the administrative skills. A joint patent was taken out for Wheatstone's five needle telegraph. To test the invention an experimental line was set up between two railway stations; one in Camden Town and one at Euston and on 25 July 1837 the first trial took place. Wheatstone, sitting at Euston, sent the first message and Cooke, in Camden, replied. It worked!

Gradually, railway companies realised the potential value of the telegraph and started to install lines between their stations. The invention soon became an invaluable part of public life. In 1840 Wheatstone suggested laying a line from Dover to Calais and in 1859 Wheatstone was asked by the Government to report on the idea of a cable across the Atlantic.

While Wheatstone and Cooke were demonstrating their telegraph, the American Samuel Morse was still thinking about his. He demonstrated his system, along a railway track as Wheatstone and Clarke had done, but seven years later, in 1844. Despite the fact that he was obviously not the real inventor Morse fought vigorously but dishonestly to be described as the sole inventor of the telegraph. He was, to a large extent, successful – particularly in the USA. (Similarly, Thomas Edison succeeded in falsely claiming to have invented the electric light.)

Wheatstone's work helped him build up a great reputation around the world. The French made him a Chevalier of the Legion of Honour. The Royal Swedish Academy of Sciences elected him a foreign member. Altogether he was given over 30 distinctions, mostly by foreign governments and societies. Eventually, even the British Government took note and, in 1868, gave him a knighthood.

Wheatstone died on a visit to Paris in 1875, while working on a receiving instrument for submarine cables.

Frank Whittle (1907-1996)

It was an Englishman who invented the world's first steam engine (Thomas Newcomen) and an Englishman (Michael Faraday) who invented the world's first electric motor. Another Englishman, Frank Whittle, invented the world's first jet engine.

Born in Coventry and trained as an aviation engineer and pilot, Frank Whittle obtained his first patent for a turbojet engine in 1930, when he was just 23.

The scientific principle behind jet propulsion is simple: every action has a reaction. If you blow air into a balloon and then let the balloon go, the balloon will race around as the air escapes through the narrow opening. The balloon's movement is the reaction to the action of the escaping air.

In Frank Whittle's jet engine air and fuel are ignited, and the escaping gases of combustion at the back of the engine make it move in the opposite direction with an equal force. The jet engine works on the same principle as the balloon whizzing round your living room.

Naturally, since Whittle had invented his jet engine in England no one was terribly interested in it. He co-founded the company Power Jets Ltd. in 1936 but it was only the start of the Second World War that triggered serious interest in his invention. Suddenly, Whittle had support from the British Government. In 1941, two years after the start of the War, the first experimental jet fighter was tested. By then, of course, German aircraft designers had recognised the importance of Whittle's invention and they too were working hard on the principle of jet propulsion. Ironically, it was the German Luftwaffe who flew the first operational jet combat aircraft.

Today, civil and military jets around the world, are powered with engines which are based on Frank Whittle's original design.

Frank Whittle received a knighthood in 1948 and received the order of merit in 1986.

William Wilberforce (1759-1833)

Slavery existed in Africa, run by Africans, long before any other country got involved (and the business of slavery continues to this day in several African countries). England, alone among the western nations, decided that slavery was morally and ethically unacceptable.

Those who love to berate England for its links to slavery should, perhaps, study history a little more closely. England was the first country in the world where slavery was actually recorded in the statute books as illegal. When, in 1833, the slave trade was abolished throughout the British Empire it was mainly thanks to an Englishman whose name was William Wilberforce.

The only son of a wealthy merchant, William Wilberforce was born on 1759 in Kingston upon Hull, Yorkshire, to Robert and Elizabeth Wilberforce. It has been said that as a child, William was small, sickly and had poor eyesight.

At only ten years of age, after the death of his father, William was forced to leave his family, friends and Grammar school behind to live 200 miles away with his wealthy uncle and aunt in Wimbolton (now called Wimbledon). Although this must have been devastating for the ten-year-old boy, the childless couple who awaited him from his journey from Hull, were loving, generous-hearted and decent people. They were also Evangelical Christians whose beliefs had an enormous impact on the young William. Their beliefs were to influence him greatly throughout most of his adult life.

William experienced a second great upheaval in his short life when his devout Church of England mother, alarmed at her son's Evangelical leanings, brought the now 12-year-old boy back to live in Hull where he attended the nearby Pocklington School. During his adolescent years, his overt commitment to his new Evangelical beliefs gradually diminished although their influence remained.

The death of several male relatives left William a wealthy man, and he used a little of his wealth in late night drinking and in playing cards with some of his fellow students when he went to Cambridge University. Despite his lack of attention to his studies, William managed to obtain his degree.

By the time he was ready to leave Cambridge, William knew what he wanted to do with his life: he wanted to become a member of parliament. In order to prepare for political life, William decided to spend some time in the public gallery at the House of Commons. It was there that he met future Prime Minister, William Pitt the Younger. Later on, this lifelong friendship was to prove extremely valuable in furthering Wilberforce's cause.

In 1780, at the young age of 21, William entered the House of Commons as MP for Hull. Four years later, William became MP for Yorkshire and in 1812, he became MP for Bramber.

William Wilberforce experienced a religious conversion in 1785. This resulted in him becoming a committed Evangelical Christian and deeply regretting his former hedonistic lifestyle. The gambling, drinking and partying were now a thing of the past. After his conversion, he devoted his life to humanitarian reform. A book, *The Rise and Progress of Religion in the Soul* by Philip Doddridge, which William read on the journey back from a holiday in Nice, is thought to have triggered his religious conversion.

It was William Wilberforce's encounter with anti-slavery campaigner, Thomas Clarkson in 1787 that was to enable him to find his destiny.

Thomas Clarkson, along with his group of anti-slave trade activists, persuaded William to fight for their cause in the House of Commons and over the next few years, William regularly introduced slavery abolition bills into the House of Commons.

After years of campaigning, the year 1807 saw William's great success: the banning of the slave trade by Parliament. England's navy immediately began to police the ban worldwide.

Not content with the abolition of slavery in his own country, William Wilberforce went on to campaign for the abolition of slavery throughout the world.

The abolition of slavery wasn't the only campaign William championed. Some of his other campaigns included work for the

Society for the Prevention of Cruelty to Animals, the Church Missionary Society and the Proclamation Society (for the suppression of vice).

In 1825, William Wilberforce retired from politics and died less than 10 years later in 1833, leaving behind his wife and children. He was 73 years of age. He died just a few days after being told that the abolition of slavery in the British Empire had been secured. It was as if his mission on earth had finally been accomplished and he was now allowed to go home.

William Wilberforce was buried on 3 August in Westminster Abbey next to his dear friend, William Pitt the Younger.

John Wilkes (1725-1797)

John Wilkes was the son of a successful malt distiller. He was educated first at a private academy in Hertford and then tutored privately at home. At the age of 22 he married Mary Meade, the heiress of the manor of Aylesbury who brought with her as a dowry a fortune and an enviable status among the local gentry.

Clearly, as a young man, Wilkes was vastly privileged. He was a member of the Hell-fire Club (which was a popular meeting place for men who enjoyed debauchery and satanism) and in order to win election to the House of Commons in 1757 he happily bribed the voters.

Once he became an MP his life seemed to change.

He started to publish a journal called *The North Briton* and in it he published a scathing attack on the Government, criticising it for signing the Treaty of Paris.

The Treaty of Paris was a result of the Seven Years' War which was, in reality, two separate wars: the continuing struggle between England and France for control in India and North America and a war in Europe between Austria and Prussia. The two wars got mixed up when England allied itself with Prussia and the French supported the Austrians. The result was that the countries involved spread themselves very thin and fighting took place all over the world. In the end, England and Prussia won the war in 1762.

The Treaty of Paris, signed in 1763, gave the English control of

French Canada, most of the territory west of the Mississippi river and most of the French West Indies. England also became the dominant power in India.

When John Wilkes, now an MP, criticised the 1763 peace treaty the Government had him arrested. Wilkes felt that the very Scottish head of the Government, John Stuart, the 3rd Earl of Bute, had betrayed England in agreeing to make over-generous peace terms with France. Wilkes was expelled from Parliament and prosecuted for seditious libel for attacking George III's speech endorsing the Paris Peace Treaty. (Even the newspaper Wilkes had started, *The North Briton*, was a satirical swipe at Bute's own newspaper called *The Briton*. (The 'North' in Wilkes' title referring to Scotland)).

Taken to court, Wilkes was found not guilty and freed. He then sued those who had arrested him for trespass. Bute was forced to resign but, dissatisfied with the court findings the Government went after Wilkes again. This time he was sued for obscene libel as well as seditious libel and officially declared an 'outlaw' in January 1764.

P.G.Wodehouse (1881-1975)

Very few authors have created great characters who require no introduction. William Shakespeare gave us Macbeth and Hamlet, Shylock and Falstaff. Charles Dickens created David Copperfield, Mr Pickwick, Uriah Heep and Oliver Twist. P.G.Wodehouse gave the world Bertie Wooster, Jeeves the valet, Lord Emsworth, Aunt Agatha, Ukridge, Mr Mulliner and Psmith. Wodehouse is almost certainly the only author in the history of literature to have created a legendary character (the Empress of Blandings) who happens to be a pig.

P. G. Wodehouse was one of the most extraordinary geniuses of the 20th century; few men or women have given, and continue to give, more undiluted joy to readers around the world and no one has written more genuinely funny books, in any language. No poet ever wrote more delightful English sentences. Wodehouse wrote intricate, delicately woven plots around which the words danced exuberantly.

Pelham Grenville Wodehouse (known as Plum) wrote over a

hundred books (including eleven novels and 35 short stories about his most famous creations, Jeeves and Bertie Wooster) and worked as a lyricist and librettist with Cole Porter, Ivor Novello, Irving Berlin and Jerome Kern on many successful Broadway shows. (Wodehouse's contribution to the theatre, and in particular, the musical, is barely remembered but he was regarded by Ira Gershwin, Oscar Hammerstein II, Cole Porter and Richard Rogers as their mentor and a most significant figure in the development of the American musical. Alan Jay Lerner wrote that Wodehouse was the pathfinder for Larry Hart, Cole Porter, Ira Gershwin and everyone who followed.)

In the way that many English names are pronounced in a curious way (Cholmondeley is pronounced Chumley, Fotheringay is pronounced Fungy and Featherstonehaugh is pronounced Fanshawe) so Wodehouse is pronounced Woodhouse. The soubriquet 'Plum' comes from the way the young Wodehouse tried, without great success, to pronounce his first Christian name.

In many ways the young Wodehouse resembled his character Bertie Wooster. He was constantly cheerful, despite numerous setbacks, and even stayed bright and funny when interned by the Nazis during the Second World War. It was to prove his undoing.

Wodehouse and his wife had stayed at their home in Le Touquet as the Germans swept through northern France. They either did not realise that they were in danger or simply didn't care. Things started to go wrong when their pet parrot, clearly a bird with good manners, attacked a German officer. The Wodehouses were arrested and taken to Berlin. When the Germans discovered the identity of their captive they put him into a hotel in Berlin and allowed (or encouraged) him to make a series of five rather bright and breezy broadcasts about life in captivity. Wodehouse saw nothing at all wrong with this, and his broadcasts were, as he intended them to be, comforting and encouraging to his English speaking audience. He was simply incapable of thinking anything bad about anyone for more than about ten seconds or so and it had never occurred to him that critics might not see the funny side of his broadcasts.

In England, people in high places took exception to his broadcasting from Berlin, mistakenly and rather stupidly assuming that this meant that he was a Nazi supporter. More sensible observers, including many of the nation's most eminent authors, realised that there was nothing whatsoever offensive in the broadcasts. George Orwell, confronting critics of Wodehouse, pointed out that nothing in the humorist's work related to life beyond about 1911. Orwell, who was a great fan of Wodehouse, and had been since the age of eight, pointed out that Bertie Wooster *et al* belonged to Edwardian England and that Wodehouse had no knowledge or understanding of modern life. (George Orwell and P.G. Wodehouse have more in common than might at first appear likely. George Orwell's father was an English upper middle class civil servant who served the British Raj in Bengal. Wodehouse's father was an English upper middle class judge who served the British Raj in Hong Kong. Orwell made his name by dramatising the problems (past, present and future) of the English working class. Wodehouse became famous by celebrating the absurdities and eccentricities of the English upper class. Sadly, Orwell was born in India and is, therefore, not eligible for inclusion in my 100 – despite the fact that few people in history were more 'English' or prouder of their country.)

The world which Wodehouse created is unique. It seems real enough, and some of the characters are doubtless based, in some way, on people Wodehouse had met. But although everything in it is consistent and convincing, it is a parallel universe, positioned at another angle to reality. In Wodehouse country it is always spring, the weather is always sunny and houses and clubs are full of young men in spats. Characters who, whether ennobled or not, went by names such as Catsmeat Potter-Pirbright, Dogface Rainsby, Bingo Little, Oofy Prosser, Gussie Fink-Nottle, Pongo Twistleton-Twistleton and Barmy Fotheringay-Phipps spent their lives having snifters at the Drones Club and stealing policemen's helmets. 'Have you thought about employment?' a prospective mother-in-law asks Bertie. 'A friend of mine once had a job,' replies Bertie, reminiscing ruefully about the disaster it had been. His own ambitions rise no higher than the job of secretary of the wine committee at the Drones Club. 'Do you always come down at this hour?' a hostess asks, fiddling with her watch, as Bertie tucks into breakfast at nine thirty. 'Oh good heavens no,' answers our young hero. 'Usually much later than this.' Wodehouse's characters live in an England that never existed, and never could, in a season of everlasting merriment. It is difficult to think of fictional characters created in the 20th century who continue to give so much sheer, uncomplicated delight to so many.

Jeeves, the butler who shimmers, floats, filters or oozes into rooms, rather than merely entering in the way that mortals do, understands all. He knows everything (his bedtime reading includes Spinoza and Nietzsche) and can make a pick-me-up capable of eradicating the worst of hangovers. He is discretion itself and, at appropriate times, can create the illusion that he isn't there at all. Bertie Wooster, on the other hand, is defined by two basic principles: never let down a chum (or even an aunt), and never scorn a woman's love, however misguided, misplaced or unwelcome it might be. It is these basic, tightly-held, principles which lead Bertie into so many scrapes and result in him almost (but never quite) tying the knot with so many entirely unsuitable females.

It is Wodehouse's writing style which makes his books what they are. Generations of authors have regarded him as their idol. Evelyn Waugh described him, simply, as 'the Master'. His fans include Dorothy Parker, John Updike, Ludgwig Wittgenstein and John le Carré. His plots are far more complex than they seem and Wodehouse created memorable characters in a way that no one before or since has managed. The girls are either sweetly dotty (describing the stars in the sky as 'God's little daisy chain') or as tough as old boots, but not as good looking. Aunts are always overbearing and demanding (as in Aunt Agatha) though sometimes possessing a slightly softer side (as in Aunt Dahlia). Women play a crucial part in his stories but they are often distant or frightening – probably because as a child Wodehouse never managed to develop a close relationship with any woman. He hardly ever saw his mother.

Older men, invariably peers and magistrates who breed pigs or collect antique silver cow creamers, are blind to Bertie Wooster's virtues. They see only a flannelled, useless and irritating fool. Pals are as idle and as half-witted as Bertie himself. When the Drones Club forms a banjo group to perform summer concerts, one of the members, playing faster than the others and therefore coming to the end of a tune before anyone else, cries out with delight that he has won by finishing first.

But it is the use of words, the mastery of the metaphor and the simile, which made Wodehouse the greatest wordsmith of the 20th century.

If you open any Wodehouse book at any page you will instantly find a stream of brilliant and original word pictures leaping at you from the page. 'Uncle Tom always looked like a pterodactyl with a secret sorrow'. An unsuitably coloured tie is described by Jeeves as 'rather sudden'. The writing, carefully crafted, meticulously reworked by a genius with a craftsman's patience, always appears utterly effortless.

Wodehouse himself, a gentle man and a lover of all animals, particularly cats and dogs, and a mad-keen cricketer (he was a good club batsman and medium pace bowler and co-founder of the Hollywood Cricket Club) was always cheerful and constantly naive; he genuinely seemed to live in an imaginary world of his own. Like many writers he lived (and loved) a rather boring, stable, ritualistic life, spreading his wings in his plots and the imaginary world he had created. He repeatedly showed himself to be unsuited to any sort of post-Edwardian world.

Early in his life he bought a Darracq motorcar with his earnings. He paid £450 for it (a huge sum at the time) and drove it into a hedge after taking a single lesson. He never drove it again and, for the rest of his life, preferred to be driven.

Wodehouse received a knighthood just before he died. The much-deserved award was long delayed. First, it was those five talks that prevented him being recognised. Then it was the Establishment. When Wodehouse was put forward for a knighthood in 1967, the then British Ambassador to the United States of America (a long forgotten stuffed shirt – and how sad for a professional diplomat to be remembered only for such ungallant and undiplomatic behaviour) objected that to give Wodehouse a gong 'would give currency to a Bertie Wooster image of the British character which we are doing our best to eradicate'. The Ambassador, who is now remembered largely for this absurd action, had totally missed the point and had failed to realise that Wodehouse's characters, although essentially English, are comic characters of genius, and have endeared themselves, their author and their home country, to much of the world. P.G. Wodehouse, one of the world's most successful authors, belatedly received his much-deserved knighthood just before he died, at the age of 93. He had very little time left to enjoy it.

The young Wodehouse was born in Guildford where his

mother was staying with her sister (Wodehouse's aunt to be). If Mrs Wodehouse had not gone into labour prematurely her son would have undoubtedly been born in Hong Kong and not eligible for this book. It is disturbing to think that 'Plum' might not have been born an Englishman.

Today, reference to his work, and his characters, appear daily throughout the world. For example, the Oxford English Dictionary contains more than 1,600 Wodehouse quotations.

Wodehouse described his own life as 'a breeze from start to finish'.

William Wordsworth (1770-1850)

He may be despised by some modern poets (the sort who don't believe in rhyme) but William Wordsworth is still one of the world's most popular poets. Born in Cockermouth, in Cumberland, the son of a lawyer, he was the leader of the English Romantic poets of the 19th century (the other Romantic poets included his great friend Samuel Coleridge, who was born at Ottery St Mary in Devon, and Percy Bysshe Shelley who was born near Horsham in Sussex).

Wordsworth was no fan of the formal and rather artificial styles preferred by the 18th century poets and believed that true poetry should be simple and sincere. He had a romantic view of love and nature and spent much of his life among the lakes and hills of the English Lake District where he had been born and brought up.

Orphaned at the age of 13 he was brought up by two uncles, who paid for an education at a good school and at Cambridge University. His first books of poetry, *Evening Walk* and *Descriptive Sketches* were inspired by a walking tour of France and Switzerland which he took in his early twenties. He was much inspired by France, which he visited in the early years of the Revolution. He stayed for a little over a year in France and had an affair with Annette Vallon who gave him an illegitimate daughter, Ann Caroline.

Wordsworth had to leave France when war was declared with England in 1793. His early poetry showed elements of anarchy and a passion for social justice (doubtless obtained from his years in revolutionary France) but he lost these passions as the years went by. On his return to England, Wordsworth set up house with his sister, first in Dorset and then in Alfoxden in Somerset.

In 1795, Wordsworth had inherited a legacy of £900 which gave him financial independence and enabled him to devote his life to literature. In the same year he met Samuel Taylor Coleridge, the author of the *Ancient Mariner*, who was living nearby in Nether Stowey, and they wrote *Lyrical Ballards* together in 1798, though most of the work in the book was Wordsworth's.

His talent was an imagination that could give real meaning to everyday country scenes and he used ordinary language (rather than the flowery, high blown stylised language preferred by poets of the 18th century) to express his feelings about events and scenes he remembered. His poems include the long autobiographical poem called *The Prelude*, which was published after his death in 1850, and the sonnet Composed upon Westminster Bridge. The lines for which he is most famous:

'I wandered lonely as a cloud
That floats on high o'er vales and hills,
When all at once I saw a crowd,
A host of golden daffodils'

appear in a poem called *The Daffodils* which he wrote in 1804 and which appeared in *Poems in Two Volumes* in 1807. The poem was not well received. Lord Byron wrote: 'Mr Wordsworth ceases to please...clothing (his ideas) in language not simple but puerile.'

After the publication of *Lyrical Ballards*, Wordsworth, his sister and Coleridge spent a year in Germany. And then in 1802, William Wordsworth married Mary Hutchinson. The couple, accompanied by Dorothy, moved to Grasmere in the Lake District where they shared a home together. Wordsworth's sister Dorothy, who had a mental breakdown, kept a now famous diary detailing their life together and wrote a journal describing a tour of Scotland which they made in 1803. After living for a while in Allan Bank, the trio finally moved to Rydal Mount which remained their home for many years.

Wordsworth became Poet Laureate in 1843 and died, at the age of 80, in 1850. His later work is usually regarded as disappointing and as not reflecting his true genius, and it took some time for his early work to receive critical approval. But today William Wordsworth is regarded as having, pretty much single-handedly, created a much-loved style of poetry.

He was, according to contemporary accounts, rather conscious of his genius and rather stiff in manner and manners. He didn't have much of a sense of humour and was rather self-centred. He never really lost himself in his poetry and there is none of the uninhibited passion seen in the work of men such as Lord Byron. But Wordsworth's sincerity and simple nature, and his indifference to wealth and status, were the foundation of his great writing.

Much of his poetry was composed in the open air. He interpreted nature with a religious view and in a letter to Lady Beaumont explained that he believed that his poems had a real role 'to console the afflicted; to add sunshine to daylight, by making the happy happier, to teach the young and the gracious of every age to see, to think, and feel, and therefore to become more actively and securely virtuous: this is their office.'

The first part of his life was that of a revolutionary manque. But for the greater part of his life he simply devoted himself to nature and to poetry and became a staunch conservative, protesting against the Kendal and Windermere Railway and opposing the Reform Bill of 1832.

John Wycliffe (1329-1384)

Today, he is more than half-forgotten but John Wycliffe played a vital role in developing English democracy. It was John Wycliffe who, when honest working men were being stomped on by the 14th century's version of today's unelected commissioners and quangocrats, started the fight against the material prosperity of the church.

Born in Yorkshire and educated at Oxford University, Wycliffe was master of Balliol College by 1360 when he was just 31 years old. But he didn't settle, resigning soon afterwards and taking on a variety of jobs, including that of an official, Government-employed pamphleteer. He was feeling increasingly unhappy about the way the world was being arranged. By the middle of the 14th century, monasteries had absorbed about a third of the land in England and the power of the church was still growing. In 1374, while rector of Lutterworth, Wycliffe travelled to Bruges to discuss ecclesiastical abuses with the Pope's ambassadors.

Nothing came of this but Wycliffe became increasingly outspoken in his attacks on the church and he won considerable support both from noblemen and from ordinary citizens. In 1376, he wrote *De Dominio Divino* in which he argued that all authority is founded in grace and that rulers (whether they are secular or ecclesiastical) who are wicked, or who abuse their power, forfeit their right to rule. He claimed that the citizens of England had a right to control the clergy – rather than the other way round.

Wycliffe's writing did not go down well with the bishops who, in 1377, summoned him before the archbishop in St Paul's, London. The meeting (intended as a trial) didn't go well and ended with a quarrel and brawl between the bishop of London and John of Gaunt (the Duke of Lancaster) who was one of Wycliffe's most powerful supporters.

The result was that Pope Gregory XI sent angry papal edicts (known as 'bulls') to the King, the university of Oxford and the bishops demanding that Wycliffe be put in prison. It took a while but eventually the English establishment succumbed to pressure from Rome and at Lambeth in 1378 proceedings were started against Wycliffe.

It was a mistake.

Wycliffe now attacked the church's constitution and declared that it would be better for the people if the Pope and the bishops were got rid of. He also questioned the right of priests to force confessions from people and to offer or deny absolution.

Up until now Wycliffe had written his attacks on the church in Latin, the language of the church and of intellectuals, but in a brilliant move he switched and started to produce leaflets and booklets written in English so that he could reach far more people. He also believed that everyone should be allowed to read The Bible and so he translated it from Latin into English. This was condemned as heretical. Not until the 16th century would an English version of The Bible be available for ordinary people to read.

Wycliffe then also organised a group of itinerant preachers (whom he described as his 'poor priests') who wandered around the country explaining his teachings. Wycliffe's priests, who wore coarse brown wool clothes and were called Lollards, spread the idea that 'all men are equal' and that posh clergymen weren't entitled to live extravagantly while ordinary folk struggled to make ends meet. Wycliffe's most important principle was that each man must hold his religion within himself. He argued that the church's established practices were mechanistic and unthinking.

In 1380, Wycliffe attacked the central dogma of transubstantiation and in 1382 Archbishop Courtenay responded by condemning Wycliffe and having his followers arrested.

Wycliffe, however, was not immediately arrested (probably because he was so popular) and he took advantage of his freedom to write a vast number of powerful and uncompromising tracts attacking the institution of the church. Although the church attempted to suppress his work, Wycliffe was now unstoppable and it was his work which eventually led to the Reformation.

Wycliffe was also a prime mover in the Peasant's Revolt. English rebels were angry that the King and those around him had grown rich at their expense. People complained, angrily, that public money was being wasted. Taxes were constantly being raised to pay for the court's extravagances. Services were deteriorating. *The Magna Carta*, though it had given rights to the people, and was a well-intentioned document, wasn't enough.

Those involved in the Peasants' Revolt of the 14th century were often illiterate and incapable of putting their feelings into words, but they were, nevertheless, conscious that they and their class were being treated unfairly.

The English rebels formed the Commons in Parliament, an assembly of outraged citizens which had no formal authority but which met simply to discuss taxes and other issues. The rebels allowed none of the King's counsellors into their Parliament. They elected a speaker and a Council of State. (There has been an office of Speaker at the House of Commons since 1376.)

This was the first stirring of English democracy. But the members of this early Parliament, although determined and searching for recognition, were not truly representative of the people and they had neither real power nor status. They sat for 74 days but when they finally dispersed and went home they left behind them no permanent organisation, no expectation of reassembling and no laws or statues. Their views and wishes were quickly overturned by the expensively clad upper classes who had moats to clean and duck houses to pay for.

The fact that their efforts had been pretty much in vain incensed the Lollards. One of Wycliffe's preachers, called John Ball, who was also known as the 'crazy priest of Kent', (even then people who opposed the establishment were dismissed as lunatics) became enormously popular. He had three quarters of all the working men of eastern, middle and southern England behind him. Despite being locked up three times he kept preaching.

Wyclifffe and Ball found support among tradesmen, craftsmen and artisans – the middle classes. New taxes lit the flames of the new revolution and led to a march on London. The leaders of the march included Wat Tyler.

The mob got angry and the next day John Ball and another rebel called Jack Straw were caught and beheaded. Subsequently over 1,500 rebels were hung or beheaded. And so, technically the Peasants' Revolt was a failure. (It's known as the Peasants' Revolt but in those days the peasants were the equivalent of today's middle classes.)

However, within the next few decades everything the peasants had demanded was given.

Wycliffe's writing and teaching had changed England. He had given freedom and power to the people and he had taken it from the King and the church.

The church didn't forgive Wycliffe.

Thirty years after his death the Council of Constance ordered that Wycliffe's bones be dug up, burned and thrown into the river. This absurd and vengeful sentence was carried out in 1428.

Extra 1

The English Chart: My Top 100 Englishmen and Englishwomen In Order Of Precedence

It was my original intention to publish the book of my chosen 100 in order of precedence. But when I found that the order of my list was changing several times a day I realised that it would be much better, and fairer all round, to publish the main list alphabetically and, purely for fun, to include my 100 in order of precedence at the back of the book. Here it is. When I chose the 100 Englishmen and Englishwomen for this book I took great care to pick the 100 who had done most for England and the world. But the list that follows is very personal. This is my view of the value of the individual contributions made by the 100 people on my list.

1. Isaac Newton
2. Charles Darwin
3. Charles Dickens
4. Oliver Cromwell
5. William Shakespeare
6. Thomas Malthus
7. Winston Churchill
8. Queen Elizabeth I
9. Francis Bacon
10. Michael Faraday
11. Alfred the Great
12. Charles Babbage
13. Joseph Lister
14. Queen Victoria
15. Robert Hooke
16. William Cobbett
17. James Cook
18. Francis Drake
19. Walter Ralegh

20. Stephen Langton
21. Humphrey Davy
22. William Petty
23. George Stephenson
24. John Snow
25. John Stuart Mill
26. Wiliam Tyndale
27. William Wilberforce
28. John Wycliffe
29. Geoffrey Chaucer
30. John Lilburne
31. Boudicca (Boadicea)
32. Daniel Defoe
33. Elizabeth Fry
34. Thomas Hobbes
35. William Harvey
36. Eadweard Muybridge
37. Richard Trevithick
38. Charles Wheatstone

39. Jethro Tull
40. Robert Peel
41. Thomas Moore
42. Edward Jenner
43. Samuel Johnson
44. Richard Cobden
45. John Dalton
46. Abraham Derby
47. Edmund Halley
48. Rowland Hill
49. Robert Cawdrey
50. Isambard Kingdom Brunel
51. John Locke
52. William Caxton
53. Charles Dodgson (Lewis Carroll)
54. Christopher Wren
55. Joseph Mallord William Turner
56. Samuel Pepys
57. Horatio Nelson
58. John Wilkes
59. Thomas Newcome
60. Jeremy Bentham
61. Edwin Chadwick
62. W. G. Grace
63. John Stuart Mill
64. William Byrd
65. William Henry Fox Talbot
66. Aphra Behn
67. Richard Arkwright
68. Thomas Paine
69. Henry Maudslay

70. John Milton
71. William Morris
72. Francis Place
73. Wat Tyler
74. Lord Byron
75. George Cayley
76. John Harrison
77. Robert Walpole
78. Peter Roget
79. Joseph Swan
80. Edith Cavell
81. William Brockeden
82. William Blake
83. Joseph Bramah
84. P.G. Wodehouse
85. Richard Burton
86. Frank Whittle
87. Edmund Spenser
88. William Hogarth
89. Thomas Cook
90. John Constable
91. Charles Chaplin
92. John Ruskin
93. Edward Elgar
94. John Donne
95. William Wordsworth
96. John Keats
97. Cecil Rhodes
98. Mrs Beeton
99. John Bunyan
100. Robert Baden-Powell

Extra 2

The Author

Vernon Coleman was an angry young man for as long as it was decently possible. He then turned into an angry middle-aged man. And now, with no effort whatsoever, he has matured into being an angry old man. He is, he confesses, just as angry as he ever was. Indeed, he may be even angrier because, he says, the more he learns about life the more things he finds to be angry about.

Cruelty, prejudice and injustice are the three things most likely to arouse his well-developed sense of ire but he admits that, at a pinch, inefficiency, incompetence and greed will do almost as well. He does not cope well with bossy people, particularly when they are dressed in uniform and attempting to confiscate his Swiss Army penknife. 'Being told I can't do something has always seemed to me sufficient reason to do it,' he says. 'And being told that I must do something has always seemed to me a very good reason not to do it.'

The author has an innate dislike of taking orders, a pathological contempt for pomposity, hypocrisy and the sort of unthinking political correctness which attracts support from *Guardian*-reading pseudo-intellectuals. He also has a passionate loathing for those in authority who do not understand that unless their authority is tempered with compassion and a sense of responsibility the end result must always be an extremely unpleasant brand of totalitarianism. He believes that multi-culturalism on a global scale is perfectly appropriate but that individual countries are best left to be individual. He regards the European Union as the most fascist organisation ever invented and looks forward to its early demise.

Vernon Coleman has written for *The Guardian* (he was a teenager at the time and knew no better), *Daily Telegraph, Sunday Telegraph, Observer, Sunday Times, Daily Mail, Mail on Sunday, Daily Express, Sunday Express, Daily Star, The Sun, News of the World, Daily Mirror, Sunday Mirror, The People, Woman, Woman's Own, Spectator, Punch, The Lady* and hundreds of other leading publications in Britain and around the world. His books have been published by Thames and Hudson, Sidgwick and Jackson, Hamlyn, Macmillan, Robert Hale, Pan, Penguin, Corgi, Arrow and several dozen other publishers in the UK and reproduced by scores of discerning publishers around the world. His novel *Mrs Caldicot's Cabbage War* was made into a film and a number of his other books have been turned into radio or television programmes. Today he publishes his books himself as this allows him to avoid contact with marketing men in silk suits and 19-year-old editorial directors called Fiona. In an earlier life he was the breakfast television doctor and in the now long-gone days when producers and editors were less wary of annoying the establishment he was a regular broadcaster on radio and television.

He has never had a proper job (in the sense of working for someone else in regular, paid employment, with a cheque or pay packet at the end of the week or month) but he has had freelance and temporary employment in many forms. He has, for example, had paid employment as: magician's assistant, postman, fish delivery van driver, production line worker, chemical laboratory assistant, author, publisher, draughtsman, meals on wheels driver, feature writer, drama critic, book reviewer, columnist, surgeon, police surgeon, industrial medical officer, social worker, night club operator, property developer, magazine editor, general practitioner, private doctor, television presenter, radio presenter, agony aunt, university lecturer, casualty doctor and care home assistant.

Today, he likes books, films, cafés and writing. He writes, reads and collects books and has a larger library than most towns. A list of his favourite authors would require another book. He has never been much of an athlete, though he once won a certificate for swimming a width of the public baths in Walsall (which was, at the time, in Staffordshire but has now, apparently, been moved elsewhere). He no longer cherishes hopes of being called upon to play cricket for England and is resigned to the fact that he will now never drive a Formula 1 racing car in anger.

He doesn't like yappy dogs, big snarly dogs with saliva dripping from their fangs or people who think that wearing a uniform automatically gives them status and rights. He likes trains, dislikes planes and used to like cars until some idiot invented speed cameras, bus lanes and car parks where the spaces are so narrow that only the slimmest, and tinniest of vehicles will fit in.

He is fond of cats, pens and notebooks and used to like watching cricket until the authorities sold out and allowed people to paint slogans on the grass. His interests and hobbies include animals, books, photography, drawing, chess, backgammon, cinema, philately, billiards, sitting in cafés and on benches and collecting Napoleana. He likes log fires and bonfires, motor racing and music by Mahler and dislikes politicians, bureaucrats and cauliflower cheese. He likes videos but loathes DVDs. His favourite 11 people in history include (in no particular order): Daniel Defoe, Napoleon Bonaparte, W. G. Grace, William Cobbett, Thomas Paine, John Lilburne, Aphra Behn, P. G. Wodehouse, Jerome K. Jerome, Francis Drake and Walter Ralegh all of whom had more than it takes and most of whom were English. (Napoleon would doubtless have been English if he'd had the chance.) What an unbeatable team they would have made. Grace and Bonaparte opening the batting and Drake and Ralegh opening the bowling. Gilles Villeneuve would be his 12th man.

Vernon Coleman lives in the village of Bilbury in Devon and enjoys malt whisky, toasted muffins and old films. He is devoted to Donna Antoinette who is the kindest, sweetest, most sensitive woman a man could hope to meet and who, as an undeserved but welcome bonus, makes the very best roast parsnips on the planet. He says that gourmands and gourmets would come from far and wide if they knew what they were missing but admits that since he and Thumper Robinson took down the road signs (in order to discourage American tourists travelling on coaches~) Bilbury has become exceedingly difficult to find.

For a catalogue of Vernon Coleman's books
please write to:

Publishing House
Trinity Place
Barnstaple
Devon EX32 9HG
England

Telephone	01271 328892
Fax	01271 328768

Outside the UK:

Telephone	+44 1271 328892
Fax	+44 1271 328768

Or visit our website:

www.vernoncoleman.com